简明会计英语教程

（第2版）

A concise course of accounting English

(The Second Edition)

主　编　牛国崎　张宏宾
副主编　贾新新　王丽英
编　者　应来喜　张宏宾　徐黎君　刘改雪
　　　　李照文　王效伟　张　辉　王四平
　　　　刘　悦　陈　冉　马　静　任立强
　　　　赵　峰　师　玲　黄　敏　侯文艳

北京理工大学出版社
BEIJING INSTITUTE OF TECHNOLOGY PRESS

版权专有　侵权必究

图书在版编目（CIP）数据

简明会计英语教程 / 牛国崎，张宏宾主编. —2版. —北京：北京理工大学出版社，2018.1（2022.8 重印）

ISBN 978-7-5682-4375-9

Ⅰ. ①简… Ⅱ. ①牛… ②张… Ⅲ. ①会计-英语-教材 Ⅳ. ①F230

中国版本图书馆 CIP 数据核字（2017）第 172175 号

出版发行 / 北京理工大学出版社有限责任公司
社　　址 / 北京市海淀区中关村南大街5号
邮　　编 / 100081
电　　话 / (010)68914775(总编室)
　　　　　 (010)82562903(教材售后服务热线)
　　　　　 (010)68948351(其他图书服务热线)
网　　址 / http://www.bitpress.com.cn
经　　销 / 全国各地新华书店
印　　刷 / 三河市天利华印刷装订有限公司
开　　本 / 787 毫米×1092 毫米　1/16
印　　张 / 15
字　　数 / 360 千字
版　　次 / 2018 年 1 月第 2 版　2022 年 8 月第 3 次印刷
定　　价 / 49.00 元

责任编辑 / 武丽娟
文案编辑 / 武丽娟
责任校对 / 孟祥敬
责任印制 / 李志强

图书出现印装质量问题，请拨打售后服务热线，本社负责调换

主编简介

牛国崎，男，汉族，1962年生，译审，教授，国际工程师协会FIDIC（菲迪克）条款专家，联合国农业发展基金（IFAD）特聘高级翻译，多年从事翻译、教学及学术研究工作。曾在国外从事翻译工作，包括交替传译和大型同声传译，涉及领域包括医学、建筑、农业、生物工程、信息技术等多个行业，对行业英语具有独到的研究和心得。近年来，主要精力转向教学与学术研究，主要讲授通信英语、物流英语、银行英语等专业英语课程，并先后出版《物流英语》《会计英语》《简明物流英语教程》等书籍。2013年，创办北京泰格经纬数控科技有限公司，任执行董事。

第2版前言 Preface(2nd)

《简明会计英语教程》第1版于2011年由北京理工大学出版社出版发行，至今已经近6个年头。本书自面世以来，受到了广大读者的好评，并被国内多所知名大学列为会计专业指定教材，受到了广大师生的一致肯定。

本教程主要面向会计专业的学生，同时也兼顾了广大会计从业人员的专业英语需求，独特的选题和简单明了的编写体例使本书成为会计专业英语中最受欢迎的教材之一，应院校教师和一般读者的要求，特于2017年7月进行修订。

本次修订重点有两个部分：一是对会计相关知识部分进行了补充、变更，使其更符合现代会计的发展动向；二是对会计英语专业术语的释义进行了全面核对和订正，以使其更符合现代会计行业的习惯性表达。

本教程发行6年来，广大读者，尤其是相关教材使用单位，包括若干大学和高职高专院校的教师们不断向编者反馈针对该教材所提出的大量修订建议，我们在此表示衷心的感谢。

囿于编者水平，错讹之处再所难免，恳请读者不吝赐教，以期下次再版时勘正之用。

本书另配有PPT课件，课件内容包括课文翻译、阅读材料、练习答案等。如需获得本书的PPT课件，请直接联系编者：email: garyline@163.com; QQ:1908636741。

牛国崎

随着2011年的到来，世界进入了全球金融危机后的第三年。经过金融危机的阵痛和洗礼，世界经济终于在各国政府合力推出的刺激措施中艰难地进入复苏阶段，与此同时，多国政府也在不断地考虑退出机制及时点的选择。通胀预期、二次探底的可能性、经济复苏的不确定性……凡此种种，都昭示着这样的推断：世界经济的复苏过程将比预想的更艰难、更复杂且更具有长期性。

金融危机给我们的警示是深刻的：人性的贪婪、金融监管机制的缺失、经济结构的失衡、过度追求产业规模而忽视内部管理、重短期量化指标而忽视长期的且可持续性的质化标准、片面追求高速度的利润指标而忽视稳定的运转机制等现象都在不断地向决策者以及监管者提醒着可能存在的巨大风险。与此同时，各种令人眼花缭乱的、复杂的金融衍生品的出现不断地放大了杠杆效应，加剧并催生潜在风险。然而，当人们以"搏傻"的心态进入市场时，当人们对风险视而不见时，当违规操作被虚假的繁荣暂时掩盖时，全球供应链这条人类经济的"多米诺骨牌"正在被越砌越长，潜在风险逐步转化成现实风险。直到有一天，雷曼兄弟——这家有着百年历史的投行巨头——在一夜间轰然倒下，代表着人性贪婪的多米诺效应瞬间发生，全球金融危机迅速在世界各主要经济体蔓延，世界经济进入了自1929年大萧条以来最大的一次经济下挫中。

金融危机爆发后，人们也越来越认识到财务管理的重要性。对于世界经济，防范金融风险要从财务管理做起；对于企业或实体，防范管理风险、运营风险、投资风险等也要从财务管理着手。作为财务管理的核心内容之一，会计学被公认是"经济的语言"，在经济活动中起着至关重要的作用。

会计在我国是一个传统行业，经过改革开放30年的发展，会计学正在逐步和国际接轨，并展现出新的活力。

随着中国全面进入"大开放"时期，中国的开放战略将从沿海地区逐步向内陆地区发展，中国经济将迎来第二个30年的持续高速的成长期，中国的GDP将在可预见的未来超过美国而成为世界第一大经济体，人民币将从现在的区域性货币逐步变成与美元、英镑等货币一样的硬通货，中国将从劳动力优势国转型为技术、管理及资金优势国，"中国制造"将过度成"中国创造"，中国在世界政治经济舞台上将成为更为重要的、不可或缺的力量之一。总之，中国将在下一个30年中完成从"大国"到"强国"的转型。

由此，我们可以预见，在未来30年的大开放中，中国与世界经济的联系将更加紧密，对外交往，尤其是经济往来将更加频繁，中国将成为世界资本角逐的重要经济战场。

在此背景下，会计学不仅要适应中国的国情，为中国经济服务，而且还要承担对外经济往来的大量相关业务。这就要求我们的会计师不仅要熟悉中国的会计制度，还要不失时机地了解并掌握国外，尤其是欧美日等国家和地区的会计制度，这样才能在国际财务交往中确保业务的顺利进行，更好地为管理及决策提供可靠而强大的财务支持。

　　但是我国会计界的现状是，懂会计专业者不懂外语，而懂外语者又不懂会计专业。我国会计从业者普遍英语水平不高，这一方面可能由于会计从业人员忙于业务而无暇顾及英语学习，另一方面可能是从业者想提高英语水平却苦于找不到适当的教材。与此同时，对外交往的增多以及考职称、考研、考公务员等硬性外语要求又显示了提高外语水平的迫切性，在此情况下，推出一本简明、实用、可学性强的会计英语教材就成了当务之急。

　　为满足市场的需求，我们编写了这本《简明会计英语教程》。

牛国崎

Unit 1	**What is accounting? 什么是会计？ / 1**
1.1a	What is the definition of accounting? 会计的定义是什么？ / 2
1.1b	What is the function of accounting? 会计的功能是什么？ / 2
1.1c	What are the methods of accounting? 会计方法有哪些？ / 3
1.1d	What is the accounting object? 什么是会计对象？ / 4
1.1e	What are the accounting elements? 什么是会计要素？ / 4
1.2	Core accounting terms 核心会计术语 / 5
1.3	Extended words 扩展词汇 / 5
1.4	Notes 注释 / 6
1.5	Reinforcement exercise 强化练习 / 7
1.6	Accounting-related knowledge 会计相关知识介绍
	什么是会计？What is accounting? / 9
1.7	Extended reading 延伸阅读
	The five account types 五种账户类型 / 9

Unit 2	**How does the double-entry system work? 复式记账法的原理是什么？ / 11**
2.1a	What is double-entry bookkeeping? 什么是复式记账？ / 12
2.1b	Why is double-entry system significant? 复式记账法的意义是什么？ / 12
2.1c	What categories do the books cover? 账簿包含哪些类别？ / 13
2.1d	What are credits and debits? 什么是贷方和借方？ / 13
2.1e	What are the advantages of the double-entry system? 复式记账法有什么优势？ / 14
2.1f	How does double-entry bookkeeping work? 复式记账法的工作原理是什么？ / 15
2.2	Core accounting terms 核心会计术语 / 17
2.3	Extended words 扩展词汇 / 17
2.4	Notes 注释 / 18
2.5	Reinforcement exercise 强化练习 / 20
2.6	Accounting-related knowledge 会计相关知识介绍
	复式记账法的记账规则 Bookkeeping rules of the double-entry system / 21
2.7	Extended reading 延伸阅读
	The pros and cons of double-entry 复式记账的正反面争论 / 22

Unit 3 How to compile the accounting documents? 如何编制会计凭证？/ 24

3.1a	What is accounting document? 什么是会计凭证？/ 25	
3.1b	How to classify the accounting documents? 如何为会计凭证分类？/ 25	
3.1c	How to compile the accounting documents? 如何编制会计凭证？/ 26	
3.1d	Why are the accounting documents significant? 会计凭证有什么意义？/ 27	
3.2	Core accounting terms 核心会计术语 / 27	
3.3	Extended words 扩展词汇 / 28	
3.4	Notes 注释 / 28	
3.5	Reinforcement exercise 强化练习 / 29	
3.6	Accounting-related knowledge 会计相关知识介绍 记账凭证的种类 Types of bookkeeping vouchers / 31	
3.7	Extended reading 延伸阅读 Accounting and accountants 会计学和会计师 / 33	

Unit 4 What is a balance sheet? 什么是资产负债表？/ 34

4.1a	What is a balance sheet? 什么是资产负债表？/ 35	
4.1b	What is the purpose of a balance sheet? 资产负债表的目的是什么？/ 36	
4.1c	How do we look at a balance sheet? 如何看待资产负债表？/ 37	
4.1d	What are assets, liabilities and owners' interest? 什么是资产、负债及所有者权益？/ 37	
4.2	Core accounting terms 核心会计术语 / 38	
4.3	Extended words 扩展词汇 / 38	
4.4	Notes 注释 / 39	
4.5	Reinforcement exercise 强化练习 / 40	
4.6	Accounting-related knowledge 会计相关知识介绍 资产负债表 A balance sheet / 42	
4.7	Extended reading 延伸阅读 Current liabilities 流动负债 / 43	

Unit 5 The format of a balance sheet 资产负债表的格式 / 44

5.1a	The heading and the body 表首和正表 / 45	
5.1b	The report-type balance sheet 报告式资产负债表 / 45	
5.1c	The account-type balance sheet 账户式资产负债表 / 47	
5.2	Core accounting terms 核心会计术语 / 48	
5.3	Extended words 扩展词汇 / 48	
5.4	Notes 注释 / 49	
5.5	Reinforcement exercise 强化练习 / 50	
5.6	Accounting-related knowledge 会计相关知识介绍 资产负债表的编制方法 The compiling method of a balance sheet / 52	

5.7	Extended reading 延伸阅读 Equity 权益 / 53

Unit 6	**How to establish the account books? 如何建账？/ 54**
6.1a	Why is book-establishing significant? 建账的意义是什么？/ 55
6.1b	What are the processes of book establishing? 建账的程序是什么？/ 55
6.1c	Three common account books 三种常用账簿 / 56
6.2	Core accounting terms 核心会计术语 / 58
6.3	Extended words 扩展词汇 / 59
6.4	Notes 注释 / 59
6.5	Reinforcement exercise 强化练习 / 61
6.6	Accounting-related knowledge 会计相关知识介绍 新办小企业如何建账？ How does a newly-started small business establish its accounts? / 63
6.7	Extended reading 延伸阅读 The general ledger 总账 / 64

Unit 7	**What is a profit statement? 什么是利润表？/ 65**
7.1a	What is a profit statement? 什么是利润表？/ 66
7.1b	What are the elements of income? 收益有哪些要素？/ 66
7.1c	What are the forms of a profit statement? 利润表有哪些形式？/ 67
7.1d	A sample single-step profit statement 单步式利润表样本 / 69
7.1e	A Sample multiple-step profit statement 多步式利润表样本 / 70
7.2	Core accounting terms 核心会计术语 / 71
7.3	Extended words 扩展词汇 / 72
7.4	Notes 注释 / 72
7.5	Reinforcement exercise 强化练习 / 74
7.6	Accounting-related knowledge 会计相关知识介绍 如何编制利润表 How to produce a profit statement / 76
7.7	Extended reading 延伸阅读 Reminders in producing a profit statement 编制利润表的提示 / 77

Unit 8	**What is a bank reconciliation statement? 什么是银行往来调节表？/79**
8.1a	What is a bank reconciliation statement? 什么是银行往来调节表？/ 80
8.1b	What are the terms on bank reconciliation? 银行往来调节方面的术语有哪些？/ 81
8.1c	How to prepare a bank reconciliation statement? 如何准备银行往来调节表？/ 82
8.1d	Tips and warnings 提示和警告 / 83
8.2	Core accounting terms 核心会计术语 / 84
8.3	Extended words 扩展词汇 / 84

8.4	Notes 注释 / 85	
8.5	Reinforcement exercise 强化练习 / 87	
8.6	Accounting-related knowledge 会计相关知识介绍 涉外会计 Foreign-related accounting / 88	
8.7	Extended reading 延伸阅读 Bank statement 银行对账单 / 89	

Unit 9 What is inventory accounting? 什么是存货核算？/ 91

9.1a	What is inventory? 什么是存货？/ 92
9.1b	What is inventory accounting? 什么是存货核算？/ 92
9.1c	What is the purpose of inventory accounting? 存货核算的目的是什么？/ 93
9.1d	What are the methods of inventory accounting? 库存核算有哪些方法？/ 93
9.2	Core accounting terms 核心会计术语 / 95
9.3	Extended words 扩展词汇 / 95
9.4	Notes 注释 / 96
9.5	Reinforcement exercise 强化练习 / 98
9.6	Accounting-related knowledge 会计相关知识介绍 各种存货核算法的比较 Comparisons between various methods of inventory accounting / 100
9.7	Extended reading 延伸阅读 Inventory turnover 存货周转 / 101

Unit 10 How to manage your accounts receivable? 如何管理应收账？/ 102

10.1a	What are accounts receivable – A/R? 什么是应收账？/ 103
10.1b	What is the nature of accounts receivable? 应收账的性质是什么？/ 103
10.1c	How do we calculate accounts receivable? 如何计算应收账？/ 104
10.1d	How do we reduce accounts receivable? 如何减少应收账？/ 107
10.2	Core accounting terms 核心会计术语 / 108
10.3	Extended words 扩展词汇 / 108
10.4	Notes 注释 / 109
10.5	Reinforcement exercise 强化练习 / 112
10.6	Accounting-related knowledge 会计相关知识介绍 企业应收账形成的原因 Causes of accounts receivable in businesses / 114
10.7	Extended reading 延伸阅读 Managing your DSO 管理您的 DSO（日销货未收款）/ 115

Unit 11 How to depreciate fixed assets? 固定资产如何折旧？/ 117

11.1a	What are fixed assets? 什么是固定资产？/ 118
11.1b	What is depreciation? 什么是折旧？/ 118

11.1c	What are the elements in planning depreciation? 计划折旧时有哪些要素？/ 119	
11.1d	What are the methods of depreciation? 折旧有哪些方法？/ 120	
11.1e	The straight-line depreciation method 直线折旧法 / 121	
11.2	Core accounting terms 核心会计术语 / 123	
11.3	Extended words 扩展词汇 / 124	
11.4	Notes 注释 / 124	
11.5	Reinforcement exercise 强化练习 / 127	
11.6	Accounting-related knowledge 会计相关知识介绍 固定资产折旧的方法 Methods of fixed assets depreciation / 129	
11.7	Extended reading 延伸阅读 Amortization and depreciation 摊销与折旧 / 130	

Unit 12 What is liability? 什么是负债？/ 133

12.1a	What is liability? 什么是负债？/ 134
12.1b	What is the significance of liabilities? 负债的意义是什么？/ 134
12.1c	What are the types of liabilities? 债务有哪些种类？/ 135
12.1d	What is the assets-liabilities ratio? 什么是资产负债比？/ 136
12.2	Core accounting terms 核心会计术语 / 138
12.3	Extended words 扩展词汇 / 138
12.4	Notes 注释 / 139
12.5	Reinforcement exercise 强化练习 / 142
12.6	Accounting-related knowledge 会计相关知识介绍 如何计算资产负债率？How to calculate the debt to assets ratio? / 143
12.7	Extended reading 延伸阅读 What is ALM? 什么是资产负债管理？/ 144

Unit 13 What is shareholders' equity? 什么是股东权益？/ 146

13.1a	What is shareholders' equity? 什么是股东权益？/ 147
13.1b	What is ROE? 什么是 ROE？/ 147
13.1c	How to calculate the ROE? 如何计算 ROE？/ 148
13.1d	Caution: ROE can be misleading! 小心：ROE 可能有误导性！/ 149
13.1e	What is the DuPont Formula? 什么是杜邦公式？/ 150
13.2	Core accounting terms 核心会计术语 / 151
13.3	Extended words 扩展词汇 / 151
13.4	Notes 注释 / 152
13.5	Reinforcement exercise 强化练习 / 154
13.6	Accounting-related knowledge 会计相关知识介绍 杜邦分析法 The DuPont Analysis / 156
13.7	Extended reading 延伸阅读

Return on equity 股本收益率/ 157

Unit 14　What is a cash flow statement?　什么是现金流量表？/ 159

- 14.1a　What is a cash flow statement? 什么是现金流量表？/ 160
- 14.1b　What is the role played by CFS? 现金流量表的作用是什么？/ 160
- 14.1c　What is the structure of a CFS? 现金流量表的结构是什么？/ 161
- 14.1d　Analyzing a sample CFS 分析现金流量样表 / 163
- 14.2　Core accounting terms 核心会计术语 / 165
- 14.3　Extended words 扩展词汇/ 165
- 14.4　Notes 注释 / 166
- 14.5　Reinforcement exercise 强化练习 / 169
- 14.6　Accounting-related knowledge 会计相关知识介绍
  如何编制现金流量表？How to prepare a cash flow statement? / 171
- 14.7　Extended reading 延伸阅读
  The preparation methods of a CFS 现金流量表的编制方法 / 172

Unit 15　What tasks does an accountant do? 会计师的工作范围是什么？/ 174

- 15.1a　What is an accountant? 什么是会计师？/ 175
- 15.1b　What tasks does an accountant do? 会计师的工作范围是什么？/ 175
- 15.1c　Why important? 为什么重要？/ 177
- 15.2　Core accounting terms 核心会计术语 / 177
- 15.3　Extended words 扩展词汇 / 178
- 15.4　Notes 注释 / 178
- 15.5　Reinforcement exercise 强化练习 / 180
- 15.6　Accounting-related knowledge 会计相关知识介绍
  什么是出纳？What is a cashier? / 182
- 15.7　Extended reading 延伸阅读
  What is a bank teller?什么是银行出纳？/ 183

Unit 16　How to calculate shareholders' dividend？如何计算股东股息？/ 185

- 16.1a　What is a dividend? 什么是股息？/ 186
- 16.1b　How does a dividend work? 股息是如何起作用的？/ 187
- 16.1c　How to calculate dividend yield and payout ratio?
  如何计算股息收益率和股息支付率？/ 187
- 16.1d　Why stock dividend instead of cash dividend?
  为什么是股票股息而不是现金股息？/ 189
- 16.2　Core accounting terms 核心会计术语 / 189
- 16.3　Extended words 扩展词汇 / 190
- 16.4　Notes 注释 / 190

16.5	Reinforcement exercise 强化练习 / 193	
16.6	Accounting-related knowledge 会计相关知识介绍 什么是股息率？What is the dividend yield? / 195	
16.7	Extended reading 延伸阅读 How to calculate the annual dividend on preferred shares? 如何计算优先股的年股息？/ 196	

Unit 17　How to maintain a healthy cash flow in a small business? 小企业如何保持健康的现金流？/ 198

17.1a	Why is a healthy cash flow vital for business survival? 为什么健康的现金流对企业生存是重要的？/ 199
17.1b	What is a stress test? 什么是压力测验？/ 200
17.1c	10 cash flow management tips 10 个现金流管理提示 / 200
17.2	Core accounting terms 核心会计术语 / 202
17.3	Extended words 扩展词汇 / 202
17.4	Notes 注释 / 203
17.5	Reinforcement exercise 强化练习 / 206
17.6	Accounting-related knowledge 会计相关知识介绍 卡桑国际的瘦身计划 Kaseng International's downsizing scheme / 208
17.7	Extended reading 延伸阅读 Perceive cash flow problems closely 密切注意现金流问题 / 209

Unit 18　What is cost accounting? 什么是成本核算？/ 212

18.1a	What are absolute costs and relative costs? 什么是绝对成本和相对成本？/ 213
18.1b	What are variable costs and fixed costs? 什么是可变成本和固定成本？/ 213
18.1c	What are the total cost and unit cost formulas? 什么是总成本和单位成本公式？/ 214
18.1d	What is the unit cost equation? 什么是单位成本等式？/ 214
18.1e	What is cost accounting? 什么是成本核算？/ 215
18.2	Core accounting terms 核心会计术语 / 216
18.3	Extended words 扩展词汇 / 216
18.4	Notes 注释 / 217
18.5	Reinforcement exercise 强化练习 / 220
18.6	Accounting-related knowledge 会计相关知识介绍 中小企业如何进行成本核算？ How to conduct cost accounting in small and medium-sized businesses? / 221
18.7	Extended reading 延伸阅读 What is a relevant cost? 什么是相关成本？/ 222

Unit 1
What is accounting?
什么是会计？

Core terms reminder
核心术语提示

accounting	会计，会计学
unit of measurement	计量单位
account	账户，户头
document	文件，单证，凭证
accounting statement	会计报表
costing	成本核算
asset	资产
liability	责任，负债
owner's interest	所有者权益
profit	利润
income	收入
expense	费用

1.1a What is the definition of accounting?

会计的定义是什么？

Accounting, with a specific currency as its major **unit of measurement**, is the task of recording, calculating, controlling, analyzing and reporting the economic activities of a given **entity** / organization, with a view to providing financial and management information.

accounting n. 会计，会计学
unit of measurement 计量单位
entity n. 实体

1.1b What is the function of accounting?

会计的功能是什么？

The major function of accounting is to:
- reflect and control the process of economic activities
- ensure the legality, trueness, accuracy and integrity of accounting information

- provide necessary financial data for economic management
- participate in **decision-making** and pursue optimal benefit

decision-making 决策

1.1c What are the methods of accounting?

会计方法有哪些？

The major special methods used in accounting are:
- setting up the **account** and **account book**
- filling in and **auditing** the accounting **document**
- **double-entry bookkeeping**
- **costing**
- property inspection
- compiling **accounting statement**
- reviewing, checking and analyzing accounting data, etc.

account *n.* 账户，户头
account book 账簿
auditing *n.* 审计
document *n.* 文件，单证，凭证
double-entry bookkeeping
　复式簿记
costing *n.* 成本核算
accounting statement 会计报表

Figure 1 *Book-keeping*
图1　簿记

1.1d What is the accounting object?

什么是会计对象？

An **accounting object** means the content that is verified and monitored within the work scope of accounting. Specifically, it means the **movements of fund** represented in the routine operational activities of a business organization; namely, movements of fund constitute the content of accounting check and accounting monitoring.

accounting object 会计对象

movements of fund 资金运动

1.1e What are the accounting elements?

什么是会计要素？

The **accounting elements** are determined by the movement and nature of the accounting object; these roughly include six **components**:

accounting element 会计要素
component *n*. 成分，组成部分

- assets
- liabilities
- owner's interest
- profit
- income
- expense

asset *n*. 资产
liability *n*. 责任，负债
owner's interest 所有者权益
profit *n*. 利润
income *n*. 收入
expense *n*. 费用

The accounting elements do not always remain the same. They may vary with the different orientation of the accounting object. The setup of the accounting elements aims at providing a basis for confirmation, **measurement** and reporting of accounting.

measurement *n*. 计量

1.2 Core accounting terms
核心会计术语

- account [ə'kaunt] n. 账户，户头
- account book 账簿
- accounting [ə'kauntiŋ] n. 会计学，会计核算
- accounting element 会计要素
- accounting object 会计对象
- accounting statement 会计报表
- accuracy ['ækjurəsi] n. 准确
- asset ['æset] n. 资产
- auditing ['ɔ:ditiŋ] n. 审计
- component [kəm'pəunənt] n. 成分，组成部分
- costing ['kɔstiŋ] n. 成本核算
- decision-making 决策
- document ['dɔkjumənt] n. 文件，单证，凭证

- double-entry bookkeeping 复式簿记
- entity ['entiti] n. 实体
- expense [ik'spens] n. 费用
- income ['inkəm] n. 收入
- integrity [in'tegriti] n. 完整
- legality [li'gæliti] n. 合法
- liability [ˌlaiə'biliti] n. 责任，负债
- movement of fund 资金运动
- owner's interest 所有者权益
- profit ['prɔfit] n. 利润
- trueness ['tru:nis] n. 真实
- parties concerned 有关各方
- unit of measurement 计量单位

1.3 Extended words
扩展词汇

- analyze ['ænəlaiz] n. 分析
- calculate ['kælkjuleit] vt. 计算
- compile [kəm'pail] vt. 编辑，编写
- confirmation [ˌkɔnfə'meiʃən] n. 确认
- constitute ['kɔnstitju:t] vt. 构成
- controlling [kən'trəuliŋ] n. 控制
- currency ['kʌrənsi] n. 货币
- ensure [in'ʃuə] vt. 确保
- financial [fai'nænʃəl] n. 财政的，财务的
- given ['givn] a. 特定的，指定的

- inspection [in'spekʃən] n. 检查，视察
- monitor ['mɔnitə] vt. 监督
- orientation [ˌɔrien'teiʃən] n. 定位
- participate [pɑ:'tisipeit] vt. 参与
- process [prə'ses] n. 过程，程序
- property ['prɔpəti] n. 财产
- pursue [pə'sju:] vt. 追求，从事
- optimal ['ɔptiməl] a. 最佳的，最理想的
- providing a basis for 为……提供依据
- recording [ri'kɔ:diŋ] n. 记录

- **reflect** [ri'flekt] *vt.* 反映
- **represent** [ˌri:pri'zent] *vt.* 代表，表示
- **specific** [spi'sifik] *a.* 特定的，具体的
- **vary with** 因……而变化
- **verify** ['verifai] *vt.* 核实
- **with a view to** 目的是

1.4 Notes 注释

1) Accounting, with a specific currency as its major unit of measurement, is the task of recording, calculating, controlling, analyzing and reporting the economic activities of a given entity/organization, with a view to providing financial and management information. 会计是以货币为主要计量单位，对特定实体/组织的经济活动进行记录、计算、控制、分析、报告，以提供财务和管理信息的工作。

  a. with a specific currency as its major unit of measurement 是由介词 with 引导的短语，在句中做状语。

  b. a given entity/organization 特定的实体/组织。Given 在此处是形容词，意为"约定的；特定的；指定的"。如：

We have to finish repairing the computer within the given time.
我们要在指定时间内把电脑修好。

  c. with a view to 是介词短语，意为"目的是……，为了……"。注意短语中的"to"是介词，不是动词不定式，后面跟动词时需要用 V-ing 形式。如：

with a view to promoting sales
目的是促进销售

2) **reflect and control the process of economic activities** 反映和控制经济活动过程

3) **ensure the legality, trueness, accuracy and integrity of accounting information** 保证会计信息的合法、真实、准确和完整

4) **provide necessary financial data for economic management** 为管理经济提供必要的财务资料

5) **participate in decision-making and pursue optimal benefit** 参与决策并谋求最佳的经济效益

6) **An accounting object means the content that is verified and monitored within the work scope of accounting.** 会计对象就是指会计工作所要核算和监督的内容。

  that is...accounting 是由 that 引导的限定性定语从句，修饰前面的名词 content。

7) **Specifically, it means the movements of fund represented in the routine operational activities of a business organization.** 具体来说，会计对象是指业务单位在日常经营活动中所表现出的资金运动。

represented...organization 是过去分词短语，在句中做定语，修饰名词短语 movements of fund，相当于定语从句 which are represented...

8) **They may vary with the different orientation of the accounting object.** 它们（会计要素）会因会计目标定位不同而变化。

    vary with 是动词短语，意为"因……而变化"。如：
Vegetable prices vary with seasons. 蔬菜价格因季节不同而变化。

1.5 Reinforcement exercise
强化练习

1. Answer the following questions in English.

    1) What is accounting?
    2) What is the major function of accounting?
    3) What are the major special methods used in accounting?
    4) What is the accounting object?
    5) What are the accounting elements?

2. Put the following into Chinese.

    1) unit of measurement
    2) record, calculate, control, analyze and report
    3) financial and management information
    4) reflect the process of economic activities
    5) legality, trueness, accuracy and integrity
    6) financial data
    7) participate in decision-making
    8) pursue optimal benefit
    9) set up the account and account book
    10) audit the accounting document
    11) double-entry bookkeeping
    12) property inspection
    13) compile the accounting statement
    14) review, check and analyze
    15) accounting check and accounting monitoring
    16) accounting object

3. Put the following into English.

    1) 核对并监督   2) 资金的运动

3) 常规经营活动
4) 构成……的内容
5) 会计要素
6) 组成部分
7) 资产
8) 负债
9) 所有者权益
10) 利润
11) 收入
12) 费用
13) 会计学
14) 货币
15) 实体
16) 成本核算

4. Subject for self-study: An accounting chart.

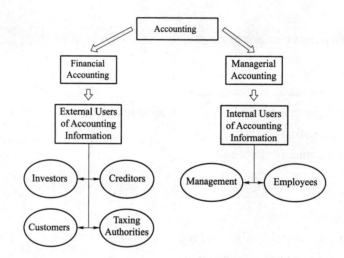

Reminder 提示

external [eks'tə:nl] *a.* 外部的
internal [in'tə:nl] *a.* 内部的
investor [in'vestə] *n.* 投资人
creditor ['kreditə] *n.* 债权人，贷方
taxing authorities 税务局

1.6 Accounting-related knowledge
会计相关知识介绍

什么是会计?
What is accounting?

会计是以货币作为主要计量单位（unit of measurement），对一定单位的经济业务进行计量、记录、汇总和分析（measurement, recording, gathering and analysis），向有关方面报导财务信息，并直接参与单位的经营管理，促使经济效益提高的一种经济信息系统和经济管理工作。

会计定义包含如下要点：首先，会计总是被用于"一定单位"，这个"一定单位"就是会计的主体。其次，会计是用来核算"经济业务"的，这个"经济业务"就是会计的客体，亦即会计对象（accounting object）。第三，会计对经济业务进行"计量、记录、汇总、分析和报导"，这就是会计的方法和程序（methods and process）。第四，会计主要采用货币计量尺度。第五，会计既向有关方面报导单位的财务信息，又参与单位的经营管理活动，这就是会计的主要职能。第六，会计既是一种经济信息系统，又是一种经济管理工作，这就是会计的本质属性。

会计是一种管理活动，是经济管理的重要组成部分。在商品货币经济条件下，它以货币为主要计量单位，并利用专门的方法和程序对单位的经济活动进行完整、连续、系统的反映和监督（reflect and monitor），旨在提供会计信息和提高经济效益。

1.7 Extended reading
延伸阅读

The five account types
五种账户类型

Double-entry accounting uses five — and only five — account types to record all the transactions that can possibly be recorded in an accounting system. There are sub-types of the following list, but all financial transactions can be recorded using these five types of accounts. The five account types are the following:

Balance sheet accounts

1. Assets   Things of value that are owned and used by the business.
2. Liabilities   Debts that are owed by the business.
3. Equity   The owner's claim to business assets.

Profit and loss accounts

4. Revenue   The amounts earned from the sale of goods and services.
5. Expenses   Costs incurred in the course of business.

You must select the proper account types when entering a transaction. Using an incorrect account type can result in a report that is incomplete or that makes no sense. The balance sheet accounts are permanent accounts that carry a balance from year to year, like checking accounts, accounts receivable, and inventory accounts. The profit and loss accounts are temporary accounts which track revenues and expenses for a yearlong fiscal period and are then closed, with balances transferred to an equity account. Using an asset, liability, or equity account type for a revenue or expense transaction will result in a report that is incorrect and improper.

Unit 2
How does the double-entry system work?
复式记账法的原理是什么?

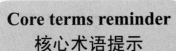
Core terms reminder
核心术语提示

double-entry bookkeeping	复式簿记,复式记账
credit	贷方
debit	借方
credit entry	贷方分录
debit entry	借方分录
ledger	分类账,总账
income statement	收益表

2.1a What is double-entry bookkeeping?

什么是复式记账？

Double-entry bookkeeping is an accounting technique which records each transaction as both a **credit** and a **debit**. **Credit entries** represent the sources of financing, and the **debit entries** represent the uses of that **financing**. Since each credit has one or more corresponding debits (and **vice versa**), the system of double-entry bookkeeping always leads to a set of balanced **ledger** credit and debit accounts. Selected entries from these ledger balances are then used to prepare the **income statement**.

double-entry bookkeeping 复式簿记，复式记账
credit n. 贷方
debit n. 借方
credit entry 贷方分录
debit entry 借方分录
financing n. 融资，筹集资金
vice versa <拉>反之亦然

ledger n. 分类账，总账

income statement 收益表

2.1b Why is double-entry system significant?

复式记账法的意义是什么？

In modern accounting the double-entry system serves as a kind of **error-detecting system**: if, at any point, the **sum** of debits does not equal the **corresponding** sum of credits, then an error has occurred.

It's easy for errors to **creep into** your financial records. It's easy to make mistakes when adding up **column** upon column of figures. Double-entry bookkeeping attempts to minimize these errors

error-detecting system 错误检查系统
sum n. 总数，和
corresponding a. 相应的

creep into 悄悄溜进

column n. 栏

Unit 2 How does the double-entry system work? 复式记账法的原理是什么? 13

by including each figure in two places, as a credit on one account and a debit on another: if the totals are in balance then you can have confidence that the calculations have been done correctly.

2.1c What categories do the books cover?
账簿包含哪些类别?

The financial books as a whole must cover the following financial categories:
- the value of goods owned by the business (**assets**)
- the **net worth** of (and **shareholders' interest** in) the company (**equity**)
- money owed (**liabilities**)
- money earned (**revenue**)
- costs (**expenses**)

asset *n.* 资产
net worth 净值
shareholders' interest 股东权益
equity *n.* 权益
liability *n.* 债务
revenue *n.* 收入
expense *n.* 费用

2.1d What are credits and debits?
什么是贷方和借方?

Credits and debits are easy to understand on a bank statement: a credit is money paid in and increases the **running total**, whereas a debit is a payment from the account and decreases it.

In your business records, the debit side, written on the left, represents the destination point of a transaction; the credit side, on the right, represents where the amount has come from. These are also called **T-accounts** because they look like a letter T with debits on the left and credits on the right.

running total 周转资金总额, 总流水

T-account "T"型账, "丁"字账

```
           Cash at Bank - Account
         DEBIT            |    CREDIT
Deposit          5,000    |
                          |  Payment        2,000
Closing Balance  3,000    |
```

Figure 1 *cash at Bank-Account*

图 1　现金银行账

（从图中可看出，借方[debit]在左边，贷方[credit]在右边，图中的两条线看上去像"T型标志"，故称为"T"型账。）

2.1e What are the advantages of the double-entry system?

复式记账法有什么优势？

The advantages of a double-entry bookkeeping system are:

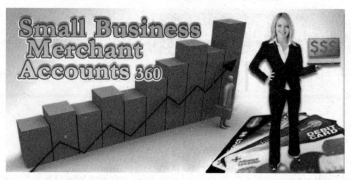

- It provides a specific means of making these **adjustments**.
- It allows you to make an **arithmetical** check on your records since the total of the debit entries must equal the total of the credit entries.
- Double entry records **form a stepping stone to** producing **annual accounts**, and can help save time and expense at the year end.
- The **financial position** of the business at any time point can be stated definitely.
- It can reduce the risk of, and help detect, any **errors** and even **fraud**.

adjustment *n.* 调整

arithmetical *a.* 算术的

form a stepping stone to 构成……的垫脚石

annual account 年度账

financial position 财务状况

error *n.* 错误，过失

fraud *n.* 欺骗，欺诈

2.1f How does double-entry bookkeeping work?
复式记账法的工作原理是什么？

As the name suggests, every transaction involves two equal and opposite entries — one DEBIT (Dr) and one CREDIT (Cr).

Total Drs should equal Crs, so it provides a **built-in error check**. Only **misclassifications** are missed — that is a Dr or Cr in the wrong place — or complete **omissions** of an entry.

We use T-accounts to record the entries — imagine them as the two opposite pages of a book.

Drs go on the left, Crs on the right. An easy way to remember this is the following diagram:

built-in 内置的
error check 错误核对
misclassification n. 误分类
omission n. 省略，忽略

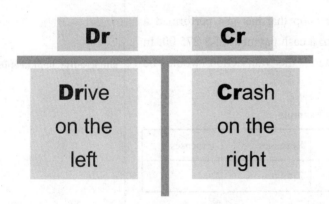

Figure 2 *Drive on the left. Crash on the right.*
图 2 左边开车。右边撞车

（本图用两个英文常用单词 drive 和 crash 的前两个字母 Dr 和 Cr 来分别表示两个会计专业词汇 debit(缩写 Dr)和 credit(缩写 Cr)。这样做是为了便于记忆左边为贷方，右边为借方的规则。）

For each transaction you must record —
- the receiving of a benefit by one account (the debit)

- the giving of a benefit by some other account (the credit)

Example:

Suppose you buy a **photocopier** for your business; the entries might be:

photocopier *n.* 复印机

- Debit

  Machinery and Equipment Account

  (the account receiving the benefit of the new machine)

- Credit

  Bank Account

  (the **credit-payments side** of the **cashbook**, the account giving the benefit in that money is flowing from it)

credit-payments side 贷付方（可单写为 credit side [贷方]和 payment side[付方]）

cashbook *n.* 现金簿

If all this seems a little **baffling** then remember the following:

baffling *a.* 令人困惑的
cash receipt 现金收入
cash payment 现金支付

Debits (left)	Credits (right)
Cash receipts	**Cash payments**
Expenses	Income
Assets	Liabilities

To illustrate, consider a repair shop that has just performed a repair service on January 4, 2010 for a cash payment of $ 275.00. In a **single-entry bookkeeping** system, the transaction would be recorded as follows:

single-entry bookkeeping 单式记账

Single Entry Example

Date	Description	Revenues	Expenses
Jan.4	Performed repair service	275.00	

In a double-entry bookkeeping system, the transaction would be recorded as follows:

Double Entry Example

Date	Accounts	Debit	Credit
Jan.4	Cash	275.00	
	Revenue		275.00

2.2 Core accounting terms
核心会计术语

- annual account 年度账
- cashbook *n.* 现金簿
- cash payment 现金支付
- cash receipt 现金收入
- asset *n.* 资产
- credit *n.* 贷方
- credit-payments side 贷付方
- credit entry 贷方分录
- credit side 贷方
- debit *n.* 借方
- debit entry 借方分录
- equity *n.* 权益
- financial position 财务状况

- financing *n.* 融资，筹集资金
- income statement 收益表
- ledger *n.* 分类账，总账
- liability *n.* 债务
- net worth 净值
- payment side 付方
- revenue *n.* 收入
- running total 周转资金总额，总流水
- shareholders' interest 股东权益
- single-entry bookkeeping 单式记账
- sum *n.* 总数，和
- T-account "T"型账，"丁"字账

2.3 Extended words
扩展词汇

- drive on the left 左边开车
- error *n.* 错误，过失
- adjustment *n.* 调整
- arithmetical *a.* 算术的
- baffling *a.* 令人困惑的
- built-in 内置的
- corresponding *a.* 相应的
- creep into 悄悄溜进
- column *n.* 栏
- crash on the right 右边撞车

- error check 错误核对
- error-detecting system 错误检查系统
- expense *n.* 费用
- form a stepping stone to 构成……的垫脚石
- fraud *n.* 欺骗，欺诈
- misclassification *n.* 误分类
- omission *n.* 省略，忽略
- photocopier *n.* 复印机
- vice versa <拉>反之亦然

2.4 Notes 注释

1) **Double-entry bookkeeping is an accounting technique which records each transaction as both a credit and a debit.** 复式记账是把每笔交易记录成贷方和借方的会计方法。

    句中 which…debit 引导一个限定性定语从句，修饰名词短语 accounting technique.

2) **Credit entries represent the sources of financing, and the debit entries represent the uses of that financing.** 贷方表示资金的来源，而借方表示这笔资金的使用。

3) **Selected entries from these ledger balances are then used to prepare the income statement.** 然后从这些分类平衡表中选择出的分录条目可用来准备收益表。

4) **In modern accounting the double-entry system serves as a kind of error-detecting system.** 在现代会计学中，复式记账法充当一种错误检查系统。

5) **if, at any point, the sum of debits does not equal the corresponding sum of credits, then an error has occurred.** 如果在任何一点上，借方之和不等于对应的贷方之和，就已经出现错误了。

6) **It's easy for errors to creep into your financial records.** 错误很容易在不知不觉中进入我们的账簿。

7) **We can make human mistakes when adding up column upon column of figures.** 在把一栏一栏的数字相加时，会出现人为的错误。

8) **Double-entry bookkeeping attempts to minimize these errors by including each figure in two places, as a credit on one account and a debit on another.** 通过把每个数字包含在两个地方,复式记账法试图把这些错误降低到最小程度。

9) **…if the totals are in balance then you can have confidence that the calculations have been done correctly.** 如果两个合计能够对上账，那么你完全可以放心，计算结果是正确的。

    句中 that 引导一个名词性从句，做名词 confidence 的同位语。

10) **the value of goods owned by the business (assets)** 企业所拥有的商品价值（资产）

11) **the net worth of (and shareholders' interest in) the company (equity)** 公司（以及股东权益）的净值（权益）

12) **money owed (liabilities)** 所欠的钱（债务）

13) **money earned (revenue)** 所挣得的钱（收入）

14) **costs (expenses)** 成本（费用）

Unit 2　How does the double-entry system work? 复式记账法的原理是什么?　19

15) **…a credit is money paid in and increases the running total, whereas a debit is a payment from the account and decreases it.** 贷方是指入账的钱，并增加总流水，而借方是从账上支付并减少总流水。

　　句中 whereas 是连词，表示"然而，尽管"。

16) **In your business records, the debit side, written on the left, represents the destination point of a transaction; the credit side, on the right, represents where the amount has come from.** 在你的企业账簿记录中，借方写在左侧，表示业务交易的目的点；贷方写在右侧，表示这笔钱从何处来。

　　句中 where…from 是宾语从句，做动词 represents 的宾语。

17) **These are also called T-accounts because they look like a letter T with debits on the left and credits on the right.** 这些被称为"T"型账，因为借方在左、贷方在右看上去像英文字母"T"。

18) **It provides a specific means of making these adjustments.** 复式记账提供做出调整的具体方法。

19) **It allows you to make an arithmetical check on your records since the total of the debit entries must equal the total of the credit entries.** 由于借方分录条目的合计必须等于贷方分录条目的合计，复式记账允许你对记账记录进行计算核对。

20) **Double entry records form a stepping stone to producing annual accounts, and can help save time and expense at the year end.** 复式记账记录成为制作年度账的垫脚石，并能够有助于在年底节省时间和费用。

21) **The financial position of the business at any time point can be stated definitely.** 企业在任何时间点的财务状况都能够得以明确地说明。

22) **It can reduce the risk of, and help detect, any errors and even fraud.** 它可以降低，并有助于检查错误甚至欺诈的风险。

23) **As the name suggests, every transaction involves two equal and opposite entries — one DEBIT (Dr) and one CREDIT (Cr).** 如其名称所示，每笔业务往来都涉及两个同等并相反的分录条目———一个"借方"（Dr）条目和一个"贷方"条目（Cr）。

24) **Total Drs should equal Crs, so it provides a built-in error check.** 借方总计应当等于贷方总计，因此它提供了内置的错误核对机制。

25) **Only misclassifications are missed — that is a Dr or Cr in the wrong place — or complete omissions of an entry.** 只有误分类的情况才会出现误算———也就是指一个分录条目的借贷方放错地方或完全漏录。

26) **We use T-accounts to record the entries — imagine them as the two opposite pages of a book.** 我们用"T"型账来记录各个分录条目———可以把它们想象成一本书的两张对开页面。

27) **For each transaction you must record — the receiving of a benefit by one account (the debit), and the giving of a benefit by some other account (the credit).** 每笔业务往来都必须记录接受收益的账（借方）以及另一个给出收益的账（贷方）。

28) **Debit: Machinery and Equipment Account (the account receiving the benefit of the new**

machine) 借方："机器设备账"（接受机器收益的账）

29) **Credit: Bank Account (the credit-payments side of the cashbook, the account giving the benefit in that money is flowing from it)** 贷方："银行账"（现金簿的借付方，亦即从该账上流出资金、给出收益的账）

30) **To illustrate, consider a repair shop that has just performed a repair service on January 4, 2010 for a cash payment of $ 275.00.** 为了加以说明，我们来看看一家修理店，它刚刚在 2010 年 1 月 4 日做了一次修理服务，收费 275 美元。

句中 that has…$ 275 是限定性定语从句，修饰其前的名词短语 repair shop。

2.5 Reinforcement exercise
强化练习

1. Answer the following questions in English.

1) What is double-entry bookkeeping?
2) Why is double-entry bookkeeping significant?
3) What categories do financial books cover?
4) What are credits and debits?
5) What are the advantages of the double-entry system?
6) How does double-entry bookkeeping work?

2. Put the following into Chinese.

1) liability
2) revenue
3) expense
4) running total
5) T-account
6) money paid in
7) destination point of a transaction
8) make an arithmetical check
9) form a stepping stone to
10) annual account
11) financial position
12) error and fraud
13) built-in error check
14) misclassification
15) cashbook
16) cash receipt
17) cash payment
18) double-entry bookkeeping

3. Put the following into English.

1) 贷方和借方
2) 贷方分录
3) 借方分录
4) 融资，筹集资金
5) 一个或多个对应的借方
6) <拉>反之亦然
7) 分类账，总账
8) 收益表
9) 错误检查系统
10) 贷方之和
11) 把每个数字包含在两处
12) 资产
13) 净值
14) 股东权益
15) 权益
16) 单式记账

4. Subject for self-study: Two bookkeeping examples.

Single Entry Example

Date	Description	Revenues	Expenses
Jan.4	Performed repair service	275.00	

Double Entry Example

Date	Accounts	Debit	Credit
Jan.4	Cash	275.00	
	Revenue		275.00

Reminder 提示

description [disˈkripʃən] *n.* 描写, 记述
perform [pəˈfɔːm] *vt.* 履行, 执行
repair service 修理服务

2.6 Accounting-related knowledge
会计相关知识介绍

复式记账法的记账规则
Bookkeeping rules of the double-entry system

所谓记账规则（bookkeeping rules），就是指记录经济业务时所应遵循的规则。运用借贷记账法（debit-credit bookkeeping）登记经济业务时，首先应根据经济业务的内容，确定它所

涉及的资产（assets）、负债（liabilities）和所有者权益（owner's interest）的变动是增加还是减少；然后，确定应将其记入有关账户的借方（credit）或贷方（debit）。

例1：企业从银行存款中提取现金500元。

这项经济业务的发生，使企业的库存现金（cash on hand）这一资产项目增加了500元，银行存款（bank deposit）这一资产项目减少了500元。因此，它涉及"现金账"（cash account）和"银行存款账"（bank deposit account）这两个账户，应登记在"现金"账户的借方和"银行存款"账户的贷方。

例2：企业从银行借入资金1 000元，归还以前所欠的应付账款。

这项经济业务的发生，使企业的短期借款（short-term loan）项目增加了1 000元，应付账款（account payable）这一项目相应地减少了1 000元。因此，它涉及"短期借款"和"应付账款"这两个账户，应登记在"短期借款"账户的贷方和"应付账款"账户的借方。

例3：企业用银行存款归还银行短期借款20 000元。

这项经济业务的发生，使企业的银行存款减少了20 000元，相应地使企业的短期借款减少了20 000元。因此，它涉及资产类"银行存款"和负债类"短期借款"这两个账户，应登记在"银行存款"账户的贷方和"短期借款"账户的借方。

总之，运用借贷记账法记账，要求对发生的每一笔经济业务，都要以相等的金额，借贷相反的方向，在两个或两个以上相互联系的账户中进行连续（continuous）、分类的登记（classified recording）。即记入一个账户的借方，同时记入一个或几个账户的贷方；或者记入一个账户的贷方，同时记入一个或几个账户的借方。记入借方的金额（the amount entered in the debit side）与记入贷方的金额（the amount entered in the credit side）必须相等。概括地说，"有借必有贷，借贷必相等"（Where there is a debit entry, there must be a credit entry; the debit entry and the credit entry must be equal.）

2.7 Extended reading
延伸阅读

The pros and cons of double-entry
复式记账的正反面争论

The single entry method of bookkeeping, whilst adequate for many purposes, will be incomplete and have shortcomings if your business grows. By contrast the double entry method of bookkeeping is a complete method. It overcomes the shortcomings, but it may be more than is needed by many small businesses.

Unit 2　How does the double-entry system work?　复式记账法的原理是什么?

Double-entry bookkeeping has been around for many years; in fact the first known work on this subject was published in the reign of Henry VII in 1494. The modern system of double-entry bookkeeping was first put into general use by Italian merchants at a time when Venice and other cities of northern Italy were Europe's main trading centres.

Drawbacks of single entry

In the single entry method you only need to make one entry to record each transaction. This system has several shortcomings. A major one is that it is hard to tell how much was spent on a particular expense (for example, motor expenses) in a given year. One way partly to overcome this is to use an analyzed cash book, but even this does not fully deal with the problem. The analyzed cash book doesn't record the amounts owing at the beginning and end of the year, only those actually paid within the year.

For example, if at the beginning of the year $130 was owed for goods delivered in the last month of the previous year, then the payments that you make during the year will include this amount. Likewise if at the end of the year $165 is owed for goods, this will not have been included in the payments made. To arrive at the correct figure of expenditure for the year, the figure of payment therefore has to be adjusted.

Advantages of double entry

The advantages of a double-entry bookkeeping system are:
- It provides a specific means of making these adjustments.
- It allows you to make an arithmetical check on your records since the total of the debit entries must equal the total of the credit entries.
- Using the personal ledgers, amounts owed by or to each person with whom you trade can be worked out easily.
- Double entry records form a stepping stone to producing annual accounts, and can help save time and expense at the year end.
- The financial position of the business at any point in time can be stated definitely.
- It can reduce the risk of, and help detect, any errors and even fraud.

Unit 3

How to compile the accounting documents?
如何编制会计凭证?

Core terms reminder
核心术语提示

accounting document	会计凭证
original document	原始凭证
bookkeeping voucher	记账凭证
bill of document	单据
cash deposit slip	现金存款单
receiving voucher	收款凭证
paying voucher	付款凭证
transfer voucher	转账凭证

3.1a What is accounting document?
什么是会计凭证？

The **accounting document** is a written proof that records a business transaction, identifies financial responsibilities and serves as the basis of bookkeeping. The accounting document includes **original document** and **bookkeeping voucher**.

accounting document 会计凭证
（亦作 accounting evidence）
original document 原始凭证
bookkeeping voucher 记账凭证

3.1b How to classify the accounting documents?
如何为会计凭证分类？

There are various types of accounting documents which can be classified by different aspects. However, these can, in terms of purpose, be classified into original document and bookkeeping voucher.

The original documents, known as **bill of document**, are the written evidences that record and prove a business transaction that has **occurred** or has been completed. They are the original basis on which accounting rests. These original documents, usually acquired and filled in at the time of business transaction, record a large amount

bill of document 单据

occur *vi.* 发生

of financial information. Therefore they carry strong legal effect and are important documents.

Invoices, **receipts**, **expense account for business travels**, **cash deposit slip** etc. are all examples of original documents.

The bookkeeping voucher is a kind of document which the accounting staff members compile after they have looked through the financial content of the original documents. The original documents come from different aspects and indicate the detailed content of a business transaction. There are various kinds and different formats for them, which means they cannot meet the requirements of bookkeeping if they are not carefully **collected** and organized. Therefore compiling the original documents into bookkeeping voucher can ensure the accuracy of book records.

The bookkeeping voucher includes **receiving voucher**, **paying voucher** and **transfer voucher**.

invoice n. 发票
receipt n. 收据
expense account for business travels 差旅费用账目
cash deposit slip 现金存款单

collect vt. 收集

receiving voucher 收款凭证
paying voucher 付款凭证
transfer voucher 转账凭证

3.1c How to compile the accounting documents?
如何编制会计凭证？

In compiling the accounting document, different companies may follow a different **approach**. However, the following points are the general **work flow** which applies to most organizations.

- **Determine** the scope of usage for the receiving voucher and paying voucher.
- Fill in the **relevant** information correctly, including date, item, brief description of a business transaction, amount that occurred during the transaction, number of sheets of the document, etc.
- **Glue** the sheets together for future reference.
- Make sure the handwriting is **legible**.

approach n. 途径
work flow 工作流程
determine vt. 决定，确定

relevant a. 相应的

glue vt. 黏合
legible a. 清晰的，易读的

3.1d Why are the accounting documents significant?

会计凭证有什么意义？

The accounting documents are important documents which records an organization's business transactions. They are significant for a company's financial management in that:

- They record the **occurrence** and **completion** of a transaction and provide original basis for accounting.
- They review the **truthfulness**, **legitimacy** and **rationality** of a transaction and provide important basis for accounting supervision.
- They identify the financial responsibilities
- They reflect the relevant relationship of economic interest and provide proof for **safeguarding** one's **legitimate interest**.

occurrence *n.* 发生
completion *n.* 完成
truthfulness *n.* 真实性
legitimacy *n.* 合法性
rationality *n.* 合理性

safeguard *vt.* 保护
legitimate interest 合法权益

3.2 Core accounting terms

核心会计术语

- ☐ **accounting document** 会计凭证（亦作 accounting evidence）
- ☐ **bill of document** 单据
- ☐ **bookkeeping document** 记账凭证
- ☐ **cash deposit slip** 现金存款单
- ☐ **expense account for business travels** 差旅费用账目
- ☐ **invoice** ['invɔis] *n.* 发票
- ☐ **legitimate interest** 合法权益
- ☐ **original document** 原始凭证
- ☐ **paying voucher** 付款凭证
- ☐ **receipt** [ri'si:t] *n.* 收据
- ☐ **receiving voucher** 收款凭证
- ☐ **transfer voucher** 转账凭证

3.3 Extended words
扩展词汇

- **approach** [əˈprəutʃ] *vt.* 收集
- **collect** [kəˈlekt] *vt.* 收集
- **completion** [kəmˈpli:ʃn] *n.* 完成
- **determine** [diˈtə:min] *vt.* 决定，确定
- **glue** [glu:] *n.* 胶水 *vt.* 黏合
- **legible** [ˈledʒəbl] *a.* 清晰的，易读的
- **legitimacy** [l iˈdʒitiməsi] *n.* 合法性
- **occur** [əˈkə:] *vi.* 发生
- **occurrence** [əˈkʌrəns] *n.* 发生
- **rationality** [ˌræʃəˈnæliti] *n.* 合理性
- **receipt** [riˈsi:t] *n.* 收据
- **relevant** [ˈrelivənt] *a.* 相应的
- **safeguard** [ˈseifˌɡɑ:d] *vt.* 保护
- **truthfulness** [ˈtru:θfulnis] *n.* 真实性
- **work flow** 工作流程

3.4 Notes
注释

1) **The accounting document is a written proof that records a business transaction, identifies financial responsibilities and serves as the basis of bookkeeping.** 会计凭证是记录业务交易、明确经济责任并作为记账依据的书面证明。

   句中 that records…bookkeeping 是由 that 引导的定语从句，修饰前面的名词性短语 written proof。

2) **There are various types of accounting documents which can be classified by different aspects.** 会计凭证是多种多样的，可以按照不同的标志进行分类。

   句中 which 引导一个限定性定语从句，修饰 accounting documents。

3) **The original documents, known as bill of document, are the written evidences that record and prove a business transaction that has occurred or has been completed.** 原始凭证，俗称单据，是用以记录、证明经济业务已经发生或完成的书面证据，是进行会计核算的原始依据。

   本句中有两个由 that 引导的从句，两个均为定语从句，其中 that record and proof…修饰名词性短语 written evidences，而 that has occurred…completed 修饰 business transaction。

4) **The bookkeeping voucher is a kind of document which the accounting staff members compile after they have looked through the financial content of the original documents.** 记账凭证，是会计人员根据审核后的原始凭证的经济内容而编制的一种凭证。

句中 which 引导一个定语从句，修饰名词 document。

5) **Determine the scope of usage for the receiving voucher and the paying voucher.** 确定收款凭证和付款凭证的使用范围。
6) **Fill in the relevant information correctly, including date, item, brief description of a business transaction, amount that occurred during the transaction, number of sheets of the document, etc.** 正确填写相关的信息，包括日期、项目、业务交易的简要介绍、交易时发生的金额、凭证页数等。
7) **Glue the sheets together for future reference.** 将凭证单粘在一起用于将来参考。
8) **Make sure the handwriting is legible.** 确保字迹清晰。
9) **They record the occurrence and completion of a transaction and provide original basis for accounting.** 它们（会计凭证）可以记录经济业务的发生和完成情况，为会计核算提供原始依据。
10) **They review the truthfulness, legitimacy and rationality of a transaction and provide important basis for accounting supervision.** 它们（会计凭证）可以检查经济业务的真实性、合法性和合理性，为会计监督提供重要依据。
11) **They identify the financial responsibilities.**（它们）可以明确经济责任。
12) **They reflect the relevant relationship of economic interest and provide proof for safeguarding one's legitimate interest.** 它们可以反映相关经济利益关系，为维护合法权益提供法律证据。

3.5 Reinforcement exercise
强化练习

1. Answer the following questions in English.

1) What is accounting document?
2) How do we classify the accounting documents?
3) What are original documents?
4) What is the bookkeeping voucher?
5) How to compile the accounting documents?
6) Why are the accounting documents significant?

2. Put the following into Chinese.

1) accounting document
2) original document
3) bookkeeping document
4) bill of document
5) written evidences
6) original basis

7) legal effect
8) invoice
9) receipt
10) expense account for business travels

3. Put the following into English.

1) 现金存款单
2) 审查
3) 财务内容
4) 收集和整理
5) 确保账簿记录的准确性
6) 收款凭证
7) 付款凭证
8) 转账凭证
9) 经济利益
10) 合法权益

4. Subject for self-study: An accounting chart.

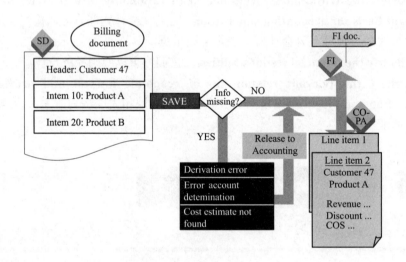

header [ˈhedə] *n.* 标题
derivation [deriˈveiʃən] *n.* 出处，来历
line item 排列项

3.6 Accounting-related knowledge
会计相关知识介绍

记账凭证的种类
Types of bookkeeping vouchers

记账凭证按其适用的经济业务，分为专用记账凭证和通用记账凭证两类。

（一）专用记账凭证（special bookkeeping voucher）

用来专门记录某一类经济业务的记账凭证。专用凭证按其所记录的经济业务是否与现金和银行存款的收付有无关系，又分为收款凭证、付款凭证和转账凭证三种。

1. 收款凭证（receiving voucher）

用于记录库存现金和银行存款收款业务的会计凭证。它是根据有关现金和银行存款收入业务的原始凭证（original voucher）填制的，是登记现金日记账、银行存款日记账以及有关明细账和总账等账簿的依据，也是出纳人员收讫款项的依据。

2. 付款凭证（paying voucher）

用于记录库存现金和银行存款付款业务的会计凭证。它是根据有关现金和银行存款支付业务的原始凭证填制的，是登记现金日记账、银行存款日记账以及有关明细账和总账等账簿的依据，也是出纳人员付讫款项的依据。

Petty Cash Voucher

Account .... Date .... / .... / ....

Amount ....

For ....

....

Signature ....

$ ......

A sample petty cash voucher
小额现金记账凭证样本

3. 转账凭证（transfer voucher）

用于记录不涉及库存现金和银行存款业务的会计凭证。它是根据有关转账业务的原始凭证填制的。转账凭证是登记总分类账及有关明细分类账的依据。

（二）通用记账凭证（general bookkeeping voucher）

用来记录各种经济业务的记账凭证。在经济业务比较简单的经济单位，为了简化凭证可以使用通用记账凭证，记录所发生的各种经济业务。

记账凭证按其包括的会计科目是否单一，分为复式记账凭证和单式记账凭证两类。

\multicolumn{4}{c}{Petty Cash Reconciliation}
Date	Item	Paid In	Paid Out
19-- April 1	Fund established	10.00	
5	Postage		1.00
9	Pens for office		2.00
13	Register tape-store		2.50
19	Repair-office equip		3.00
28	Paper clips-office		1.25
Total		10.00	9.75
Cash remaining			.25
		10.00	10.00

A petty cash reconciliation statement
小额现金对账表

1. 复式凭证（double-entry voucher）

将每一笔经济业务事项所涉及的全部会计科目及其发生额均在同一张记账凭证中反映的一种凭证。优点是可以集中反映一项经济业务的科目对应关系，便于了解有关经济业务的全貌，减少凭证数量，节约纸张等。缺点是不便于汇总计算每一个会计科目的发生额。

2. 单式凭证（single-entry voucher）

每一张记账凭证只填列经济业务事项所涉及的一个会计科目及其金额的记账凭证。

优点为内容单一，便于汇总计算每一会计科目的发生额，便于分工记账。

缺点为制证工作量大，且不能在一张凭证上反映经济业务的全貌，内容分散，也不便于查账。

（三）记账凭证的基本内容

1. 记账凭证的名称
2. 填制记账凭证的日期

3. 记账凭证的编号
4. 经济业务事项的内容摘要
5. 经济业务事项所涉及的会计科目及其记账方向
6. 经济业务事项的金额
7. 记账标记
8. 所附原始凭证张数
9. 会计主管、记账、审核、出纳、制单等有关人员的签章

3.7 Extended reading
延伸阅读

Accounting and accountants
会计学和会计师

To put it simply, accounting is about keeping track of the money. Accounting is how businesses monitor income, expenses, and assets over a given period of time. Accounting often is referred to as "the language of business" because of its role in maintaining and processing all relevant financial information that an entity or company requires for its managing and reporting purposes. Accounting is a field of specialization critical to the functioning of all types of organizations.

Accounting is also a body of principles and conventions, as well as an established general process for capturing financial information related to an organization's resources. Accounting is a service function that provides information of value to all operating units and to other service functions, such as the headquarters offices of a large corporation.

Accountants learn about accounting and engage in a wide variety of activities besides the basic bookkeeping of preparing financial statements and recording business transactions. Accountants also compute costs and efficiency gains from new technologies, participate in strategies for mergers and acquisitions, quality management, develop and use information systems to track financial performance, tax strategy, and health care benefits management. Good accountants are vital to a company's success.

Unit 4
What is a balance sheet?
什么是资产负债表？

Core terms reminder
核心术语提示

balance sheet	资产负债表
current asset	流动资产
current liability	流动负债
liability	责任，负债
inventory	库存，存货
account receivable	应收账
account payable	应付账
liquidation	清算
short term debt	短期借款
sales tax payable	应付税金

4.1a What is a balance sheet?
什么是资产负债表？

For an individual person, he can clearly calculate how much **property** he has as long as he lists all the items he owns less the money he owes to others. His **net asset** is what he owns minus what he owes. The same situation also applies to an organization though it often appears more **extensive** in scale and more complex in content.

property *n.* 财产
net asset 净资产

extensive *a.* 广泛的

A **balance sheet** is a kind of accounting statement which lists and displays all the items (assets) an organization owns and the total amount of money it owes (liabilities) at a certain time point (e.g. as ended June 30, 2009). It lists all items of an organization at a certain time as per the **correlation** between assets, liabilities and **owners' interest** (or **shareholders' interest**).

A balance sheet is a **static** accounting statement.

balance sheet 资产负债表

correlation *n.* 相互关系
owners' interest 所有者权益
shareholders' interest 股东权益
static *a.* 静态的

4.1b What is the purpose of a balance sheet?

资产负债表的目的是什么？

A balance sheet provides the **panorama** of assets, liabilities and owners' interest, providing the total amount of assets at a given time and indicating the financial resources owned or controlled by an organization as well as their **distribution**. It serves as important information for analyzing an organization's production and operation **capacity**.

panorama *n.* 全景，全景画

distribution *n.* 分配

capacity *n.* 容量，能力

Balance sheet

Assets		
Cash	$	9 000
Accounts receivable	$	10 500
Inventory	$	300 000
Total assets	$	319 500
Liabilities		
Short term debt	$	10 200
Accounts payable	$	20 400
Sales tax payable	$	30 100
Bank loan due	$	15 000
Total liabilities	$	75 700
Owner's equity	$	8 000
Total liabilities and owner's equity	$	83 700

Figure 1 *A sample balance sheet*
图 1 资产负债样表

4.1c How do we look at a balance sheet?
如何看待资产负债表？

The basic structure of a balance sheet is —
Asset = liabilities + owners' interest

Whatever status an organization is in, this accounting **equation** always remains **identical**. The left side reflects the resources it owns; the right side reflects the claims that various **obligees** may make to such resources.

equation *n.* 等式
identical *a.* 同一的，恒等的
obligee *n.* 权力人，债权人

4.1d What are assets, liabilities and owners' interest?
什么是资产、负债及所有者权益？

Assets are **substantiated** economic benefit or service potential which can, at present or in the future, be measured with a currency. Assets are classified as fixed assets and current assets.

Fixed assets are those assets acquired by an organization for its

asset *n.* 资产
substantiate *vt.* 使具体化

fixed assets 固定资产

own use. Fixed assets are usually not for sale and are used for a considerable length of time. Land, buildings, equipment, vehicles are examples of fixed assets.

Current assets are those assets that an organization does not intend to hold for more than a year. **Inventories**, **accounts receivable** and cash are examples of current assets.

Liabilities are what an organization owes. **Liquidation** of such liabilities leads to outflow of resources (or shrinkage of assets). Liabilities include **current liabilities** and other liabilities.

In popular terms, owners' interest is the economic interest that the owners enjoy with regard to an organization's asset. Its sum is the **balance** of assets minus liabilities. In Britain, the term "net assets" (or "**net worth**" in the States) is often used to **denote** the owners' interest.

current assets 流动资产
inventory n. 库存
accounts receivable 应收账目
liability n. 责任，负债
liquidation n. 清算
current liabilities 流动负债
in popular terms 通俗地讲
balance n. 平衡，余额
net worth 资产净值
denote vt. 指示，表示

4.2 Core accounting terms
核心会计术语

- **accounts receivable** 应收账目
- **asset** ['æset] n. 资产
- **balance** ['bæləns] n. 平衡，余额
- **balance sheet** 资产负债表
- **current assets** 流动资产
- **current liabilities** 流动负债
- **fixed assets** 固定资产
- **inventory** ['invəntri] n. 库存
- **liability** [,laiə'biliti] n. 责任，负债
- **liquidation** [,likwi'deiʃən] n. 清算
- **net asset** 净资产
- **net worth** 资产净值
- **obligee** ['ɔblidʒi:] n. 权力人，债权人
- **owners' interest** 所有者权益
- **shareholders' interest** 股东权益

4.3 Extended words
扩展词汇

- **capacity** [kə'pæsiti] n. 容量，能力
- **correlation** [,kɔri'leiʃən] n. 相互关系
- **denote** vt. 指示，表示
- **distribution** [,distri'bju:ʃən] n. 分配
- **equation** [i'kweiʃən] n. 等式
- **extensive** [iks'tensiv] a. 广泛的

Unit 4　What is a balance sheet?　什么是资产负债表?　　39

- **identical** [aiˈdentikəl] *a.* 同一的，恒等的
- **in popular terms** 通俗地讲
- **inventory** [ˈinvəntri] *n.* 库存
- **panorama** [ˌpænəˈrɑːmə] *n.* 全景，全景画
- **property** [ˈprɔpəti] *n.* 财产
- **static** [ˈsteitik] *a.* 静态的
- **substantiate** [sʌbsˈtænʃieit] *vt.* 使具体化

4.4　Notes　注释

1) **For an individual person, he can clearly calculate how much property he has as long as he lists all the items he owns less the money he owes to others.** 对于个人来说，只要能列出他所拥有的所有物品以及他欠别人的，他就可以清楚地计算出他拥有多少财产。

 a. 本句出现了三个从句，how much property he has 是宾语从句，做动词 calculate 的宾语；he owns 是定语从句，其前省略了关系词 that，修饰先行词 items；而 he owes to others 也是省略关系词 that 的定语从句，修饰先行词 money。

 b. less 在这里是介词，意为"减去"。如：

 （1）Five less two is three. 五减二等于三。

 （2）a year less two days 一年差两天

2) **A balance sheet is a kind of accounting statement which lists and displays all the items (assets) an organization owns and the total amount of money it owes (liabilities) at a certain time point (e.g. as ended June 30, 2009).** 资产负债表是一种会计报表，它列出并显示在某个时间点（如截至 2009 年 6 月 30 日）企业所拥有的所有物品（资产）以及所欠的总金额（负债）。

 句中 which lists…point 是定语从句，修饰先行词 statement。需要注意的是，该从句中又包含另外两个省略关系词 that 的定语从句，即 (that) an organization owns 和 (that) it owes，分别修饰其前的先行词 items 和 money。

3) **It lists all items of an organization at a certain time as per the correlation between assets, liabilities and owners' interest (or shareholders' interest).** 它根据资产、负债以及所有者权益（或股东权益）之间的相互关系列出了企业的所有项目。

 as per 意为"按照，依照"，是常用的商务英语，相当于 according to，如：

 a. We shall deliver the goods as per the date set in the agreement.

 我们将根据协议书中所确定的日期交货。

 b. As per our telephone conversation, I am forwarding you our product catalogues.

 根据我们的电话谈话，我现在把我方的产品目录传给您。

4) **A balance sheet provides the panorama of assets, liabilities and owners' interest, providing the total amount of assets at a given time and indicating the financial resources owned or controlled by an organization as well as their distribution.** 资产负债表提供了资产、负债、所有者权益的全貌，它提供了某一日期资产的总额，表明企业拥有或控制的经济资源及其分布情况。

  a. providing 和 indicating 均为 V-ing 形式引导的伴随性状语。

  b. owned or controlled…distribution 是过去分词短语，在句中做定语，修饰前面的名词性词组 financial resources.

5) **Whatever status an organization is in, this accounting equation always remains identical.** 不论公司处于怎样的状态，这个会计平衡式永远是恒等的。

  Whatever status an organization is in 是状语从句，相当于 No matter what status…in. 在英语语法中，由 whatever, whoever, whenever 等词引导的从句均可以用 no matter what (who, when)来替代。如：

a. Whoever you are, you have to obey the rules.

不管你是谁，你都得遵守规则。

（参照：No matter who you are…）

b. Just contact me whenever you feel like it.

你想联系我的时候就联系我吧。

（参照：…no matter when you feel like it.）

6) **The left side reflects the resources it owns; the right side reflects the claims that various obligees may make to such resources.** 左边反映的是公司所拥有的资源；右边反映的是公司的不同权利人对这些资源的要求。

  本句有两个定语从句，前一个是 it owns，前面省略关系词 that，修饰先行词 resources；后一个是 that…resources，修饰先行词 claims。

7) **Assets are substantiated economic interest or service potential which can, at present or in the future, be measured with a currency.** 资产是现在或未来可以用货币单位计量的经济利益或服务潜力的具体化。

  Which 在句中引导一个定语从句，修饰先行词 economic interest or service potential。

8) **Its sum is the balance of assets minus liabilities.** 其金额为资产减去负债后的余额。

  句中 minus 是介词，和前文中出现的 less 相同，也是"减去"的意思。

4.5 Reinforcement exercise

强化练习

1. Answer the following questions in English.

1) What is a balance sheet?   2) What is the purpose of a balance sheet?

3) How do we look at a balance sheet?
4) What are assets?
5) What are fixed assets? Give examples.
6) What are current assets? Give examples.
7) What are liabilities?
8) What is owner's interest?

2. Put the following into Chinese.

1) property
2) extensive in scale
3) complex in content
4) assets
5) fixed assets
6) current assets
7) liabilities
8) owners' interest (or shareholders' interest)
9) financial resources
10) production and operation capacity
11) accounting equation
12) obligee
13) substantiated economic benefit
14) service potential

3. Put the following into English.

1) 土地、建筑物、设备、车辆
2) 库存
3) 应收账
4) 清算
5) 资源外流
6) 资产缩水
7) 流动负债及其他负债
8) 经济利益
9) 资产减去负债的余额
10) 净资产（净值）

4. Subject for self-study: A sample balance sheet.

Balance sheet

Assets

Cash	$	9 000
Accounts receivable	$	10 500
Inventory	$	300 000
Total assets	$	**319 500**

Liabilities

Short term debt	$	10 200
Accounts payable	$	20 400
Sales tax payable	$	30 100
Bank loan due	$	15 000
Total liabilities	$	**75 700**
Owner's equity	$	**8 000**
Total liabilities and owner's equity	$	**83 700**

accounts receivable 应收账
inventory ['invəntri] *n.* 库存
total assets 总资产
short term debt 短期债务
accounts payable 应付账
sales tax payable 应付销售税
due [dju:] *a.* 应付的
bank loan due 应付银行贷款
total liabilities 总负债
equity ['ekwiti] *n.* （股东）利益，权益
owner's equity 所有者权益

4.6 Accounting-related knowledge
会计相关知识介绍

资产负债表
A balance sheet

资产负债表（balance sheet）是反映企业在某一特定日期财务状况的报表。由于它反映的是某一时点的情况，所以，又称为静态报表（static statement）。资产负债表主要提供有关企业财务状况（financial position）方面的信息。通过资产负债表，可以提供某一日期资产的总额（total assets）及其结构（structure），表明企业拥有或控制的资源及其分布情况，即有多少资源是流动资产（current assets）、有多少资源是长期投资（long-term assets）、有多少资源是固定资产（fixed assets）等；可以提供某一日期的负债总额（total liabilities）及其结构，表明企业未来需要用多少资产或劳务清偿债务以及清偿时间，即流动负债有多少、长期负债有多少、长期负债中有多少需要用当期流动资金进行偿还等；可以反映所有者（owner）所拥有的权益（interest），据以判断资本保值、增值的情况以及对负债的保障程度。

资产负债表的主要内容
1. 资产（assets）
按资产的流动性大小不同，分为流动资产和非流动资产（non-current assets）两类。

流动资产类由货币资金、交易性金融资产、应收账款、预付账款、其他应收款、存货和待摊费用等项目组成。非流动资产类由可供出售金融资产、长期股权投资、固定资产、无形资产和长期待摊费用等项目组成。

2. 负债（liabilities）

按负债的流动性不同，分为流动负债和非流动负债（non-current liabilities）两类。

流动负债类由短期借款、应付账款、预收账款、应付职工薪酬、应交税费、应付股利、其他应付款、预提费用等项目组成。非流动负债类由长期借款和应付债券组成。

3. 所有者权益（owner's interest）

按所有者权益的来源不同，由实收资本、资本公积、盈余公积和未分配利润等项目组成。

4.7 Extended reading
延伸阅读

Current liabilities
流动负债

In accounting, current liabilities are considered liabilities of the business that are to be settled in cash within the fiscal year or the operating cycle, whichever period is longer.

An operating cycle is the average time that is required to go from cash to cash in producing revenues.

For example, accounts payable for goods, services or supplies that were purchased for use in the operation of the business and payable within a normal period of time would be current liabilities.

Bonds, mortgages and loans that are payable over a term exceeding one year would be fixed liabilities or long-term liabilities. However, the payments due on the long-term loans in the current fiscal year could be considered current liabilities if the amounts were material.

The proper classification of liabilities is essential when considering a true picture of an organization's fiscal health.

Unit 5
The format of a balance sheet
资产负债表的格式

Core terms reminder
核心术语提示

report-type balance sheet	报告式资产负债表
account-type balance sheet	账户式资产负债表
annual balance sheet	年度资产负债表
net receivables	净应收账
total equity	总权益
preferred stock equity	优先股权益
common stock equity	普通股权益
plant and equipment	厂房和设备
accumulated depreciation	累计折旧

5.1a The heading and the body
表首和正表

The format of a balance sheet may vary with such factors as nature of an organization, the trade it is in, its objectives, **among others**. **Nevertheless**, a balance sheet generally consists of two parts: the **heading** and the **body**.

The heading summarizes name of statement, the compiling organization, date, **serial number**, name of currency, **unit of measurement** and so on.

The body is the **principal part** of a balance sheet. It lists and displays **each and every** item that accounts for the financial position of an organization. There are generally two types of format for the body of a balance sheet: the report-type balance sheet and account-type balance sheet.

among others 除了别的以外，其中
nevertheless ad. 尽管如此，不过
heading n. 标题，表首
body n. 主体，正文，正表

serial number 序号，编号
unit of measurement 计量单位
principal a. 主要的
principal part 主要部分，主体
each and every 每一个

5.1b The report-type balance sheet
报告式资产负债表

The **report-type balance sheet** (Figure 1) adopts the **upper and lower structure**. The upper half lists and displays the assets, while the lower half liabilities and owner's equity. There are two types of the specific arrangement of statement: The first type is arranged on the basis of the principle of "*assets = liabilities + owner's equity*," while the second type of "*assets − liabilities = owner's equity*."

report-type balance sheet 报告式资产负债表
upper and lower structure 上下结构

Smith Brothers Energy Partners

- *All amounts in millions of US dollars*

Annual Balance Sheet

BS-2102
As ended December 31, 2009

Items	Dec. 09	Dec. 08	Dec. 07
Assets			
Current assets			
Cash	10.6	10.0	0.7
Net receivables	168.2	125.8	87.4
Inventories	24.6	24.0	18.2
Other current assets	26.8	34.9	15.0
Total current assets	230.3	194.7	121.3
Net fixed assets	1,238.1	994.1	896.0
Other Non-current Assets	27.0	22.2	6.9
Total assets	1,495.4	1,211.0	1,024.2
Liabilities and shareholders' equity			
Current liabilities			
Accounts payable	140.0	152.0	84.9
Short-term debt	120.0	120.0	79.9
Other current liabilities	158.6	172.3	169.8
Total current liabilities	418.6	444.3	334.6
Long-term debt	409.4	250.0	270.0
Other Non-current Liabilities	67.2	61.0	54.4
Total liabilities	895.2	755.3	659.0
Shareholders' equity			
Preferred stock equity	0.0	0.0	0.0
Common stock equity	600.2	455.7	365.2
Total equity	600.2	455.7	365.2

Figure 1 *A report-type balance sheet with the upper and lower structure*
图 1 具有上下结构的报告式资产负债表

---

all amounts in millions of US dollars 所有金额以百万美元计
annual *a.* 每年的
annual balance sheet 年度资产负债表
as ended 截止
item *n.* 项目

net receivables 净应收账

total current assets 总流动资产
net fixed assets 净固定资产
other non-current assets 其他非流动资产
total assets 总资产

current liabilities 流动负债
accounts payable 应付账
short-term debt 短期债务

long-term debt 长期债务
other non-current liabilities 其他非流动债务
total liabilities 总负债

shareholders' equity 股东权益
preferred stock equity 优先股权益
common stock equity 普通股权益
total equity 总权益

Unit 5 The format of a balance sheet 资产负债表的格式

As shown in Figure 1, the total liabilities and total equity of Smith Brothers Energy Partners as ended December 2009, for instance, are **respectively** $ 895.2 m and $ 600.2 m, **adding up to** $ 1,495.4 m of total assets. This is a good example of "assets = liabilities + owner's equity."

respectively *ad.* 分别地
add up to 合计为

5.1c The account-type balance sheet
账户式资产负债表

The **account-type balance sheet** (Figure 2) adopts the left-right structure. Listed on the left are the assets and on the right, the liabilities and owner's interest.

account-type balance sheet 账户式资产负债表

Balance sheet

Assets		Liabilities	
Current assets		Current liabilities	
Cash	$ 50 000	Short-term debt	$ 30 000
Accounts receivable	$ 40 000	Accounts payable	$ 50 000
Merchandise inventory	$ 100 000	Salaries	$ 110 000
Total current assets	$ 190 000	Total current liabilities	$ 190 000
		Long-term debt	$ 20 000
Plant & equipment	$ 30 000	Total liabilities	$ 210 000
Less: Accumulated depreciation	$ (2 000)	Owner's equity	$ 8 000
Total assets	$ 218 000	Total liabilities & owner's equity	$ 218 000

accounts receivable 应收账
merchandise *n.* 商品

Figure 2 *A report-type balance sheet with the left-right structure*
图 2 具有左右结构的账户式资产负债表

Whatever format is **adopted**, this accounting equation must remain identical where the total of all the items under ASSETS **equals to** the total of all the items under LIABILITIES plus OWNER'S EQUITY. In China the account type is adopted for the balance sheet.

adopt *vt.* 采纳，采取

equal to 等于

5.2 Core accounting terms
核心会计术语

- **accounts payable** 应付账
- **accounts receivable** 应收账
- **account-type balance sheet** 账户式资产负债表
- **accumulated depreciation** 累计折旧
- **annual balance sheet** 年度资产负债表
- **common stock equity** 普通股权益
- **current assets** 流动资产
- **current liabilities** 流动负债
- **inventory** ['invəntri] *n.* 库存
- **shareholders' equity** 股东权益
- **long-term debt** 长期债务
- **merchandise** ['mə:tʃəndaiz] *n.* 商品
- **net receivables** 净应收账
- **net fixed assets** 净固定资产
- **other current assets** 其他流动资产
- **other current liabilities** 其他流动负债
- **other non-current assets** 其他非流动资产
- **other non-current liabilities** 其他非流动债务
- **plant and equipment** 厂房和设备
- **preferred stock equity** 优先股权益
- **report-type balance sheet** 报告式资产负债表
- **short-term debt** 短期债务
- **total assets** 总资产
- **total equity** 总权益
- **total liabilities** 总负债
- **total current assets** 总流动资产
- **unit of measurement** 计量单位

5.3 Extended words
扩展词汇

- **add up to** 合计为
- **adopt** [ə'dɔpt] *vt.* 采纳，采取
- **among others** 除了别的以外，其中
- **annual** ['ænjuəl] *a.* 每年的
- **as ended** 截止
- **body** ['bɔdi] *n.* 主体，正文，正表
- **cash** [kæʃ] *n.* 现金
- **each and every** 每一个
- **equal to** 等于
- **heading** ['hediŋ] *n.* 标题，表首
- **item** ['aitəm] *n.* 项目
- **less** [les] *prep.* 减去
- **nevertheless** [ˌnevəðə'les] *ad.* 尽管如此，不过

- **principal** ['prinsipəl] *a* 主要的
- **principal part** 主要部分，主体
- **respectively** [ri'spektivli] *ad.* 分别地
- **serial number** 序号，编号
- **upper and lower structure** 上下结构

5.4 Notes 注释

1) **The format of a balance sheet may vary with such factors as nature of an organization, the trade it is in, its objectives, among others.** 在诸多因素中，资产负债表的格式会因公司性质、其所处的行业、公司目标等因素而不同。

   句中 the trade it is in 是名词性短语，包含一个定语从句，省略关系词 that，完整的表达应为 the trade (that) it is in。

2) **The upper half lists and displays the assets, while the lower half liabilities and owner's interest.** 上半部分列示资产，下半部分列示负债和所有者权益。

   句中 while…interest 是省略语，省略了谓语动词 lists and displays。

3) **The first type is arranged on the basis of the principle of "assets = liabilities + owner's equity," while the second type of "assets – liabilities = owner's equity."** 第一种按"资产= 负债+所有者权益"的原理排列；第二种按"资产–负债=所有者权益"的原理排列。

   同上句，while…equity 亦为省略语，省略谓语动词 + 介词结构：is arranged on the basis of。

4) **Smith Brothers Energy Partners** 史密斯兄弟能源合伙人公司

   这个内容是资产负债表的表首内容之一，一般来说，表首的相关内容有——

   a. 公司名称　　　如：Smith Brothers Energy Partners
   　　　　　　　　　　史密斯兄弟能源合伙人公司
   b. 日期　　　　　如：As ended December 31, 2009
   　　　　　　　　　　2009 年 12 月 31 日截止
   c. 计量单位　　　如：All amounts in millions of US dollars
   　　　　　　　　　　所有金额以百万美元计
   d. 报表名称　　　如：Annual Balance Sheet 年度资产负债表
   e. 表号　　　　　如：BS-2102

5) **shareholders' equity** 股东权益

   在会计英语中 owner's interest 或 owner's equity（所有者权益）以及 shareholders' equity 具有相同的实质意义，均为"所有者权益"的意思，只是习惯表达法不同。

6) **preferred stock equity** 优先股权益

   优先股是相对于普通股（common stock）而言的。主要指在利润分红及剩余财产分配的权利方面，优先于普通股。优先股也是一种没有期限的有权凭证，优先股股东一般不能在中途向公司要求退股（少数可赎回的优先股例外）。

7) **common stock equity** 普通股权益

   普通股和优先股相对应，是指在公司的经营管理和盈利及财产的分配上享有普通权利的股份，表示在满足所有债权偿付要求以及在优先股东的收益权与求偿权得到优先满足后对企业盈利和剩余财产的索取权，它构成公司资本的基础，是股票的一种基本形式，也是发行量最大、最为重要的股票。目前在上海和深圳证券交易所上市交易的股票，都是普通股。

8) **As shown in Figure 1, the total liabilities and total equity of Smith Brothers Energy Partners as ended December 2009, for instance, are respectively $ 895.2 m and $ 600.2 m, adding up to $ 1 495.4 m of total assets.** 如图 1 所示，史密斯兄弟能源合伙人公司截至 2009 年 12 月的总负债和总权益分别为 8.952 亿美元和 6.002 亿美元，合计为 14.954 亿美元。

   句中，adding up to…是 V-ing 短语，在句中做伴随性状语。

9) **Listed on the left are the assets and on the right, the liabilities and owner's interest.** 左边列示资产，右边列示负债和所有者权益。

   a. 这是两个并列的倒装句，正句应当写为 The assets are listed on the left and…。

   b. 句子的后半部分是省略句，全句应为…and listed on the right are the liabilities and owner's interest.

10) **Whatever format is adopted, this accounting equation must remain identical where the total of all the items under ASSETS equals to the total of all the items under LIABILITIES plus OWNER'S EQUITY.** 不管采取什么格式，资产各项目的合计等于负债和所有者权益各项目的合计这一会计等式必须保持不变。

    a. Whatever format is adopted 相当于 No matter what format is adopted.

    b. 句中 where 是连词，不是疑问词，亦不是关系词，意为"在此处，在……地方"。

5.5 Reinforcement exercise
强化练习

1. Answer the following questions in English.

1) What are the two parts that a balance sheet consist of?
2) What is the function of the heading?
3) What is the function of the body?
4) What are the two types of format for the body of a balance sheet?
5) What is the structure of the report-type balance sheet?
6) What is the structure of the account-type balance sheet?
7) How do you understand the format of a balance sheet?

2. Put the following into Chinese.

1) heading   2) body

3) serial number
4) unit of measurement
5) principal part
6) report-type balance sheet
7) upper and lower structure
8) all amounts in millions of US dollars
9) annual balance sheet
10) as ended
11) current assets
12) net receivables
13) inventory
14) total current assets
15) net fixed assets
16) other non-current assets

3. Put the following into English.

1) 负债及股东权益
2) 流动负债
3) 应付账
4) 短期债务
5) 其他流动负债
6) 长期债务
7) 其他非流动债务
8) 总负债
9) 股东权益
10) 优先股权益
11) 普通股权益
12) 总权益
13) 合计为
14) 账户式资产负债表
15) 应收账
16) 商品
17) 厂房和设备
18) 累计折旧

4. Subject for self-study: A sample balance sheet.

Medilark Medical supplies Co.

Annual balance sheet

As at December 31, 2009
(In thousands of US dollars)

Current assets		Liabilities	
Cash & cash equivalent	5 000	Accounts payable	25 000
Marketable securities	25 000	Accrued liability	10 000
Accounts receivable	40 000	Notes payable	5 000
Notes receivable	25 000	Unearned revenue	6 000
Inventory	45 000	Current portion of	
Prepaid expenses	2 500	long-term debt	1 500
		Current portion of capital	
		lease obligations	600
Total current assets	142 500		
Fixed assets		*Total current liability*	48 100
Investment	7 500		
Machinery & equipment	60 000	Long-term debt	18 750
Buildings & land	200 000	Deferred income tax	
Intangible assets	75 000	liability	500
		Long-term capital lease	
		obligations	7 500
Total fixed assets	342 500		
		Total long-term liabilities	26 750
Total assets	485 000		
		Shareholders' equity	
		Preferred stock	20 000
		Common stock	90 150
		Retained earnings	300 000
		Total shareholders' equity	410 150
		Total shareholders' equity	
		and liability	485 000

Reminder 提示

cash equivalent 现金等价物
marketable securities 有价证券
accounts receivable 应收账
notes receivable 应收票据
prepaid expenses 预付费用
machinery & equipment 机器和设备
buildings & land 建筑物和土地
intangible assets 无形资产
accounts payable 应付账
accrued liability 应计债务
notes payable 应付票据
unearned revenue 预收收入
current portion of long-term debt 长期债务的当前部分
current portion of capital lease obligations 资本租赁债务的当前部分
long-term debt 长期债务
deferred income tax liability 递延所得税负债
long-term capital lease obligations 长期资本金债务
retained earnings 留存收益

5.6 Accounting-related knowledge
会计相关知识介绍

资产负债表的编制方法
The compiling method of a balance sheet

会计报表的编制，主要是通过对日常会计核算记录的数据加以归纳、整理，使之成为有用的财务信息。中国企业资产负债表各项目数据的来源，主要通过以下五种方式取得。

1. 根据总账科目余额直接填列

如"应收票据"（notes receivable）项目，根据"应收票据"总账科目的期末余额（end-of-period balance）直接填列；"短期借款"（short-term loan）项目，根据"短期借款"总账科目的期末余额直接填列。

2. 根据总账科目余额计算填列

如"货币资金"项目,根据"现金""银行存款""其他货币资金"科目的期末余额合计数计算填列。

3. 根据明细科目(classification item)余额计算填列

如"应付账款"(accounts payable)项目,根据"应收账款"(accounts receivable)、"预付账款"(prepaid accounts)科目所属相关明细科目的期末贷方余额计算填列。

4. 根据总账科目和明细科目余额分析计算填列

如"长期借款"(long-term loan)项目,根据"长期借款"总账科目期末余额,扣除"长期借款"科目所属明细科目中反映的、将于一年内到期的长期借款部分,分析计算填列。

5. 根据科目余额减去其备抵项目后的净额填列

如"短期投资"(short-term investment)项目,根据"短期投资"科目的期末余额,减去"短期投资跌价准备"备抵科目余额后的净额填列;又如,"无形资产"(intangible assets)项目,根据"无形资产"科目的期末余额,减去"无形资产减值准备"备抵科目余额后的净额填列。

5.7 Extended reading
延伸阅读

Equity
权 益

The net assets shown by the balance sheet equals the third part of the balance sheet, which is known as the shareholders' equity. Formally, shareholders' equity is part of the company's liabilities: they are funds "owing" to shareholders (after payment of all other liabilities); usually, however, "liabilities" is used in the more restrictive sense of liabilities excluding shareholders' equity. The balance of assets and liabilities (including shareholders' equity) is not a coincidence. Records of the values of each account in the balance sheet are maintained using a system of accounting known as double-entry bookkeeping. In this sense, shareholders' equity by construction must equal assets minus liabilities, and are a residual.

- Numbers of shares authorized, issued and fully paid, and issued but not fully paid
- Par value of shares
- Reconciliation of shares outstanding at the beginning and the end of the period
- Description of rights, preferences, and restrictions of shares
- Treasury shares, including shares held by subsidiaries and associates
- Shares reserved for issuance under options and contracts

A description of the nature and purpose of each reserve within owners' equity.

Unit 6
How to establish the account books?
如何建账？

Core terms reminder
核心术语提示

account book	账册
binding account book	订本式账簿
cash journal	现金日记账
bank deposit journal	银行存款日记账
general ledger	总分类账，总账
monetary resources	货币资金
note receivable	应收票据
deferred expense	待摊费用
cumulative depreciation	累计折旧
subsidiary ledger account	辅助分类账，明细分类账
classified accounting	分类核算

Unit 6 How to establish the account books? 如何建账?

6.1a Why is book-establishing significant?
建账的意义是什么？

The **account books** are the carrier with which accounting is recorded, and a fundamental link in the accounting work. Only **by virtue of** the books, can accounting information be collected, **sorted up**, processed, stored and provided.

book *n.* 账册
account book 账册
by virtue of 依靠，由于
sort up 整理，分类

While establishing the accounting books, different organizations may need different books, depending on such factors as size of the organization, nature of business, the extent of **computerization**, etc.

computerization *n.* 计算机化

6.1b What are the processes of book establishing?
建账的程序是什么？

The basic book-establishing processes are:

Step 1: Prepare various account books that are needed. Note that all **loose sheets** must be **bound up into a book**.

Step 2: Write on the account books name of organization, name of account book, **volumes**, serial number, starting date, bookkeeping person and other related information.

loose sheet 活页
bind *vt.* (bound) 装订
bind up into a book 装订成册

volume *n.* 册数

Step 3: Establish the ledger accounts on the **ledger paper** according to the sequence and names in the **charts of accounts**.

Step 4: Start using the **binding account book** by giving **ordinal numeration** from the first page to the last page.

ledger paper 总账账页
chart of account 会计科目表
binding account book 订本式账簿
ordinal numeration 顺序编号

6.1c Three common account books
三种常用账簿

There are various account books used in accounting, and three are the most commonly used:
- Cash journal and bank deposit journal
- General ledger
- Subsidiary ledger

1. Cash journal and bank deposit journal

Cash journal is a kind of special journal used to record **receipt** and disbursement of cash. The cash journal must use the binding account book, and its format of **account sheet** often adopts the three **column** type of **receipt (debtor)**, **disbursement (creditor)** and **balance**.

The **bank deposit journal** is a special journal used to record receipt and disbursement of bank deposits. Like the cash journal, it must also use the binding book, and adopt the three column type of receipt (debtor), disbursement (creditor) and balance.

cash journal 现金日记账
receipt n. 接收，收入
account sheet 账页
column n. 栏，栏目
receipt (debtor) 收入（借方）
disbursement (creditor) 支出（贷方）
balance n. 余额
bank deposit journal 银行存款日记账

2. The general ledger

The **general ledger**, or ledger in short, records all the economic business, according to the **subjects** in the ledger. It makes **general classified accounting**, and provides **all-inclusive accounting information**. The accounting

ledger n. 分类账，总账
general ledger 总分类账，总账

subject n. （会计的）科目
general classified accounting 总分类核算
all-inclusive accounting information 总括核算资料

information provided by the ledger is the principal basis with which the accounting statements are compiled. Any organization must establish the ledger account.

The ledger accounts that an organization normally establishes usually involve, but are not limited to, the following items:

- cash
- bank deposit
- other **monetary resources**
- short-term debt
- **notes receivable**
- **accounts receivable**
- inventory
- **deferred expenses**
- long-term investment
- fixed assets
- **cumulative depreciation**
- **intangible assets**

The ledger account can be registered on a case-to-case basis in terms of each **bookkeeping voucher** or a **collection of the vouchers**.

monetary resources 货币资金
notes receivable 应收票据
accounts receivable 应收账款
deferred expenses 待摊费用
cumulative depreciation 累计折旧
intangible assets 无形资产
bookkeeping voucher 记账凭证
collection of the vouchers 汇总记账凭证

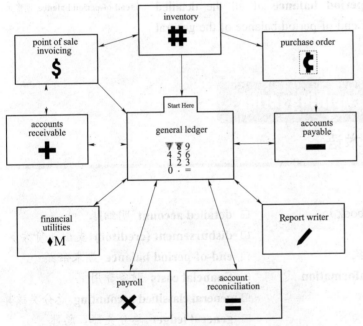

Figure 1 *A practical general ledger chart*
图1 实用总分类账图

3. Subsidiary ledger account

The **subsidiary ledger account**, **detailed account** or **itemized account** in short, is established on the basis of detailed and classified subjects. It is used to register a certain category of economic activity, to make **classified accounting** and to provide the information thereof.

In an organization, the subsidiary ledger account is established

subsidiary ledger account 辅助分类账，明细分类账
detailed account 明细账
itemized account 明细账
classified accounting 分类核算

according to the management needs of the organization itself as well as the needs of external departments that may require the information of the organization.

The subsidiary ledger accounts that an organization normally establishes usually involve, but are not limited to, the following items:

- Short-term investment
- Accounts receivable
- Deferred expenses
- Long-term investment
- Fixed assets
- Short-term debt
- Accounts payable
- **Salary payable**
- **Tax payable**
- **Overheads**
- **Financial costs**

salary payable 应付工资
tax payable 应缴税金
overheads 管理费用
financial costs 财务费用

Whatever method is used to classify the subsidiary ledger account, the total of **end-of-period balance** of all the detailed accounts shall equal the total of end-of-period balance of the general ledger account.

end-of-period balance 期末余额

6.2 Core accounting terms
核心会计术语

- **account book** 账册（亦作 book）
- **account sheet** 账页
- **account receivable** 应收账款
- **all-inclusive accounting information** 总括核算资料
- **balance** [ˈbæləns] n. 余额
- **bank deposit journal** 银行存款日记账
- **book** n. 账册（亦作 account book）
- **bookkeeping voucher** 记账凭证
- **binding account book** 订本式账簿
- **cash journal** 现金日记账
- **chart of account** 会计科目表
- **classified accounting** 分类核算
- **collection of the vouchers** 汇总记账凭证
- **cumulative depreciation** 累计折旧
- **deferred expenses** 待摊费用

- **detailed account** 明细账
- **disbursement (creditor)** 支出（贷方）
- **end-of-period balance** 期末余额
- **financial costs** 财务费用
- **general classified accounting** 总分类核算
- **general ledger** 总分类账，总账
- **intangible assets** 无形资产
- **itemized account** 明细账
- **ledger** [ˈledʒə] n. 分类账，总账
- **ledger paper** 总账账页
- **monetary resources** 货币资金
- **notes receivable** 应收票据
- **overhead** [ˈəuvəhed] n. 管理费用
- **receipt** [riˈsi:t] n. 接收，收入
- **receipt (debtor)** 收入（借方）
- **salary payable** 应付工资

- subject ['sʌbdʒikt] n.（会计）科目
- subsidiary ledger account 辅助分类账，明细分类账
- tax payable 应缴税金

6.3 Extended words 扩展词汇

- bind [baind] vt. (bound) 装订
  bind into a book 装订成册
- by virtue of 依靠，由于
- column ['kɔləm] n. 栏，栏目
- computerization [kəm,pju:tərai'zeiʃən] n. 计算机化
- loose sheet 活页
- ordinal numeration 顺序编号
- sort up 整理，分类
- volume ['vɔlju:m] n. 册数

6.4 Notes 注释

1) **Only by virtue of the books, can accounting information be collected, sorted up, processed, stored and provided.** 只有借助会计账册，才能对会计信息进行收集、整理、加工、储存和提供。

    这是一个倒装句，英语语法规定，当 only 前置时，句子的主谓语需要倒装。如：
    Only when delivery is made, can payment be made.
    只有交货后，才能付款。

2) **While establishing the accounting books, different organizations may need different books, depending on such factors as size of the organization, nature of business, the extent of computerization, etc.** 不同的企业在建账时所需要的账簿是不相同的，它取决于企业的规模、业务性质、电子化程度等因素。

    depending on…是 V-ing 引导的伴随性状语。

3) **Note that all loose sheets must be bound up into a book.** 注意所有活页必须装订成册。

    句中 bound 是动词 bind 的过去式和过去分词。

4) **Write on the account books name of organization, name of account book, volumes, serial number, starting date, bookkeeping person and other related information.** 在账簿上，写明单位名称、账簿名称、册数、编号、启用日期以及记账人员等相关信息。

5) **Establish the ledger accounts on the ledger paper according to the sequence and names in the charts of accounts.** 按照会计科目表的顺序、名称，在总账账页上建立总账账户。

6) **Start using the binding account book by giving ordinal numeration from the first page to the last page.** 启用订本式账簿，从第一页起到最后一页止顺序编定号码。

7) **Cash journal is a kind of special journal used to record receipt and disbursement of cash.** 现金日记账是专门用来记录现金收支业务的一种特种日记账。

  used to…是过去分词结构，在句中做定语，修饰其前面的名词 journal。

8) **…and its format of account sheet often adopts the three column type of receipt (debtor), disbursement (creditor) and balance.** ……其账页格式一般采用"收入"（借方）、"支出"（贷方）和"余额"三栏式。

9) **The general ledger, or ledger in short, records all the economic business, according to the subjects in the ledger.** 总分类账，简称总账，根据总分类科目开设账户，用来登记全部经济业务。

10) **It makes general classified accounting, and provides all-inclusive accounting information.** 总分类账进行总分类核算并提供总括核算资料。

11) **The accounting information provided by the ledger is the principal basis with which the accounting statements are compiled.** 总分类账所提供的核算资料，是编制会计报表的主要依据。

  a. 句中 provided by…是过去分词短语，在句中做定语，修饰其前的名词 information。
  b. with which…是介词 + 关系词结构，在句中引导一个定语从句，修饰其前的名词 basis。

12) **The ledger account can be registered on a case-to-case basis in terms of each bookkeeping voucher or a collection of the vouchers.** 总账可以根据记账凭证逐笔登记，也可以根据汇总记账凭证进行登记。

13) **The subsidiary ledger account, detailed account or itemized account in short, is established on the basis of detailed and classified subjects.** 明细分类账，简称明细账，根据明细分类科目所开设。

  句中 detailed account 和 itemized account 均为 subsidiary ledger account 的简称。

14) **It is used to register a certain category of economic activity, to make classified accounting and to provide the information thereof.** 明细分类账用来登记某一类经济业务，进行明细分类核算并提供明细核算资料。

  句中，the information thereof 相当于 the information of the classified accounting，这里使用 thereof 可以避免重复。

15) **In an organization, the subsidiary ledger account is established according to the management needs of the organization itself as well as the needs of external departments that may require the information of the organization.** 在企业里，明细分类账的设置是根据企业自身管理需要和外界各部门对企业信息资料的需要来设置的。

Unit 6 How to establish the account books? 如何建账?

句中 that may require…是限定性定语从句，修饰其前面的名词 departments。

16) **Whatever method is used to classify the subsidiary ledger account, the total of end-of-period balance of all the detailed accounts shall equal the total of end-of-period balance of the general ledger account.** 明细账无论按怎样的分类方法，各个账户明细账的期末余额之和应与其总账的期末余额相等。

Whatever method is…相当于 No matter what method is…

6.5 Reinforcement exercise 强化练习

1. Answer the following questions in English.

1) Why is book-establishing significant?
2) What are the three commonly-used account books?
3) What is cash journal?
4) What is bank journal?
5) What is the general ledger?
6) What is the subsidiary ledger account?

2. Put the following into Chinese.

1) financial costs
2) general classified accounting
3) general ledger
4) intangible assets
5) itemized account
6) ledger paper
7) monetary resources
8) notes receivable
9) overhead
10) receipt
11) receipt (debtor)
12) salary payable
13) subject
14) subsidiary ledger account
15) tax payable
16) ordinal numeration
17) bind into a book
18) ordinal numeration

3. Put the following into English.

1) 账册
2) 账页
3) 应收账
4) 总括核算资料
5) 余额
6) 银行存款日记账
7) 记账凭证
8) 订本式账簿
9) 现金日记账
10) 会计科目表

11) 分类核算
12) 汇总记账凭证
13) 累计折旧
14) 待摊费用

15) 明细账
16) 支出（贷方）
17) 期末余额

4. Subject for self-study: A ledger chart.

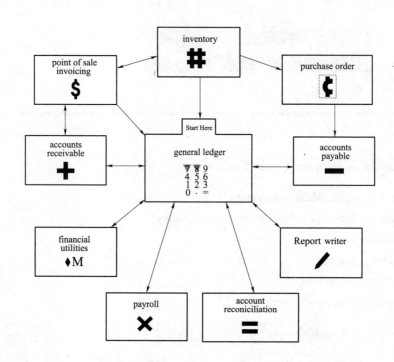

report writer 写报告者
account reconciliation 账目核对
payroll *n.* 工资单
financial utilities 财务实用程序
point of sale invoicing 销售点出发票

6.6 Accounting-related knowledge
会计相关知识介绍

新办小企业如何建账？
How does a newly-started small business establish its accounts?

多数新开办的小企业由于规模小、资金紧张、缺乏经验，尤其是缺乏财务管理经验，往往不知道该从何下手建立会计账户。下面是一些具体的建议。

可通过盘点确定以下数据：库存现金（cash on hand）、银行存款（bank deposit）、存货（inventory）各项目、固定资产（fixed assets）及其折旧，其中固定资产折旧（depreciation），可通过固定资产购入凭证作折旧期限及已提折旧年限确定。

可通过出纳/财务的有效记录，或通过对账单核对（reconciliation of bank statement）等方法，确定各项往来款项，如应收/应付账款（accounts receivable/payable）、其他应收/应付账款、预收/预付账款。

通过合作协议等资料确定原始股本（original capital）投入额。

至于其他无法确定的项目数据（除未分配利润外），应与经营管理者协商确定。

所有数据取得后，应填列在"资产负债表"（balance sheet）相应的项目，差额均为"未分配利润"（unappropriated profit）。

关于内部账的做法，一般有以下三个要求。
1）清楚明晰各账项的往来及具体数字，以反映企业的真实财务状况（financial position）。
2）由于内部账项的主要作用是配合企业管理，所以成本数据应尽量细化。
3）出于使用者的角度不同（内账的使用者主要是老板），故固定资产折旧/长期待摊费用（long-term deferred expenses）的摊销（amortization）等，应与使用者协商分摊期限，并记入备忘录，用以备查。

关于账本及开设科目
1）内账主要是内部使用，所以，手续可相应简化，所有资料和数据妥善保管即可。登账工作一般比较烦琐，做内账时一般只记往来账（current account），其他如存货、费用都不设账本，改为 EXCEL 跟进。
2）至于具体的开设科目，每个企业都有自己的特点，视需求而定，一般不可缺少的有：

资金类（funds）、往来账项（current accounts）、费用（expenses）、固定资产（fixed assets）、存货（inventory）、权益（equity）、损益（profit and loss）等类别。

6.7 Extended reading
延伸阅读

The general ledger
总 账

The general ledger is a collection of the group of accounts that supports the value items shown in the major financial statements. It is built up by posting transactions recorded in the sales daybook, purchases daybook, cash book and general journals daybook. The general ledger can be supported by one or more subsidiary ledgers that provide details for accounts in the general ledger. For instance, an accounts receivable subsidiary ledger would contain a separate account for each credit customer, tracking that customer's balance separately. This subsidiary ledger would then be totalled and compared with its controlling account (in this case, accounts receivable) to ensure accuracy as part of the process of preparing a trial balance.

There are seven basic categories in which all accounts are grouped:
1) assets
2) liability
3) owner's equity
4) revenue
5) expense
6) gains (profits)
7) losses

The balance sheet and the income statement are both derived from the general ledger. Each account in the general ledger consists of one or more pages. The general ledger is where posting to the accounts occurs. Posting is the process of recording amounts as credits (right side), and amounts as debits(left side), in the pages of the general ledger. Additional columns to the right hold a running activity total (similar to a checkbook).

Unit 7
What is a profit statement?
什么是利润表?

Core terms reminder
核心术语提示

利润表	profit statement
收益表	income statement
收支表	income and expense statement
损益表	profit and loss statement
经营情况表	operating statement
单步式利润表	single-step profit statement
多步式利润表	multiple-step profit statement

7.1a What is a profit statement?

什么是利润表？

A **profit statement** is a financial statement that summarizes the revenues, costs and expenses **incurred** during a specific period of time — usually a fiscal quarter or year. These records show the ability of a company to **generate profit** by increasing revenue and reducing costs.

A profit statement is also known as a **profit and loss statement** (P&L), an **income statement**, an **income and expense statement** or an **operating statement**.

The balance sheet, profit statement and statement of cash flows are the most important financial statements produced by a company. While each is important **in its own right**, they are meant to be analyzed together.

profit statement	利润表
incur *vt.*	导致，承受
generate profit	产生利润
profit and loss statement	损益表
income statement	收益表
income and expense statement	收支表
operating statement	经营情况表
in one's own right	凭本身的能力（身份）

7.1b What are the elements of income?

收益有哪些要素？

The elements of income are generally divided into four categories:
- revenues
- expenses
- gains
- losses

Revenues are **inflows** or **enhancements** of financial assets of your business. They may also be **settlements** of your liabilities from delivering or producing goods and services, or engaging in other activities that constitute your company's **ongoing** major or central operation.

revenue *n.*	收入
expense *n.*	费用，开支
gain *n.*	获得，收益
loss *n.*	损失
inflow *n.*	流入，输入
enhancement *n.*	增进，增加
settlement *n.*	解决，决算
ongoing *a.*	正在进行的

Expenses, on the other hand, are **outflows** of assets or **incurrences** of liabilities from delivering or producing goods and services, or carrying out other activities that constitute your company's ongoing major or central operations.

When gains are reported, they represent increases in net assets from **peripheral** or **incidental transactions** and from all other transactions, events and **circumstances** affecting your company, except those resulting from revenues or investments by owners.

Losses report decreases in your company's net assets.

outflow *n.* 流出，输出
incurrence *n.* 导致，蒙受，造成

peripheral *a.* 外围的
incidental *a.* 伴随的，偶然的
peripheral transaction 外围交易
incidental transaction 附带交易，非经常性交易
circumstance *n.* 环境，情况

7.1c What are the forms of a profit statement?

利润表有哪些形式？

The profit statement traditionally has been prepared in either **single-step form** or **multiple-step form**.

Under the single-step form, you should place all of your revenues and gains that are identified as operating items first on the profit statement, followed by all expenses and losses identified as operating items. The **difference** between **total revenues** and **total expenses** represents income from your operations. If there are no **non-operating, irregular,** or **extraordinary items**, this difference is also equal to your net income. A single-step profit statement is generally used by service organizations.

single-step form 单步式表格
multiple-step form 多步式表格
difference *n.* 差额
total revenue 总收入
total expense 总费用
non-operating item 营业外项目
irregular item 非正常项目
extraordinary item 特别项目

| HUNTER COMPANY |
| Income Statement |
| For the Year Ending December 31, 20X9 |

Revenues		
Net sales		$ 653,000
Expenses and losses		
Cost of goods sold	$ 283,000	
Selling expenses	142,000	
General & administraive	170,000	
Loss on sale of land	2,000	
Interest expense	7,000	604,000
Income before tax		$ 49,000
Income tax expense		10,000
Net income		$ 39,000

Figure 1 *A single-step income statement*
图 1 单步式收益表

When using the multiple-step form, your profit statement is divided into **separate sections**, and various **subtotals** are reported that reflect different levels of profitability.

separate section 单独的部分
subtotal *n*. 小计

| HUNTER COMPANY |
| Income Statement |
| For the Year Ending Decembr 31, 20X9 |

Revenues				
Sales				$660,000
Less: Sales discounts			$ 5,000	
Sales returns & allowances			2,000	7,000
Net sales				$653,000
Cost of goods sold				
Beginning inventory, Jan.1			$120,000	
Add: Purchases		$230,000		
Freight-in		10,000		
		$240,000		
Less: Purchase discounts	$ 2,400			
Purchase returns & allowances	3,600	6,000		
Net purchases			234,000	
Goods available for sale			$354,000	
Less: Ending inventory, Dec.31			71,000	
Cost of goods sold				283,000
Gross profit				$370,000
Selling expenses				
Advertising		$ 70,000		
Freight-out		4,000		
Depreciation		28,000		
Utilities		11,000		
Salaries		29,000	142,000	
General & administrative				
Salaries		$ 63,000		
Depreciation		17,000		
Utilities		22,000		
Insurance		44,000		
Rent		24,000	170,000	
Other				
Loss on sale of land		$ 2,000		
Interest expense		7,000	9,000	321,000
Income before tax				$ 49,000
Income tax expense				10,000
Net income				$ 39,000

Figure 2 *A multiple-step income statement*
图 2 多步式收益表

7.1d A sample single-step profit statement
单步式利润表样本

The basic format of the single-step profit statement is as follows.

First Line

On the first line at the top of the profit/income statement, the name of the business appears.

Second Line

The second line reads profit/income statement.

Last Line

The last line tells the reader the period of time covered by the profit/income statement. This period covered can be a month, a quarter, six months or a year. This is different from a balance sheet where a date, not a period of time is **specified**.

(You can use the **interactive table** provided to create an income statement for your company.)

specify *vt.* 指定，限定

interactive table 交互式表格

XYZ COMPANY
STATEMENT OF INCOME
FOR THE YEAR ENDED DECEMBER 31, 2009

SINGLE - STEP INCOME STATEMENT	
Revenue:	
Net sales..	0
Interest income..	0
Gain on sale of equipment..	0
Total Revenue..	
Costs and expenses:	
Cost of goods sold..	0
Selling expenses..	0
General and administrative expenses..	0
Interest expense..	0
Income taxes..	0
Total cost and expenses..	
Net income..	

Figure 3 *An interactive table*
图 3　交互式表格

7.1e A Sample multiple-step profit statement
多步式利润表样本

Net Sales Revenue from **net sales** shows your **total sales** for the income statement period less any **sales discounts** or **returns** and **allowances**. Sales returns and allowances and sales discounts should be subtracted from gross sales in arriving at net sales revenue. When the sales price is increased to cover the cost of freight to the customer and the customer is billed accordingly, **freight charges** paid by the company should also be subtracted from sales in arriving at net sales. Freight charges not passed to the buyer are recognized as selling expenses.

net sales revenue 净销售收入
net sales 净销售额
total sales 总销售额
sales discount 销售折扣
sales return 销货退回
sales allowance 销售折让

freight charge 运货费

XYZ COMPANY
STATEMENT OF INCOME
FOR THE YEAR ENDED DECEMBER 31, 2009

MULTI - STEP INCOME STATEMENT			
	EXPENSE	REVENUE	INCOME
Sales..			
Sales returns and allowances..			
Sales discounts..			
Cost of goods sold			
Beginning inventory..			
Purchases..			
Freight-in..			
Cost of goods available for sale..			
Less ending inventory..			
Gross profit on sales..			

Unit 7　What is a profit statement?　什么是利润表？

Operating Expenses				
Selling Expenses				
Sales salaries..				
Advertising expense..				
Other selling expense..				
General and Administrative Expenses				
Officer's salaries..				
Office salaries..				
Payroll taxes..				
Insurance..				
Depreciation..				
Misc. general expenses..				
Operating income..				
Other Income				
Interest income..				
Gain on sale of equipment..				
Other Expense				
Interest expense..				
Income before taxes..				
Income taxes				
Net Income				

[Reset Values]　　　　　　　　　　[Calculate Totals]

Figure 4　A multi-step income statement
图 4　多步式收益表

7.2 Core accounting terms
核心会计术语

- **expense** [ik'spens] *n.* 费用，开支
- **extraordinary item** 特别项目
- **freight charge** 运货费
- **gains and losses** 损益
- **generate profit** 产生利润
- **income statement** 收益表
- **income and expense statement** 收支表
- **incidental transaction** 附带交易，非经常性交易
- **irregular item** 非正常项目
- **multiple-step form** 多步式表格
- **net sales** 净销售额
- **net sales revenue** 净销售收入
- **non-operating item** 营业外项目
- **operating statement** 经营情况表
- **peripheral transaction** 外围交易，外围业务往来
- **profit and loss statement** 损益表
- **profit statement** 利润表
- **sales allowance** 销售折让

- **sales discount** 销售折扣
- **sales return** 销货退回
- **single-step form** 单步式表格
- **statement of cash flows** 现金流量表
- **total expense** 总费用
- **total revenue** 总收入
- **total sales** 总销售额
- **revenue** [ˈrevənjuː] n. 收入

7.3 Extended words 扩展词汇

- **circumstance** [ˈsəːkəmstəns] n. 环境，情况
- **difference** [ˈdifərəns] n. 差额
- **enhancement** [inˈhɑːnsmənt] n. 增进，增加
- **gain** [gein] n. 获得，收益
- **inflow** [ˈinfləu] n. 流入，输入
- **loss** [lɔs] n. 损失
- **incidental** [ˌinsiˈdentl] a. 伴随的，偶然的
- **incur** [inˈkəː] vt. 招致，承受
- **incurrence** [inˈkəːrəns] n. 招致，蒙受，造成
- **in one's own right** 凭本身的能力（身份）
- **interactive table** 交互式表格
- **ongoing** [ˈɔngəuiŋ] a. 正在进行的
- **outflow** [ˈautfləu] n. 流出，输出
- **peripheral** [pəˈrifərəl] a. 外围的
- **separate section** 单独的部分
- **settlement** [ˈsetlmənt] n. 解决，决算
- **specify** [ˈspesifai] vt. 指定，限定
- **subtotal** [ˈsʌbˌtəutl] n. 小计

7.4 Notes 注释

1) **A profit statement is a financial statement that summarizes the revenues, costs and expenses incurred during a specific period of time — usually a fiscal quarter or year.** 利润表是总结在特定时间段——通常为一个财政季度或财政年度期间所发生的收入、成本及支出的财务报表。

   a. 句中 that 引导一个限定性定语从句，修饰先行词 statement。

   b. incurred 是过去分词，引导一个定语，修饰其前 revenues 等三个并列名词，相当于定语从句 which are incurred。

2) **These records show the ability of a company to generate profit by increasing revenue and reducing costs.** 这些记录显示公司通过增加收入并降低成本来产生利润的能力。

3) **A profit statement is also known as a profit and loss statement (P&L), an income statement, an income and expense statement or an operating statement.** 利润表又称为损益表（P&L）、

收益表、收支表或经营情况表。

4) **The balance sheet, profit statement and statement of cash flows are the most important financial statements produced by a company.** 资产负债表、利润表和现金流量表是公司制作的最为重要的财务报表。

　　句中 produced by…是由过去分词引导的定语，修饰名词 statement。

5) **While each is important in its own right, they are meant to be analyzed together.** 尽管每一个报表自身都很重要，但是三个报表要在一起分析使用才更有意义。

6) **Revenues are inflows or enhancements of financial assets of your business.** 收入是贵公司财务资产的流入或增加。

7) **They may also be settlements of your liabilities from delivering or producing goods and services.** 这些收入也可以是从递送或生产商品及提供服务所发生的债务结算而来。

8) **…or engaging in other activities that constitute your company's ongoing major or central operation.** 或因从事构成公司正在进行的重大或中心经营业务的其他活动所发生的债务结算而来。

　　句中 that…operation 是限定性定语从句，修饰先行词 activities。例句 9 中 that 从句的语法作用同本句。

9) **Expenses, on the other hand, are outflows of assets or incurrences of liabilities from delivering or producing goods and services, or carrying out other activities that constitute your company's ongoing major or central operations.** 另一方面，费用是资产的流出，或从递送商品或服务所发生的负债，或是从履行构成公司正在进行的重大或中心经营业务的其他活动所发生的负债。

10) **When gains are reported, they represent increases in net assets from peripheral or incidental transactions.** 在报告收益时，它们表示从外围交易或附带交易中获得的净资产增长。

11) **…and from all other transactions, events and circumstances affecting your company.** ……以及从影响贵公司的所有其他业务往来、事件或环境中所获得的净资产增长。

　　句中 affecting…是 V-ing 短语，在句中作定语，修饰名词短语 events and circumstances, 相当于定语从句 which affect…

12) **…except those resulting from revenues or investments by owners.** ……（这种增长）不包括从企业主自身的收入或投资中所产生的增长。

13) **Under the single-step form, you should place all of your revenues and gains that are identified as operating items first on the profit statement, followed by all expenses and losses identified as operating items.** 在使用单步式表格时，你应当先把认定为经营项目的所有收入和收益放在利润表上，随后填上认定为经营项目的所有费用及亏损。

　　a. 句中 that…statement 是限定性定语从句，修饰名词短语 revenues and gains。
　　b. followed by…是过去分词短语，在句中做伴随性状语。

14) **The difference between total revenues and total expenses represents income from your operations.** 总收入和总支出之间的差额就表示营业收益。

15) **If there are no non-operating, irregular, or extraordinary items, this difference is also equal to your net income.** 如果没有营业外项目、非正常项目或特别项目，这个差额也等于净收益。

16) **…and various subtotals are reported that reflect different levels of profitability.** ……而

且要报告反映不同盈利水平的各种小计。

　　句中 that...profitability 是限定性定语从句后置，正句应为...and various subtotals that... profitability are reported.

17) **This is different from a balance sheet where a date, not a period of time is specified.** 这不同于特定日期，而不是一段时间的资产负债表。

　　句中 where 引导一个限定性定语从句，修饰名词短语 balance sheet，这里 where 相当于介词加关系词结构 in which。

18) **Net Sales Revenue from net sales shows your total sales for the income statement period less any sales discounts or returns and allowances.** 从净销售额中算出的净销售收入表示收益表期内的总销售额扣减销售折扣、销货退回或销售折让余额。

19) **Sales returns and allowances and sales discounts should be subtracted from gross sales in arriving at net sales revenue.** 要从毛销售额中减去销货退回、销售折让或销售折扣才能得出净销售收入。

20) **When the sales price is increased to cover the cost of freight to the customer and the customer is billed accordingly, freight charges paid by the company should also be subtracted from sales in arriving at net sales.** 当利用提高销售价格来抵消给客户的运费成本，并且客户也已经相应地收到了账单，公司所支付的运货费也要在计算净销售额时扣除掉。

　　句中 paid by the company 是过去分词短语，在句中做定语，修饰名词短语 freight charges，相当于定语从句 which have been paid...

21) **Freight charges not passed to the buyer are recognized as selling expenses.** 没有转移到买方一边的运货费要算作售货费用。

　　句中 not passed to the buyer 是过去分词短语，修饰名词短语 freight charges，相当于定语从句 which have not been passed...

7.5 Reinforcement exercise
强化练习

1. Answer the following questions in English.

1) What is a profit statement? And what are the other names for it?
2) What are the three most important financial statements produced by a company?
3) What are the elements of a income/profit statement? Explains them respectively.
4) What are the two forms of a profit statement? Explain.

2. Put the following into Chinese.

1) profit statement　　　　　　　　　　2) incur costs and expenses

3) fiscal quarter or year
4) generate profit
5) increase revenue and reduce costs
6) profit and loss statement
7) income statement
8) income and expense statement
9) operating statement

10) statement of cash flows
11) gains and losses
12) inflows of assets
13) enhancements of financial assets
14) settlements of liabilities
15) major or central operation
16) outflows of assets

3. Put the following into English.

1) 负债的发生
2) 外围业务往来
3) 附带业务往来，非经常性业务往来
4) 单步式表格
5) 多步式表格
6) 经营项目
7) 总收入
8) 总费用
9) 营业外项目

10) 非正常项目
11) 特别项目
12) 销售收入
13) 净销售额
14) 总销售额
15) 销售折扣
16) 销货退回
17) 销售折让
18) 运货费

4. Subject for self-study: A chart of multiple-step income statement.

```
                         HUNTER COMPANY
                          Income Statement
                   For the Year Ending Decembr 31, 20X9
Revenues
  Sales                                                    $660,000
  Less: Sales discounts                        $ 5,000
        Sales returns & allowances               2,000        7,000
  Net sales                                                $653,000
Cost of goods sold
  Beginning inventory, Jan.1                             $120,000
  Add: Purchases                     $230,000
       Freight-in                      10,000
                                     $240,000
  Less: Purchase discounts  $ 2,400
        Purchase returns & allowances  3,600    6,000
  Net purchases                                           234,000
  Goods available for sale                               $354,000
  Less: Ending inventory, Dec.31                           71,000
  Cost of goods sold                                                 283,000
Gross profit                                                        $370,000
Selling expenses
  Advertising                         $ 70,000
  Freight-out                            4,000
  Depreciation                          28,000
  Utilities                             11,000
  Salaries                              29,000  $142,000
General & administrative
  Salaries                            $ 63,000
  Depreciation                          17,000
  Utilities                             22,000
  Insurance                             44,000
  Rent                                  24,000   170,000
Other
  Loss on sale of land                $  2,000
  Interest expense                       7,000     9,000   321,000
Income before tax                                         $ 49,000
  Income tax expense                                         10,000
Net income                                                $ 39,000
```

Reminder 提示

beginning inventory 期初存货
purchases 采购品，进货
freight-in 进货运费
goods available for sale 本期待销商品
ending inventory 期末存货
freight-out 销货运费
utility *n.* [juːˈtiliti] 公共设施
loss on sale of land 出售土地亏损

7.6 Accounting-related knowledge
会计相关知识介绍

如何编制利润表
How to produce a profit statement

依照目前我国企业利润表（profit statement）的格式和内容，利润表的编制方法如下：

（一）利润表反映企业在一定期间内利润/亏损（profit/loss）的实际情况

利润表中"本月数"栏反映各项目的本月实际发生数；在编报中期财务会计报告（financial accounting report）时，填列上年同期累计实际发生数；在编报年度财务会计报告时，填列上年全年累计实际发生数，并将"本月数"栏改成"上年数"栏。如果上年度利润表与本年度利润表的项目名称和内容不相一致，应对上年度利润表项目的名称和数字按本年度的规定进行调整，填入本表"上年数"栏。在编报中期和年度财务会计报告时，应将"本月数"栏改成"上年数"栏。

利润表"本年累计数"（accumulated total for the current year）栏反映各项目自年初（beginning of the year）起至报告期末（end of report period）止的累计实际发生数（accumulated ascertained total）。

（二）利润表各项目的填列方法

1)"主营业务收入"（main business income）项目，反映企业经营主要业务所取得的收入总额。本项目应根据"主营业务收入"科目的发生额分析填列。

2)"主营业务成本"（main business cost）项目，反映企业经营主要业务发生的实际成本。本项目应根据"主营业务成本"科目的发生额分析填列。

3)"主营业务税金及附加"(tax money and surtax for main business)项目，反映企业经营主要业务应负担的营业税（sales tax）、消费税（consumption tax）、城市维护建设税（urban maintenance and construction tax）、资源税（resource tax）、土地增值税（land value increment tax）和教育费附加（surtax for education fees）等。本项目应根据"主营业务税金及附加"科目的发生额分析填列。

4)"其他业务利润"(profit from other business)项目，反映企业除主营业务以外取得的收入，减去所发生的相关成本、费用以及相关税金及附加等的支出后的净额。本项目应根据"其他业务收入""其他业务支出"科目的发生额分析填列。

5)"营业费用"(operating expenses)项目，反映企业在销售商品和商品流通企业在购入商品等过程中发生的费用。本项目应根据"营业费用"科目的发生额分析填列。

6)"管理费用"(administrative expenses, overhead)项目，反映企业发生的管理费用。本项目应根据"管理费用"科目的发生额分析填列。

7)"财务费用"(finance cost)项目，反映企业发生的财务费用。本项目应根据"财务费用"科目的发生额分析填列。

8)"投资收益"(return on investment)项目，反映企业以各种方式对外投资所取得的收益。本项目应根据"投资收益"科目的发生额分析填列；如为投资损失，以"—"号填列。

9)"补贴收入"(subsidy revenue)项目，反映企业取得的各种补贴收入以及退回的增值税等。本项目应根据"补贴收入"科目的发生额分析填列。

10)"营业外收入"(non-operating income)项目和"营业外支出"(non-operating expenses)项目，反映企业发生的与其生产经营无直接关系的各项收入和支出。这两个项目应分别根据"营业外收入"科目和"营业外支出"科目的发生额分析填列。

11)"利润总额"(total profit)项目，反映企业实现的利润总额。如为亏损总额，以"—"号填列。

12)"所得税"(income tax)项目，反映企业按规定从本期损益中减去的所得税。本项目应根据"所得税"科目的发生额分析填列。

13)"净利润"(net profit)项目，反映企业实现的净利润。如为净亏损，以"—"号填列。

7.7 Extended reading
延伸阅读

Reminders in producing a profit statement
编制利润表的提示

In compiling a profit statement, special attention must be paid to the following items.

1. Cost of Goods Sold

Whether you're a merchandising or manufacturing enterprise, you must determine the cost of goods relating to sales for the period. This is the sum of your beginning inventory, net purchases, and all other buying, freight, and storage costs relating to the acquisition of goods. Your net purchases balance is developed by subtracting purchase returns and allowances and purchase discounts from gross purchases. Your cost of sold goods can then be calculated by subtracting your ending inventory from your cost of goods available for sale. When you manufacture your goods, additional elements enter into the cost. Aside from material costs, you will incur labor and overhead costs to convert raw materials to finished goods. A manufacturing company has three inventories rather than one: raw materials, goods in process, and finished goods.

2. Operating Expenses

Operating expenses may be reported in two parts: selling expenses as well as general and administrative expenses. Your selling expenses include items such as sales salaries and commissions as well as related payroll taxes, advertising and store displays, store supplies used, depreciation of store furniture and equipment, and delivery expenses. Your general and administrative expenses include salaries as well as related payroll taxes, office supplies used, depreciation of office furniture and fixtures, telephone, postage, business licenses and fees, legal and accounting services, and contributions.

Note: For manufacturing companies, charges related jointly to both production and administrative functions should be allocated in some equitable manner between manufacturing overhead and operating expenses.

3. Other Revenues and Gains

This section usually includes items identified with the peripheral activities of your company. Examples include revenue from financial activities (i.e., rents, interest and dividends) and gains from the sale of assets (i.e., equipment or investments).

4. Other Expenses and Losses

This section parallels other revenues and gains; however, the items result in deductions from, rather than increases to, your operating income. Examples include interest expense and losses from the sale of assets.

5. Income Tax on Continuing Operations

Your total income tax expense for a period is allocated to various components of your income. One amount is computed for income from your continuing operations, and separate computations are made for any irregular or extraordinary items you may find.

Unit 8
What is a bank reconciliation statement?
什么是银行往来调节表?

Core terms reminder
核心术语提示

银行往来调节表	bank reconciliation statement
银行对账单余额	bank balance as per bank statement
公司账簿余额	bank balance as per the accounting systems
银行对账单	bank statement
账户余额	account balance

8.1a What is a bank reconciliation statement?
什么是银行往来调节表？

A bank **reconciliation statement** is a form that allows individuals or companies to compare their **respective** bank account records to the bank's records of the individual/company's **account balance** in order to **uncover** any possible **discrepancies**.

Discrepancies could include:
- cheques recorded as a lesser amount than what was **presented** to the bank
- money received but not lodged, or payments taken from the bank account without the company's knowledge

A bank reconciliation done regularly can reduce the number of errors in an accounts system and make it easier to find missing **purchases** and **sales invoices**.

reconciliation *n.* 调和，调节，核对
reconciliation statement 往来调节表
respective *a.* 各自的
account balance 账户余额
uncover *vt.* 揭示
discrepancy *n.* 误差，出入
present *vt.* 呈送，提交
lodge *vt.* 存放，寄放

purchases *n.* [复] 购买的东西，进货
sales invoice 销售发票

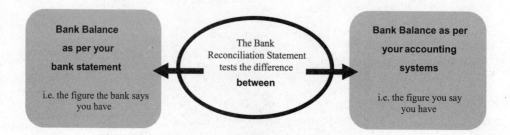

Unit 8　What is a bank reconciliation statement? 什么是银行往来调节表？　81

8.1b What are the terms on bank reconciliation?
银行往来调节方面的术语有哪些？

The **terms** frequently used on bank reconciliation are —

1. **Deposits in transit**

These are deposits that are in the company's cashbooks but not in the **bank statement**. The reason is that there is delay between when the cash gets recorded on the books and when the bank records the deposit.

2. **Outstanding checks**

These are checks that have been **deducted** from the cashbooks but not the bank statement. The reason is that there is a delay between when the check gets recorded on the books and when the bank records the check.

3. **Bank charges**

An expense for bank services that is listed on the bank statement but is not recorded on the company's books.

4. **Non-sufficient fund checks (NSF checks)**

A customer payment by check that has been recorded as a deposit on the books but was not **collectible** because of insufficient funds in the account of the customer.

term *n.* 术语

deposits in transit 未达存款

bank statement 银行对账单

outstanding check 未兑现支票

deduct *vt.* 扣除，减去

bank charge 银行收费

non-sufficient fund check 存款不足支票

collectible *a.* 可收集的，可代收的

8.1c How to prepare a bank reconciliation statement?

如何准备银行往来调节表？

Compare the balances of the bank statement and the cashbook as at the end of the **accounting period** you are checking. If they **disagree**, then a bank reconciliation will be needed. **Proceed** as follows.

Step 1: **Check off** each payment listed in the cashbook against the bank statement. **Tick** each one in pencil in the cashbook, and on the bank statement. As you will see, items on the credit side of your cashbook appear on the debit side of the bank statement, and vice versa.

Step 2: Can you see on the statement any **standing orders** (STOs), **direct debits** (DDRs) or bank charges? These items may not have been recorded in your cashbook as yet.

Step 3: Take a sheet of A4 paper and begin by writing: "**balance as per bank statement**".

Step 4: Record the "balance as per bank statement", with the amount. Then list all the **errors and omissions** on the bank's part, in groups, for example listing **unpresented cheques** first, and then any **unshown lodgements**.

Step 5: **Reconcile** if the sums do not equal by rechecking **addition and subtraction**; check to make sure the balance was **carried forward** correctly from one page to another in your **check register**.

Step 6: When you have listed all the errors and omissions, write against your final figure: "**corrected (or adjusted) bank statement balance**".

accounting period 会计期，会计年度
disagree vt. 不同意，不一致
proceed vi. 继续
check off 核对
tick vt. 打勾，勾记
standing order (STO) 定期支付指令
direct debit (DDR) 直接借计
balance as per bank statement 银行对账单余额
error and omission 错误和漏录
unpresented cheque 未提交的支票
unshown lodgement 未显示的存入款项
reconcile vt. 使和谐，调节，核对
addition and subtraction n. 加法和减法
carry forward 结转
check register 支票登记簿
corrected bank statement balance 已修正银行对账单余额
adjusted a. 已调整的

Unit 8　What is a bank reconciliation statement? 什么是银行往来调节表？

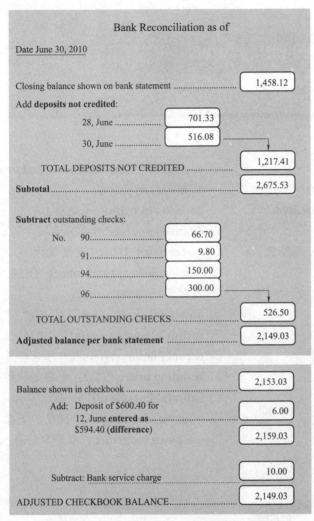

Figure 1　*A sample bank reconciliation statement*
图1　银行往来调节表样本

closing balance 结清余额，期末余额
credit *vt.* 存入
deposits not credited 未存入存款

subtotal *n.* 小计

adjusted balance per bank statement 调整后的银行对账单余额

enter as 把……记作
difference *n.* 差额

bank service charge 银行手续费
adjusted chequebook balance 调整后的支票簿余额

8.1d　Tips and warnings
提示和警告

Get in the habit of reconciling your **checking account** as soon as your statement arrives, whether by **snail mail** or email. The longer you put it off, the harder it is. If you cannot **reconcile your account**, a visit to the bank will get you free help to find the errors.

checking account 支票账户
snail mail 平信
reconcile one's account 核对账户，调节账户

8.2 Core accounting terms
核心会计术语

- account balance 账户余额
- accounting period 会计期，会计年度
- adjusted balance per bank statement 调整后的银行对账单余额
- adjusted chequebook balance 调整后的支票簿余额
- balance as per bank statement 银行对账单余额
- bank charges 银行收费
- bank service charge 银行手续费
- bank statement 银行对账单
- carry forward 结转
- checking account 支票账户
- check register 支票登记簿
- closing balance 结清余额，期末余额
- corrected bank statement balance 已修正银行对账单余额
- deposits in transit 未达存款
- deposits not credited 未存入存款
- direct debit (DDR) 直接借计
- non-sufficient fund check (NSF check) 存款不足支票
- outstanding check 未兑现支票
- reconcile one's account 核对账户，核账
- reconciliation statement 往来调节单
- standing order (STO) 定期支付指令
- subtotal ['sʌb,təutl] n. 小计
- unpresented cheque 未提交的支票
- unshown lodgement 未显示的存入款项

8.3 Extended words
扩展词汇

- addition and subtraction n. 加法和减法
- adjusted [ə'dʒʌstid] a. 已调整的
- as per 根据，按照
- check off 核对
- collectible [kə'lektəbl] a. 可收集的，可代收的
- credit ['kredit] vt. 存入
- deduct [di'dʌkt] vt. 扣除，减去
- difference ['difərəns] n. 差额
- disagree [,disə'gri:] vt. 不同意，不一致
- discrepancy [dis'krepənsi] n. 误差，出入
- enter as 把……记作
- error and omission 错误和漏录
- lodge [lɔdʒ] vt. 存放，寄放
- present [pri'zent] vt. 呈送，提交
- proceed [prə'si:d] vi. 继续
- purchases ['pə:tʃəsiz] n. [复] 购买的东西，进货
- reconcile ['rekənsail] vt. 使和谐，调节，核对

Unit 8　What is a bank reconciliation statement?　什么是银行往来调节表?

- **reconciliation** [ˌrekənsiliˈeiʃən] *n.* 调和，调节，核对
- **respective** [risˈpektiv] *a.* 各自的
- **sales invoice** *n.* 销售发票
- **snail mail** 平信
- **subtract** [səbˈtrækt] *vt.* 减去
- **term** [tə:m] *n.* 术语
- **tick** [tik] *vt.* 打勾，勾记
- **uncover** [ʌnˈkʌvə] *vt.* 揭示

8.4　Notes　注释

1) **A bank reconciliation statement is a form that allows individuals or companies to compare their respective bank account records to the bank's records of the individual/company's account balance in order to uncover any possible discrepancies.** 银行往来调节表是让个人或公司拿他们各自的银行账户记录来和银行的个人/公司账户记录相对照，以便发现可能出现的任何出入的一种表格。

　　句中 that allows...引导一个限定性定语从句，修饰其前的名词 form。

2) **cheques recorded as a lesser amount than what was presented to the bank** 记录的金额少于实际交给银行的金额的支票

3) **money received but not lodged** 收到钱款却未存入（银行）

4) **payments taken from the bank account without the company's knowledge** 从银行账户上把款划走，而公司却不知道

5) **A bank reconciliation done regularly can reduce the number of errors in an accounts system and make it easier to find missing purchases and sales invoices.** 经常进行银行往来调节可以减少账户系统出错的数量，并能更容易地发现漏掉的进货和销售发票。

6) **These are deposits that are in the company's cashbooks but not in the bank statement.** 这是指登记在公司账上，却没有登记在银行对账单上的存款。

　　句中 that are...引导一个非限定性定语从句，修饰其前的名词 deposit。

7) **The reason is that there is delay between when the cash gets recorded on the books and when the bank records the deposit.** 原因是现金在公司账簿上登记时以及银行在登记存款时，中间出现了延迟。

　　句中 that there is...引导一个表语从句，做 is 的表语。

8) **These are checks that have been deducted from the cashbooks but not the bank statement.** 这是指已经从现金簿上扣除，却没从银行对账单中扣除的支票。

  句中 that have...引导一个限定性定语从句，修饰其前的名词 checks。

9) **The reason is that there is a delay between when the check gets recorded on the books and when the bank records the check.** 原因是支票在公司账簿上登记时以及银行在登记支票时，中间出现了延迟。

  本句结构同"注 7)"。

10) **An expense for bank services that is listed on the bank statement but is not recorded on the company's books.** （这是指）列在银行对账单上，却没有记在公司账簿上的一项银行手续费用。

  句中 that is listed...引导一个非限定性定语从句，修饰其前的名词短语 expense。

11) **A customer payment by check that has been recorded as a deposit on the books but was not collectible because of insufficient funds in the account of the customer.** （这是指）客户的支票付款已经在公司账簿上记作存款，却由于客户账户上资金不足而无法代收。

  句中 that has...引导一个限定性定语从句，修饰其前的名词 payment。

12) **As you will see, items on the credit side of your cashbook appear on the debit side of the bank statement, and vice versa.** 正如你所见，记在贵公司账簿贷方的项目会出现在银行对账单的借方，反之亦然。

13) **Can you see on the statement any standing orders (STOs), direct debits (DDRs) or bank charges?** 你能在对账单上看到任何定期支付指令、直接借计或银行收费吗？

  a. standing order："定期支付指令"或"长期自动转账委托"。又名 banker's order（定期银行汇票），是你给银行下的订单，这个订单是你和银行之间签订的。用来告诉银行定期划款给某个账户（这个账户不知道你的密码，只能被动地接受），而且每次所划的款项是固定不变的，如房租、按揭贷款等。

  b. direct debit："直接借计"。这是一种支付协议，是你和商家之间签订的，商家会按照约定的日期从你账户里划款，他的划款行为是主动的（因为你给他提供密码），所以每次划的款数可以不固定，如水电费等。

14) **Get in the habit of reconciling your checking account as soon as your statement arrives, whether by snail mail or email.** 养成对账单一到，就马上核对支票账的习惯，不论是用平信还是用电子邮件。

  Snail mail：平邮，蜗牛邮件。这指由邮递员分发传递的传统信件，因其速度缓慢，像蜗牛爬行一样，故得名。

Unit 8　What is a bank reconciliation statement?　什么是银行往来调节表？

8.5 Reinforcement exercise
强化练习

1. Answer the following questions in English.

1) What's a bank reconciliation statement?
2) What situation could give rise to discrepancies?
3) What are deposits in transit?
4) What are outstanding checks?
5) What are non-sufficient fund checks (NSF checks)?

2. Put the following into Chinese.

1) bank reconciliation statement
2) account balance
3) discrepancies
4) missing purchases
5) sales invoices
6) bank balance as per your bank statement
7) bank balance as per your accounting systems
8) deposits in transit
9) outstanding checks
10) bank charges
11) non-sufficient fund checks (NSF checks)
12) deduct from the cashbooks
13) record on the books
14) collectible
15) accounting period
16) check off

3. Put the following into English.

1) 定期支付指令
2) 直接借计
3) 错误和漏录
4) 未提交的支票
5) 未显示的存入款项
6) 加法和减法
7) 结转
8) 支票登记簿
9) 已修正银行对账单余额
10) 结清余额，期末余额
11) 未存入存款
12) 银行手续费
13) 支票账户
14) 核对账户，对账
15) 银行对账单余额
16) 银行对账单

4. Subject for self-study: A Bank reconciliation chart.

Bank Account Reconciliation

Bank account*　　　First Security Bank

Statement balance:　　2780.68　　Date: 01/31/2010
Include transactions after statement date

Service charge: _____　　MISC. DEDUCTIONS
Interest earned: _____　　MISC. INCOME
Other charges: _____　　CASH DISCOUNTS

Reminder 提示

security [siˈkjuəriti] *n.* 安全，保险
First Security Bank 第一保险银行
transaction [trænˈzækʃən] *n.* 交易，业务往来
MISC. = miscellaneous [misiˈleinjəs] *a.* 其他的，杂项的
deduction [diˈdʌkʃən] *n.* 扣除，减除
interest earned 已取得利息
discount [ˈdiskaunt] *n.* 折扣

8.6 Accounting-related knowledge
会计相关知识介绍

涉外会计
Foreign-related accounting

涉外会计（foreign-related accounting）是以货币（currency）为主要计量单位（measurement unit），针对该类企业的经济活动，按照会计法规（accounting regulations）、会计准则和国际

惯例（international practices），采取复式记账方法来反映和监督各类涉外经济活动的一种专业会计。主要包括在进出口企业、三资企业、对外承包工程企业、对外劳务输出企业、对外运输、国际货代等涉外企业中，从事外币交易、进出口业务核算的监管、进出口纳 (退、免)税、涉外业务融资、外汇风险规避以及出纳等财务工作。

涉外会计的特点主要表现在：

1. 需设置记录外币交易的复币式账户（double-currency account），以达到同时核算人民币与外币的目的。

2. 需进行汇兑损溢的会计处理。外币与人民币的比价经常波动（fluctuation），因而常会出现汇兑损溢问题。

3. 涉及大量的国际贸易实务知识。由于进出口业务会涉及不同的价格条件下的交易条件及价值构成，故存在如何对销售收入予以确认、计算以及如何协调所产生的差异的问题。

4. 涉及常用的国际金融知识。通常在使用外币结算时，就涉及外汇管理、汇率制度、外汇报价等相关知识。

5. 涉及较多的税收知识。主要指在组织货物进出境时交纳的海关税金（customs tariffs），货物出口后的申报出口退税等。

6. 涉及相关的海关管制知识。涉外企业在组织货物通关时，必须遵守海关相关的管理制度。

7. 需进行经济效益的复币指标考核。要考虑政策环境、汇率政策、国际经济环境等多方面的因素变动。

8.7 Extended reading
延伸阅读

Bank statement
银行对账单

An account statement or a bank statement is a summary of all financial transactions occurring over a given period of time on a deposit account, a credit card, or any other type of account offered by a financial institution.

Bank statements are typically printed on one or several pieces of paper and either mailed directly to the account holder's address, or kept at the financial institution's local branch for pick-up. Certain ATMs offer the possibility to print, at any time, a condensed version of a bank statement.

Historically, bank statements were produced quarterly or even annually. Since the introduction of computers in banks in the 1960s, bank statements are generally produced every month. Lesser frequencies are nowadays reserved for accounts with small transaction volumes, such as investments or savings accounts. Depending on the financial institution, bank statements may include certain features such as the cancelled cheques (or their images) that cleared through the account during the statement period, promotional inserts or important notices about changes in fees or interest rates. Thanks to online banking, financial institutions offer virtual statements, also known as paperless statements or e-statements. Due to identity theft concerns, a virtual statement may be seen as a safer alternative against physical theft as it does not contain tangible personal information, and does not require extra safety measures of disposal such as shredding. However, a virtual statement is easier to obtain for the thief who is an expert on online banking.

Unit 9
What is inventory accounting?
什么是存货核算？

Core terms reminder
核心术语提示

存货核算	inventory accounting
存货成本核算	inventory costing
先进先出法	FIFO Method
后进先出法	LIFO Method
加权平均法	Weighted Average Method
个别识别法	Specific Identification Method

9.1a What is inventory?

什么是存货？

Inventory refers to **stocks** of anything necessary to do business. **Raw materials**, **goods in process** and **finished goods** all represent various forms of inventory.

Inventories are considered **current assets** in that they usually are sold within a year or within a company's **operating cycle**. Furthermore, inventories make up the most valuable current assets for most businesses.

stock *n.* 库存
raw material 原材料
goods in process 在制品
finished goods 成品
current assets 流动资产
operating cycle 经营周期

9.1b What is inventory accounting?

什么是存货核算？

Inventory accounting is the process of **determining** and **keeping track of** the inventory costs.

Inventory costs refer to all the costs a company incurs to obtain **merchandise**, including the actual merchandise costs as well as costs of **shipping**, receiving, holding and **handling**.

determine *vt.* 决定，确定
keep track of 跟踪

merchandise *n.* 商品，货物
shipping *n.* 发运
handling *n.* 搬运

9.1c What is the purpose of inventory accounting?
存货核算的目的是什么？

Proper inventory accounting enables companies to represent their net income accurately. To do so, accountants must use the **appropriate** methods for **measuring** inventory, because inaccurate inventory amounts or values can make a company seem more profitable than it really is and can **misrepresent** a company in its financial statements.

appropriate *a.* 适当的
measure *vt.* 测量，衡量
misrepresent *vt.* 误传，虚报

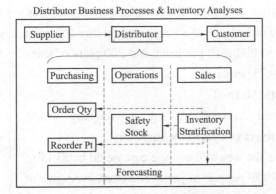

Figure 1　*A practical inventory management chart*
图 1　实用存货管理图

9.1d What are the methods of inventory accounting?
库存核算有哪些方法？

A **starting point** for inventory accounting is to determine the cost of merchandise that has been sold within a given accounting period, which is referred to as the "**cost of goods sold**". However,

starting point 起点
cost of goods sold 售出商品成本，销货成本

there are a few methods used in measuring such costs.

1. Specific Identification Method

If a company knows the cost of every individual item that is sold, then it is operating under the Specific Identification Method. This method works well when the **inventory level** a company is holding is limited, the value of its **inventory items** is high, and each inventory item is relatively unique.

Suppose a **retailer** buys its inventory from a **wholesaler** and pays $3,000 for 300 pairs of jeans. **Hence**, the cost per pair is $10. If the cost never changes, then inventory costing is simple. Every pair of jeans costs the exact same amount. Because of **inflation** as well as **discounts** and sales, however, prices tend to **fluctuate**. For instance, this retailer might buy 100 pairs of jeans on Monday for $1,000 ($10 per pair), and 200 pairs of jeans on Friday for $2,150 ($10.75 per pair).

2. Weighted Average Method

Under the Weighted Average Method, a company would determine the **weighted average cost** of the inventory.

In the example above, the weighted average cost would be $3,150 / 300 pairs which equals $10.50 per pair of jeans. Therefore, every pair of jeans would have the inventory price of $10.50, **regardless of** whether they were actually bought in the $10 purchase or the $10.75 purchase.

This weighted average would remain unchanged until the next purchase occurs, which would result in a new weighted average cost to be calculated.

3. FIFO Method

First in First Out (FIFO) is a **stock rotation policy** that items are processed in order of arrival. A **queue implements** this.

Therefore, the inventory that remains is from **the most recent purchases**. So for the given example,

---

Specific Identification Method 个别识别法

inventory level 库存量

inventory item 库存品

retailer *n.* 零售商
wholesaler *n.* 批发商
hence *ad.* 因此

inflation *n.* 通货膨胀
discount *n.* 折扣
fluctuate *vi.* 波动

Weighted Average Method 加权平均法
weighted average cost 加权平均成本

regardless of 不管，不论

FIFO Method 先进先出法

stock rotation policy 库存周转策略

queue *n.* 行列
implement *vt.* 实施，贯彻
the most recent purchases 最近的进货

the first 100 jeans that are sold will reduce inventory and increase cost of goods sold at a rate of $10 per pair. The next 200 sold will have an inventory price of $10.75 per pair. It is **irrelevant** whether customers actually buy the older pairs of jeans first.

irrelevant *a.* 不相关的

4. LIFO Method

Last in First Out (LIFO) is a stock rotation policy that **the most recently arrived items** are processed first. A **stack** implements this.

Under LIFO, the inventory that remains is always the oldest inventory. So for the given example, the first 200 jeans that are sold will reduce inventory and increase cost of goods sold at a rate of $10.75 per pair. Again, It does not matter if customers actually buy the newer pair of jeans first.

LIFO Method 后进先出法
the most recently arrived item 最新到的货
stack *n.* 堆

9.2 Core accounting terms
核心会计术语

- ☐ **cost of goods sold** 售出商品成本,销货成本
- ☐ **current assets** 流动资产
- ☐ **FIFO Method** 先进先出法
- ☐ **inventory item** 库存品
- ☐ **inventory level** 库存量
- ☐ **inventory accounting** 存货核算
- ☐ **inventory costing** 存货成本核算
- ☐ **LIFO Method** 后进先出法
- ☐ **operating cycle** 经营周期
- ☐ **Specific Identification Method** 个别识别法
- ☐ **stock rotation policy** 库存周转策略
- ☐ **the most recent purchases** 最近的进货
- ☐ **the most recently arrived item** 最新到的物品
- ☐ **Weighted Average Method** 加权平均法

9.3 Extended words
扩展词汇

- ☐ **appropriate** [əˈprəupriit] *a.* 适当的
- ☐ **determine** [diˈtəːmin] *vt.* 决定,确定
- ☐ **discount** [ˈdiskaunt] *n.* 折扣
- ☐ **finished goods** 成品
- ☐ **fluctuate** [ˈflʌktjueit] *vi.* 波动
- ☐ **goods in process** 在制品
- ☐ **handling** [ˈhændliŋ] *n.* 搬运
- ☐ **hence** [hens] *ad.* 因此

- **implement** ['implimənt] *vt.* 实施，贯彻
- **inflation** [in'fleiʃən] *n.* 通货膨胀
- **irrelevant** [i'relivənt] *a.* 不相关的
- **keep track of** 跟踪
- **measure** ['meʒə] *vt.* 测量，衡量
- **merchandise** ['mə:tʃəndaiz] *n.* 商品，货物
- **misrepresent** ['mis,repri'zent] *vt.* 误传，虚报
- **queue** [kju:] *n.* 行列，队列
- **raw material** 原材料
- **regardless of** 不管，不论
- **retailer** [ri:'teilə] *n.* 零售商
- **shipping** ['ʃipiŋ] *n.* 发运
- **stack** [stæk] *n.* 堆
- **starting point** 起点
- **stock** [stɔk] *n.* 库存
- **wholesaler** ['həulseilə] *n.* 批发商

9.4 Notes 注释

1) **Inventory refers to stocks of anything necessary to do business.** 存货是指商品交易所必需的所有库存品。

   句中 necessary to do business 是形容词短语后置，做定语，修饰其前的名词短语 stocks of anything。

2) **Inventories are considered current assets in that they usually are sold within a year or within a company's operating cycle.** 存货被看作流动资产，表现在存货通常是在一年内或在公司的一个营业周期内售出。

   句中 in that 意为"由于，因为，表现在……，在这一点上"。

3) **Inventory accounting is the process of determining and keeping track of the inventory costs.** 存货核算是确定和跟踪存货成本的过程。

   句中 determing 和 keeping 是两个并列的 V-ing 形式，共同做介词 of 的宾语。

4) **Inventory costs refer to all the costs a company incurs to obtain merchandise, including the actual merchandise costs as well as costs of shipping, receiving, holding and handling.** 存货成本是指公司为了获得商品所发生的所有费用，包括商品本身的实际成本以及运输成本、收货成本、持有成本及搬运成本。

   本句 a company incurs 是限定性定语从句，其前省略关系词 that, 修饰名词 costs。

5) **…because inaccurate inventory amounts or values can make a company seem more profitable than it really is and can misrepresent a company in its financial statements.** ……因为不准确的存货量和价值可以让公司的赢利看上去超过其实际情况，并且会虚报公司的财务报表。

6) **A starting point for inventory accounting is to determine the cost of merchandise that has been sold within a given accounting period, which is referred to as the "cost of goods sold".** 存货核算的起点就是要确定在特定会计年度内售出商品的成本，这被称为"售出商品

成本"。

本句包含两个定语从句,第一个是 that has…period,第二个是 which is…,前者是限定性从句,修饰名词 merchandise,后者是非限定性从句,对整个句子进行补充说明。

7) **This method works well when the inventory level a company is holding is limited, the value of its inventory items is high, and each inventory item is relatively unique.** 当一个公司所持有的存货量有限、存货品的价值高并且每个存货品相对独特时,这个方法会起作用。

句中 a company is holding 是限定性定语从句,前面省略了关系 that,修饰名词短语 inventory level。

8) **In the example above, the weighted average cost would be $3,150 / 300 pairs which equals $10.50 per pair of jeans.** 在上面的例子中,该加权平均成本将是$3,150 / 300 条,等于每条牛仔裤$10.50。

句中 which 引导一个非限定性定语从句,对整句内容进行补充说明。

9) **…regardless of whether they were actually bought in the $10 purchase or the $10.75 purchase.** ……不论这些牛仔裤事实上是$10 进的货还是$10.75 进的货。

句中 whether 引导一个宾语从句,做介词 of 的宾语。

10) **This weighted average would remain unchanged until the next purchase occurs, which would result in a new weighted average cost to be calculated.** 该加权平均成本在下一次进货前会保持不变,这会(在下一次进货时)产生出新计算出来的加权平均成本。

句中 which 引导一个非限定性定语从句,对整句内容进行补充说明。

11) **First in First out (FIFO) is a stock rotation policy that items are processed in order of arrival.** 先进先出(FIFO)是物品按到货顺序进行处理的一个库存周转策略。

句中 that items…不是定语从句,而是名词 policy 的同位语。

12) **A queue implements this.** 排列式实施的就是这个方法(FIFO 法)。

13) **Therefore, the inventory that remains is from the most recent purchases.** 因此,留下来的存货就是最近的进货。

句中 that remains 是限定性定语从句,修饰其前的名词 inventory.

14) **So for the given example, the first 100 jeans that are sold will reduce inventory and increase cost of goods sold at a rate of $10 per pair.** 所以,就所给的例子而言,售出的头 100 条牛仔裤会减少库存量并按每条$10 的价格增加售货成本。

句中 that are sold 是限定性定语从句,修饰其前的名词 jeans.

15) **It is irrelevant whether customers actually buy the older pairs of jeans first.** 客户是否实际上先购买旧牛仔裤,这点是不相关的。

16) **Last in First out (LIFO) is a stock rotation policy that the most recently arrived items are processed first.** 后进先出法(FIFO)是指先对最新到货的物品进行处理的库存周转策略。

句中 that 引导一个限定性定语从句,修饰其前的名词 policy.

17) **Under LIFO, the inventory that remains is always the oldest inventory.** 在 LIFO 法中,留下来的存货总是最旧的存货。

句中 that remains 是限定性定语从句，修饰其前的名词 inventory。

18) **So for the given example, the first 200 jeans that are sold will reduce inventory and increase cost of goods sold at a rate of $10.75 per pair.** 所以，就所给的例子而言，售出的头 200 条牛仔裤会减少库存量并按每条$10.75 的价格增加售货成本。

句中 that are sold 是限定性定语从句，修饰其前的名词 jeans。

19) **Again, it does not matter if customers actually buy the newer pair of jeans first.** 同样，客户是否实际上先购买新牛仔裤，这一点无关紧要。

句中 if 引导一个宾语从句，做动词 matter 的宾语。

9.5 Reinforcement exercise
强化练习

1. Answer the following questions in English.

1) What is inventory?
2) What are inventory costs?
3) What is inventory accounting?
4) What is the Specific Identification Method?
5) What is the Weighted Average Method?
6) What is the FIFO method?
7) What is the LIFO method?

2. Put the following into Chinese.

1) inventory accounting
2) inventory costing
3) FIFO Method
4) LIFO Method
5) Weighted Average Method
6) Specific Identification Method
7) inventory
8) raw material
9) goods in process
10) finished goods
11) current assets
12) operating cycle
13) keeping track of the inventory costs
14) incur costs
15) obtain merchandise costs of shipping, receiving, holding and handling

3. Put the following into English.

1) 净收入
2) 衡量存货
3) 虚报公司的财务报表
4) 确定商品成本
5) 在特定会计年度内
6) 存货量

Unit 9 What is inventory accounting? 什么是存货核算?

7) 存货品
8) 零售商和批发商
9) 通货膨胀
10) 折扣
11) 波动的价格
12) 库存周转策略
13) 增加销货成本
14) 减少库存量
15) 最新到的物品
16) 最近的进货

4. Subject for self-study: An inventory analysis chart.

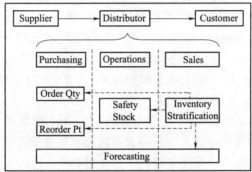

distributor [dis'tribjutə] *n.* 库存
business processes 业务程序
Qty = quantity 数量
Reorder Pt 再订购跟踪 (Pt = private tracker)
safety stock 安全库存
stratification [ˌstrætifi'keiʃən] *n.* 层化
forecasting ['fɔːkɑːstiŋ] *n.* 预测

9.6 Accounting-related knowledge

会计相关知识介绍

各种存货核算法的比较
Comparisons between various methods of inventory accounting

1. 月末加权平均法在计算机会计信息系统中不适用

加权平均法（Weighted Average Method）指在月末进行一次加权平均单价（unit price）计算，平时无法从数据库（database）"账簿"（books）中得到结存存货的单价，在计算机条件下当暂估入库进行时无法进行存货的核算，所以月末加权平均法在计算机会计信息系统中不具有可操作性。

2. 采用 FIFO 和 LIFO 方法的利与弊

采用"先进先出法"（FIFO）和"后进先出法"（LIFO）这两种方法，平时数据库"账簿"中有结存单价。因此，当暂估存货入库时可以实时得到相应的入库价格。但是，在物价变动时期，对财务的影响比较显著。采用先进先出法，当物价上涨时，会高估（overestimate）企业当期利润和存货的库存价值（stock value）；物价下跌时会低估（underestimate）收益和资产（income and assets）。采用后进先出法，结果正好相反。在物价变动的一定时期，采用某一方法对企业可能有利，但当形势逆转时，则会对企业有不良影响。

3. 个别计价法的局限性

采用个别计价法（Specific Identification Pricing Method）时，平时账簿中也可能随时得到暂估存货的入库成本，可以掌握发出存货成本和实际库存情况（actual inventory status）。但这种方法要求根据采购批别，挂上标签，分别存放，分别保管，以便发出时能够识别是哪个批次购进的。对于普通存货，若采用这种方法，会计核算不成问题，但仓库部门工作量太大，仓储、保管费用太高。个别计价法只适合于量少、价高的贵重物品。

4. 移动加权平均法

移动加权平均法（Moving Weighted Average Method）是计算机会计信息系统可采用的最优方法（optimum method）。采用移动加权平均法，每次收入存货后，立即根据现有存货的总价值（total value）和总数量（total quantity）计算出新的单位成本（unit cost）。每发出一批存货都要根据发出存货的数量和前一次进货时计算的平均单位成本（average unit cost）确定发出存货成本和结存存货的价值，这种方法能及时提供存货的成本资料。在手工条件下移动加权平均成本法因计算工作相当烦琐、计算量太大而很少采用，但在计算机条件下，计算机高速计算的优势正好弥补了这一缺陷，使移动加权平均法在实际工作中具有可操作性，并且对暂估入库存货的成本的确定非常有利。

通过分析可知，移动加权平均法所确定的存货单价在一定程度上应该说是最接近暂估存货实际单价的，而且这一方法在计算机条件下可以充分发挥其长处，克服其弱势，移动加权平均法是计算机会计信息系统中确定暂估存货入账价值的最佳选择。

9.7 Extended reading
延伸阅读

Inventory turnover
存 货 周 转

In accounting, the inventory turnover is an equation that measures the number of times inventory is sold or used over in a period such as a year. The equation equals the cost of goods sold divided by the average inventory. Inventory turnover is also known as inventory turns, stockturn, stock turns, turns, and stock turnover.

Inventory Turnover Equation:

$$\text{Inventory Turnover} = \frac{\text{Cost of Goods Sold}}{\text{Average Inventory}}$$

The formula for inventory turnover:

$$\text{Average Inventory} = \frac{\text{Beginning Inventory} + \text{Ending Inventory}}{2}$$

Application in Business

A low turnover rate may point to overstocking, obsolescence, or deficiencies in the product line or marketing effort. However, in some instances a low rate may be appropriate, such as where higher inventory levels occur in anticipation of rapidly rising prices or shortages. A high turnover rate may indicate inadequate inventory levels, which may lead to a loss in business. Assume cost of sales is $70,000, beginning inventory is $10,000, and ending inventory is $9,000. The inventory turnover equals 7.37 times ($70,000/$9,500).

It should be noted that some compilers of industry data use sales as the numerator instead of cost of sales. Cost of sales yields a more realistic turnover ratio, but it is often necessary to use sales for purposes of comparative analysis. Cost of sales is considered to be more realistic because of the difference in which sales and the cost of sales are recorded. Sales are generally recorded at market value, i.e. the value at which the marketplace paid for goods or services provided by the firm. In the event that the firm had an exceptional year and the market paid a premium for the firm's goods and services, then the numerator may be an inaccurate measure. However, cost of sales is recorded by the firm at what the firm actually paid for the materials available for sale. Additionally, firms may reduce prices to generate sales in an effort to cycle inventory. In this article, the terms "cost of sales" and "cost of goods sold" are synonymous.

Unit 10
How to manage your accounts receivable?
如何管理应收账？

Core terms reminder
核心术语提示

应收账	A/R — account receivables
应收账款平均回收天数	DSO — Days Sales Outstanding
净月结30天	Net 30 / Net 30 Days
回收资金	to recover money
按卖方细分	to break down by vendor
销货分类控制账	sales ledger
销货簿	sales journal
应收账总额	accounts receivable total
应收账余额	accounts receivable balance
应收账均值	accounts receivable average
应收账数额	accounts receivable amount
账龄报告	aging report

Unit 10　How to manage your accounts receivable? 如何管理应收账？　　103

10.1a　What are accounts receivable – A/R?

什么是应收账？

　　If a company has **receivables**, this means it has made a sale but has yet to collect the money from the purchaser. To understand **account receivables (A/R)** on your company's balance sheet, it simply is any amount customers owe the company. It is considered a **current asset** if the amount is due within one year. The actual process of bookkeeping can get quite difficult depending on the **size** of your company.

receivable n. 应收账

account receivables (A/R) 应收账

current asset 流动资产

size n. 尺寸，规模

10.1b　What is the nature of accounts receivable?

应收账的性质是什么？

　　Account receivables are a crucial part of every business because it deals directly with **collecting money** owed to the business. Businesses need to recognize that not all account receivables will be

collect money 集资，收款

paid. As a **business owner**, it is a good idea to be aware of this process of account receivable because there always is the chance could happen to you. You have to be prepared for when it happens so you will have a better chance of **recovering** some or all of your money owed.

business owner 企业主

recover *vt.* 回收，收回
to recover money 回收资金

10.1c How do we calculate accounts receivable?
如何计算应收账？

The following steps are useful hints in calculating account receivables.

Step 1

Gather all accounts receivable information for the entire year. Your accounts should be **broken down** by vendor. In your **sales ledger** or **journal**, you should have **accounts receivable totals** for the month for each vendor.

break down 分解，细分
be broken down by vendor 按卖方细分
sales ledger 销货账，销货分类控制账
sales journal 销货日记账，销货簿
accounts receivable total 应收账总额

Unit 10 How to manage your accounts receivable? 如何管理应收账？

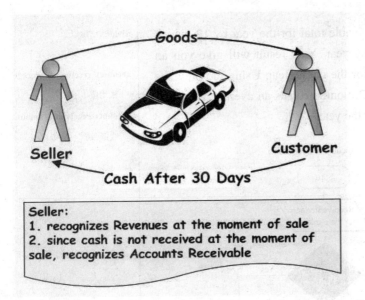

Step 2

Add accounts receivable totals for each vendor you've **billed** during a particular month but haven't been paid. Perform this task for all your vendors in every **calendar month**. When you're done with this task, you should have an **accounts receivable balance** for each month of the year.

Step 3

Add your accounts receivable balance for all 12 months. If you have accounts receivable of $200 for all 12 months, your total accounts receivable for the entire year will equal $2,400.

bill *vt.* 开票，记账

calendar month 历月

accounts receivable balance 应收账余额

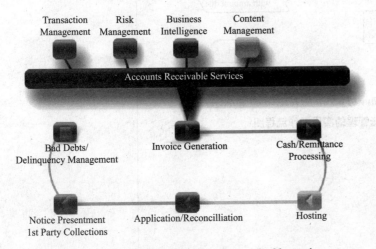

Figure 1 *Practical diagram for accounts receivable services*
图 1   应收账服务示意图

Step 4

Divide your accounts receivable total for the year by 12, which represents the 12 months of the year. Your result will give you an **accounts receivable average** for the entire year. Using the previous example, dividing $2,400 by 12 months equals an average **accounts receivable amount** of $200 for the year.

divide vt. 除以

accounts receivable average 应收账均值

accounts receivable amount 应收账数额

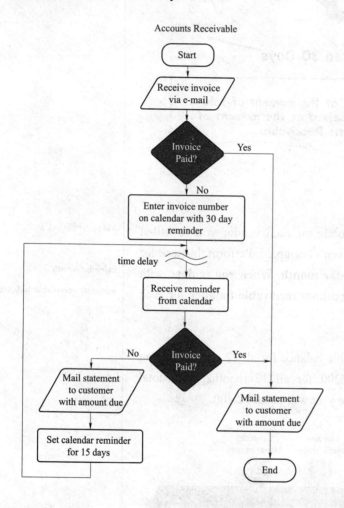

Figure 2 *Practical workflow of accounts receivable management*
图 2 应收账管理的实用工作流程图

10.1d How do we reduce accounts receivable?
如何减少应收账？

Cash is always king. Businesses must be mindful of **payroll** and the **day-to-day operations** of an organization. It is crucial that every company has someone who is tasked with **monitoring** and reducing account receivables. Here are five steps to ensure that accounts receivable **turns into cash** in a timely manner.

Step 1
Choose a software tool that allows simple reporting (called an **Aging Report**) of A/R (account receivables). This tool should be able to report **cash outstanding** in 30-day **intervals** (**Net 30**) from the date of sale or the date the service was delivered. A report that is **exportable** into an **Excel format** is helpful.

Step 2
Combine A/R into similar categories. Individual **payers** behave differently than organizations. Commercial payers may have different **schedules** than government payers. Viewing receivables as groups allows the A/R Manager to develop a strategy for reducing certain types of accounts receivable.

Step 3
Address the oldest and largest A/R first. Accounts that are over 120 days old are more important than a 30-day-old account. Finding the biggest dollar value in the oldest **time frame** means **tackling** the A/R with the highest risk of loss.

Step 4
Contact **front line managers** in the organization to develop processes that reduce the **Days Sales Outstanding** (DSO) based on findings with specific vendors. It may be current policy to allow three to four weeks to pass before payer information makes it from the Front Line Manager to the A/R Manager. Processing this information immediately may reduce DSO by three to four weeks.

---

payroll *n.* 薪水册
day-to-day operation 日常经营
monitor *vt.* 监督

turn into cash 变成现金，变现

aging report 账龄报告

cash outstanding 未付现金，未达现金
interval *n.* 间隔
Net 30 净月结 30 天
exportable *a.* 可输出的
Excel format （微软 OFFICE 办公软件中的）Excel 电子表格格式
payer *n.* 付款人
schedule *n.* 时间表，进度表

address *vt.* 从事，处理

time frame 时间框架
tackle *vt.* 处理，解决

front line manager 一线经理
Days Sales Outstanding (DSO) 日销货未收款；应收账款平均回收天数

Step 5

Communicate Collection Issues **with** vendors. Often written or verbal communication stating the facts of a particular situation will **generate** the conversation needed to **convert** accounts receivable **into** cash.

communicate *vt.* 通信，沟通
communicate with 与……沟通
generate *vt.* 产生，发生
convert *vt.* 使转换
to convert...into 把……转换成

10.2 Core accounting terms
核心会计术语

- **accounts receivable amount** 应收账数额
- **accounts receivable average** 应收账均值
- **accounts receivable balance** 应收账余额
- **accounts receivable total** 应收账总额
- **aging report** 账龄报告
- **bill** *vt.* 开票，记账
- **break down by vendor** 按卖方细分
- **account payable** 应付账
- **account receivables (A/R)** 应收账
- **cash outstanding** 未付现金，未达现金
- **collect money** 集资，收款
- **current asset** 流动资产
- **Days Sales Outstanding** (DSO) 日销货未收款；应收账款平均回收天数
- **Net 30** 净月结30天
- **payer** ['peiə] *n.* 付款人
- **payroll** ['peirəul] *n.* 薪水册
- **receivables** [ri'si:vəblz] *n.* 应收账
- **sales journal** 销货日记账，销货簿
- **sales ledger** 销货账，销货分类控制账
- **turn into cash** 变成现金，变现

10.3 Extended words
扩展词汇

- **address** [ə'dres] *vt.* 从事，处理
- **break down** 分解，细分
- **calendar month** 历月
- **business owner** 企业主
- **communicate** [kə'mju:nikeit] *vt.* 通信，沟通
- **communicate with** 与……沟通
- **convert** [kən'və:t] *vt.* 使转换
- **convert...into** 把……转换成
- **day-to-day operation** 日常经营
- **divide** [di'vaid] *vt.* 除以
- **Excel format** （微软OFFICE办公软件中的）Excel电子表格格式
- **exportable** ['ekspɔ:təbl] *a.* 可输出的
- **front line manager** 一线经理
- **generate** ['dʒenə,reit] *vt.* 产生，发生
- **interval** ['intəvəl] *n.* 间隔

Unit 10 How to manage your accounts receivable? 如何管理应收账? 109

- **monitor** ['mɔnitə] *vt.* 监督
- **recover** [ri'kʌvə] *vt.* 回收，收回
- **schedule** ['ʃedju:l; (US)'skedʒul] *n.* 时间表，进度表
- **size** [saiz] *n.* 尺寸，规模
- **tackle** ['tækl] *vt.* 处理，解决
- **time frame** 时间框架
- **vendor** ['vendɔ:] *n.* 卖方，厂商

10.4 Notes 注释

1) **If a company has receivables, this means it has made a sale but has yet to collect the money from the purchaser.** 如果一个公司有应收账，这就意味着公司已经售货但还没有从买方收到货款。

   句中 it has... 是宾语从句，其前省略 that，做动词 means 的宾语。

2) **To understand account receivables (A/R) on your company's balance sheet, it simply is any amount customers owe the company.** 要理解贵公司资产负债表上的应收账，简单地讲这就是客户欠公司的金额。

   句中 customers owe the company 是限定性定语从句，其前省略关系词 that，修饰先行词 amount。

3) **It is considered a current asset if the amount is due within one year.** 如果金额应在一年内支付，应收账就被看成是流动资产。

   单词 due 的意思很多，其中有"应付的，到期的"的意思，如：
   a. to pay the interest due 支付到期利息
   b. the date due 到期日期
   c. the amount due 应付金额
   d. This note will become due. 这张票据就要到期了。

4) **Account receivables are a crucial part of every business because it deals directly with collecting money owed to the business.** 应收账是每个企业至关重要的一部分，因为它直接涉及收回企业的被欠钱款。

   句中 owed to the business 是过去分词短语，在句中作定语，修饰其前的名词 money，相当于定语从句 (that is) owed...

5) **Businesses need to recognize that not all account receivables will be paid.** 企业必须认识到，并不是所有的应收账都能被支付。

   句中 that 引导一个宾语从句，做动词 recognize 的宾语。

6) **As a business owner, it is a good idea to be aware of this process of account receivable because there always is the chance this could happen to you.** 作为企业主，清楚应收账的程序是明智的，因为应收账发生在任何企业主身上的概率都存在。

   句中 this could happen to you 是定语从句，其前省略 that，修饰名词 chance。

7) **You have to be prepared for when it happens so you will have a better chance of recovering some or all of your money owed.** 应收账发生时，要有所准备，这样就会有更大的机会回收被欠的一些或全部钱款。

8) **Your accounts should be broken down by vendor.** 应按卖方来细分应收账。

9) **In your sales ledger or journal, you should have accounts receivable totals for the month for each vendor.** 在销货分类控制账或销货簿中，应该为每个卖方计算出当月的应收账总计。

10) **Add accounts receivable totals for each vendor you've billed during a particular month but haven't been paid.** 对于特定月份内已记账但还没有付款的每个卖方，要把其应收账总计相加。

  句中 you've billed 是限定性定语从句，其前省略 that，修饰名词 vendor。

11) **Perform this task for all your vendors in every calendar month.** 在每个历月都要为所有的卖方做这项工作。

12) **When you're done with this task, you should have an accounts receivable balance for each month of the year.** 这项工作完成时，你就应该得到当年每个月的应收账结余。

13) **Divide your accounts receivable total for the year by 12, which represents the 12 months of the year.** 把应收账总计除以 12，12 表示当年的 12 个月。

  句中 which 引导一个非限定性定语从句，对句子进行补充说明。

14) **Your result will give you an accounts receivable average for the entire year.** 计算结果会给出整年的应收账均值。

15) **Using the previous example, dividing $2,400 by 12 months equals an average accounts receivable amount of $200 for the year.** 使用前面的例子，把$2 400 除以 12 个月就等于当年平均应收账金额$200。

  句中 using 是 V-ing 短语，作伴随性状语；dividing 引导另一个 V-ing 短语，做主语。

16) **Cash is always king.** 现金总是为王。

17) **Businesses must be mindful of payroll and the day-to-day operations of an organization.** 公司必须留意单位的薪水册及日常经营情况。

18) **It is crucial that every company has someone who is tasked with monitoring and reducing account receivables.** 每个公司应该派人监督并降低应收账，这一点至关重要。

  这是一个形式主语的句子，it 是形式主语，代表后面的 that 从句（真实主语），who 引导一个限定性定语从句，修饰先行词 someone。

19) **Here are five steps to ensure that accounts receivable turns into cash in a timely manner.** 这里有五个步骤来确保应收账及时变现。

  句中 that 引导一个宾语从句，做动词 ensure 的宾语。

20) **Choose a software tool that allows simple reporting (called an Aging Report) of A/R

Unit 10　How to manage your accounts receivable?　如何管理应收账？　　111

(account receivables). 选择一套能够进行简单 A/R（应收账）报告（即"账龄报告"）的软件工具。

　　句中 that 引导一个限定性定语从句，修饰先行词 tool。

21) **This tool should be able to report cash outstanding in 30-day intervals (Net 30) from the date of sale or the date the service was delivered.** 这个工具应当能够报告从销货日算起，或从服务提交日算起 30 天间隔（净月结 30 天）的未偿付现金。

　　Net 30 days：净月结 30 天。即无论是本月当中哪天出的货，付款期都从当月的最后一天开始计算 30 天后付款。这样无形中实际付款时间要在送货后 30～60 天。

22) **A report that is exportable into an Excel format is helpful.** 可以输出为 Excel 表格格式的报告会有帮助。

　　句中 that 引导一个定语从句，修饰先行词 report。

23) **Combine A/R into similar categories.** 把 A/R 组合成相似类别。

24) **Individual payers behave differently than organizations.** 个人付款人和单位付款人（在付款时）表现方式不同。

25) **Commercial payers may have different schedules than government payers.** 在付款时间安排方面，商业付款人可能会比政府付款人有所区别。

26) **Viewing receivables as groups allows the A/R Manager to develop a strategy for reducing certain types of accounts receivable.** 把应收账看成组别，能够使 A/R 经理形成降低某类应收账的策略。

27) **Address the oldest and largest A/R first.** 先处理账龄最长、金额最大的 A/R。

28) **Accounts that are over 120 days old are more important than a 30-day-old account.** 超过 120 天的账要比 30 天的账更重要。

　　句中 that 引导一个限定性定语从句，修饰先行词 accounts。

29) **Finding the biggest dollar value in the oldest time frame means tackling the A/R with the highest risk of loss.** 在账龄最长的时间框架中找出最大的美元价值就意味着着手处理损失风险最高的 A/R。

　　句中有两个 V-ing 短语，前一个是 finding…，做主语，后一个是 tackling…，做动词 mean 的宾语。

30) **Contact front line managers in the organization to develop processes that reduce the Days Sales Outstanding (DSO) based on findings with specific vendors.** 联系公司的一线经理，以便根据具体卖方的发现结果来形成降低应收账款平均回收天数（DSO）的程序。

　　a. 句中 that…vendors 引导一个限定性定语从句，修饰先行词 processes。

　　b. based on…是过去分词短语引导的定语，修饰名词短语 Days Sales Outstanding。

c. DSO: 应收账款平均回收天数,是 Days Sales Outstanding 的缩写,指一家企业把账目变成现金的平均时间。

31) **It may be current policy to allow three to four weeks to pass before payer information makes it from the Front Line Manager to the A/R Manager.** 宽限三、四周时间好让付款人的信息能够从一线经理转到 A/R 经理手中,这可能是通行的策略。

32) **Processing this information immediately may reduce DSO by three to four weeks.** 立即处理这些信息可以把 DSO 降低三、四周时间。

33) **Communicate collection issues with vendors.** 和卖方沟通收款事项。

34) **Often, vendors may not be aware of any issues with accounts payable.** 卖方经常意识不到应付账的任何事项。

35) **Often written or verbal communication stating the facts of a particular situation will generate the conversation needed to convert accounts receivable into cash.** 说明特定情况事实的书面或口头沟通经常能引发把应收账转换成现金所必要的交谈。

　　句中 needed 是过去分词,引导一个定语,修饰其前的名词 conversation,相当于定语从句 which is needed。

10.5 Reinforcement exercise
强化练习

1. Answer the following questions in English.

1) What is the definition of accounts receivable?
2) What is the nature of accounts receivable?
3) How do you understand DSO?
4) How do you understand Net 30?

2. Put the following into Chinese.

1) A/R — account receivables　　　　2) DSO — Days Sales Outstanding

3) Net 30
4) recover money
5) break down by vendor
6) sales ledger
7) sales journal
8) accounts receivable total
9) accounts receivable balance
10) accounts receivable average
11) accounts receivable amount
12) aging report

3. Put the following into English.

1) Cash is king.
2) day-to-day operation
3) monitor and reduce account receivables
4) turn into cash in a timely manner
5) cash outstanding
6) in 30-day intervals (Net 30)
7) individual payers
8) commercial payers
9) government payer
10) view receivables as groups
11) reduce certain types of accounts receivable
12) in the oldest time frame

4. Subject for self-study: An account receivable workflow chart.

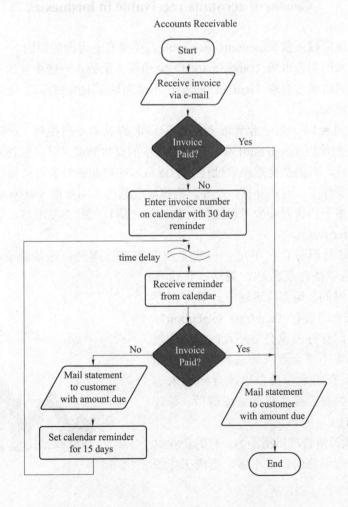

Reminder 提示

enter invoice number 输入发票号
remainder [ri'meində] *n.* 剩余, 余数
Mail statement to customer with amount due 把标有应付金额的报表邮寄给客户

10.6 Accounting-related knowledge
会计相关知识介绍

企业应收账形成的原因
Causes of accounts receivable in businesses

  造成企业出现应收账款（accounts receivable）主要有五方面的原因。
  一是供大于求的买方市场（buyer market）竞争压力所致。一些企业出于竞争的需要，为了扩大产品销售和市场占有率（market share），不适当地采取赊销方式（credit sale），导致企业应收账款大量增加。
  二是制度不健全。一些企业管理者侧重于日常的成本支出控制（cost and expenditure control），对现金的流出（cash outflow）有较为严格的审批制度，但对应收账款及赊销管理制度的制定不够重视。有的企业赊销审批程序不规范，在对赊销对象资信情况（qualification）缺乏充分了解的条件下，贸然发货。此外，销售与收款的不同步性（desynchronization）使得企业营销人员侧重于销售而较少考虑清收欠款，加之清收欠款力度不够，导致企业应收账款不能及时收回（recover）。
  三是合同签订及履行存在不足。一些企业在签订合同时，未能就合同条款（contract terms）进行严格审核，在品种、规格、售价、代垫费用、交货时间、地点、运输方式等方面存在诸多漏洞。在合同履行（contract execution）过程中，发货部门有时出现交货不及时、品种规格数量出错、质量不符合要求等违约（breach of contract）行为，有的企业擅自更改合同而未与对方进行磋商，给对方拖欠货款造成借口，导致企业应收账款增加。
  四是应收账款日常管理措施不力。有的企业财务部门与销售、仓储部门沟通不够，造成工作脱

节；对客户所欠的应收账款数额（amount）、账龄（aging）及增减（increase/decrease）情况不明，风险意识薄弱；没有根据客户欠款情况进行分类建档，对逾期应收账款（accounts receivable overdue）未能及时清收，导致企业出现呆账（uncollectible accounts）、坏账（bad debts）。

五是社会商业信用（business credit）问题。由于我国实行市场经济体制时间较短，经济立法不健全，一些不法分子利用可乘之机恶意诈骗货款的现象时有发生。在执法上，受地方保护、关系网及执法人员素质等多方面影响，执行难是众所周知的事实。

应收账款是企业的一项重要流动资产（current assets），也是一项风险较大的资产。完善应收账款管理机制，对加快货款回收（recovery of goods payment）、防范财务风险（finance risks）、提高经营效益具有重要意义。

10.7 Extended reading
延伸阅读

Managing your DSO
管理您的 DSO（日销货未收款）

DSO stands for Days Sales Outstanding.

It is a commonly used measure for the invoicing collection process. Investopedia defines DSO as "A measure of the average number of days that a company takes to collect revenue after a sale has been made".

If you are strictly a cash business, then your DSO will be "0". If you generate invoices for your customers and give them credit terms (some number of days before they are supposed to pay) then you will have an accounts receivable balance and thus a DSO. You can use the DSO number to measure the efficiency of your collections. Since DSO is so popular you can also use it as a gauge against other companies in your industry.

Benefit of reinforced management of DSO
- Minimized delinquencies
- Increased cash flow & recoveries
- Decrease in bad debt
- Elimination of unapplied credits
- Minimized operating cost

Calculating your Days Sales Outstanding

The calculation is as follows.

$$DSO = \frac{\text{Accounts Receivables}}{\text{Invoiced Sales in Period}} \times \text{Days in period}$$

Here is a simple example of how to calculate DSO.

A company started June with $700 in receivables (Invoices still not paid from May and earlier).

Lets say the company had sales of $1,100 in June.

- The company got cash for $100 that was not cash for invoices. Some one came into their office and gave them $100 for a widget that never got invoiced.
- They generated invoices with Net 30 day terms (customer has 30 days to pay) for the other **$1,000**. These are "credit sales". The total Credit/Invoice Sales for June will be $1,000 (not $1,100 since they got cash for $100 and never invoiced it, the DSO on that cash is 0).
- During the month they got payments on invoices of $500.
- So $700+$1,000-$500=$1,200 for their accounts receivable at the end of June. 700 that was still open + $1,000 in new invoices — $500 in payments.

NOTE: It does not matter what invoices the $500 got applied to or even if it gets applied for the DSO calculation. It just matters what the A/R is at the end of June.

Their accounts receivable at the end of June would be $1,200. The DSO for the month of June would be $1,200/$1,000 × 30 (# of days in June) = 36.

A 36 day average to get paid is not too bad. Generally speaking, if your DSO is under 40 (assuming Net 30 day credit terms) you are fairly efficient at collecting your money.

DSO measures efficiency not effectiveness.

In a future article, we will show you the problems with DSO. Your goal is to get paid faster and there are other performance indicators that can be used, along with DSO, to get a clearer picture of your collections effectiveness.

Unit 11
How to depreciate fixed assets?
固定资产如何折旧？

Core terms reminder
核心术语提示

折旧	depreciation
摊销	amortization
损耗	depletion
固定资产	fixed asset
流动资产	current asset
有形资产	tangible asset
无形资产	intangible asset
折旧费用	depreciation expense
残值	residual value
账面值	book value
冲减值，折余值	WDV (written-down value)
纯账面价值	NBV (net book value)

11.1a What are fixed assets?

什么是固定资产？

Fixed assets are a long-term, **tangible asset** held by an organization and not expected to be converted into cash in the current or upcoming **fiscal year**. Buildings, **real estate**, equipment and furniture are good examples of fixed assets.

Fixed assets are sometimes collectively referred to as "**plant**".

Fixed assets are also known as a **non-current asset** or as property, plant, and equipment (**PP&E**). This can be compared with **current assets** such as cash or bank accounts, which are described as **liquid assets**. In most cases, only tangible assets are referred to as fixed.

fixed assets 固定资产
tangible asset 有形资产

fiscal year 财政年度
real estate 房地产

plant n. （全部）设备，厂房
non-current asset 非流动资产
PP&E 财产、厂房和设备，固定资产
current asset 流动资产
liquid asset 流动资产，可变现资产

11.1b What is depreciation?

什么是折旧？

Depreciation is the process by which a company allocates an asset's cost over the duration of its **useful life**. Each time a company prepares its financial statements, it records a **depreciation expense** to allocate a portion of the cost of the buildings, machines or equipment it has purchased to the current fiscal year.

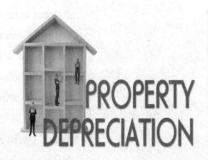

The purpose of recording depreciation as an expense is to spread the **initial price** of the asset over its useful life. For **intangible assets** —

depreciation n. 贬值，折旧

useful life 生命周期，有效期，使用寿命

depreciation expense 折旧费用

initial price 最初成本
intangible assets 无形资产

such as **brands** and **intellectual property** — this process of allocating costs over time is called **amortization**. For natural resources — such as **minerals**, **timber** and **oil reserves** — it's called **depletion**.

brand *n.* 品牌
intellectual property 知识产权
amortization *n.* 摊销，摊还，分期偿付
mineral *n.* 矿物
timber *n.* 木材
oil reserves 石油储备
depletion *n.* 损耗，耗损，折耗

Brands are intangible assets.

11.1c What are the elements in planning depreciation?

计划折旧时有哪些要素？

In depreciating an asset, three elements must first be determined.
- the initial cost of the asset
- the **expected useful life** of the asset
- the estimated value of the asset at the end of its useful life

The **initial cost** of the asset is the cost to purchase the asset along with any amounts spent to get the asset ready to use. Sales taxes, **freight**, and **installation** costs are examples of some of the costs that can be included in the cost of the asset for depreciation purposes.

expected useful life 预期使用寿命

initial cost 最初成本，开办费，创办费

freight *n.* 运费
installation *n.* 安装

Machines have a useful life of seven years.

The **expected useful life** should be determined at the time the asset is placed in service. Generally speaking, most **machinery and equipment** have a useful life of seven years, while automobiles and **light duty trucks** have a useful life of five years. These guidelines are used for **income tax** purposes; companies may use different guidelines for financial reporting purposes.

expected useful life 预期使用寿命
machinery and equipment 机器设备
light duty truck 轻型卡车
income tax 所得税

Light duty trucks have a useful life of five years.

The **expected value** at the end of a fixed asset's useful life is typically referred to as the **residual value**. In order to properly calculate depreciation, the residual value must be determined at the time the asset is placed into service.

expected value 期望值，预期值
residual value 残值

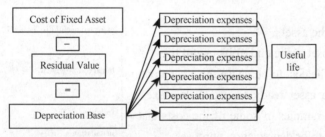

11.1d What are the methods of depreciation?

折旧有哪些方法？

Determining the best method for depreciating tangible fixed assets can be difficult. Three methods are most common.
- the **straight-line method**

straight-line method 直线法

- the **units-of-production method**
- the **double declining balance method**

This unit discusses the straight-line method only.

Data

A business purchases a new machine for $75,000 on 1 January 2003. It is estimated that the machine will have a residual value of $10,000 and a useful economic life of (5) years. The business has an accounting year end of 31 December.

units-of-production method 单位生产法

double declining balance method 双倍余额递减法

11.1e The straight-line depreciation method
直线折旧法

Using the straight line depreciation method, the calculation of the annual **depreciation charge** is as follows.

$$dpn = (C-R) / N$$

where:

dpn=Annual straight-line depreciation charge

C=Cost of the asset

R=Residual value of the asset

N=Useful economic life of the asset (years)

So the calculation is:

dpn= ($75,000–$10,000) / 5

dpn=$13,000

In the accounts of the business a depreciation charge of $13,000 will be **expensed** in the **profit and loss account** for each of the five years of the asset's useful economic life.

depreciation charge 折旧费

expense vt. 花费，支出

profit and loss account 损益账

In the annual balance sheet, the machine would be shown at its **original cost** less the **total accumulated depreciation** for the asset **to date**.

Example of how this would be disclosed in the accounts

At the end of the third year of ownership of the machine, the financial accounts of the business would include the following items in relation to the machine:

In the Profit and Loss Account:

  Depreciation of Machinery — Charge: $13,000

In the Balance Sheet at 31 December 2005:

	$	$
Machine at Cost	75,000	
less: Accumulated Depreciation	39,000	
Machine at net **book value**		36,000

The figure for accumulated depreciation of $39,000 at 31 December 2005 represents three years' worth of depreciation at $13,000 per year.

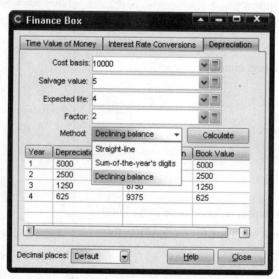

An On-Line Finance Box for Depreciation
在线折旧财务包

The cost of the machine ($75,000) less the accumulated depreciation charged on the machine ($39,000) is known as the **"written-down value" (WDV)** or **"net book value" (NBV)**.

It should be **noted** that WDV or NBV is simply an accounting value that is the result of a decision about which method is used to calculate depreciation. It does not necessarily mean that the machine is actually worth more or less than the WDV or NBV.

11.2 Core accounting terms
核心会计术语

- **amortization** *n.* 摊销，摊还，分期偿付
- **book value** 账面值
- **current assets** 流动资产
- **depletion** [dɪˈpliːʃən] *n.* 损耗，耗损，折耗
- **depreciation** [dɪˌpriːʃɪˈeɪʃən] *n.* 贬值，折旧
- **depreciation expense** 折旧费用
- **depreciation charge** 折旧费
- **double declining balance method** 双倍余额递减法
- **expected useful life** 预期使用寿命
- **expected value** 期望值，预期值
- **fiscal year** 财政年度
- **fixed assets** 固定资产
- **income tax** 所得税
- **initial cost** 最初成本，开办费，创办费
- **initial price** 最初成本
- **intangible assets** 无形资产
- **liquid assets** 流动资产，可变现资产
- **machinery and equipment** 机器设备
- **NBV** 纯账面价值（net book value）
- **non-current asset** 非流动资产
- **original cost** 原始成本，原价，原置成本
- **PP&E** 财产、厂房和设备，固定资产（property, plant and equipment）
- **profit and loss account** 损益账
- **residual value** 残值
- **straight-line method** 直线法
- **tangible asset** 有形资产
- **total accumulated depreciation** 总累计折旧
- **units-of-production method** 单位生产法
- **useful life** 生命周期，有效期，使用寿命
- **WDV** 减去折旧的资产价值，冲减值，折余值（written-down value）

11.3 Extended words
扩展词汇

- **brand** [brænd] *n.* 品牌
- **expense** [ikˈspens] *vt.* 花费，支出
- **fiscal** [ˈfiskəl] *a.* 财政的，会计的
- **freight** [freit] *n.* 运费
- **initial** [iˈniʃəl] *a.* 最初的，初始的
- **installation** [ˌinstəˈleiʃən] *n.* 安装
- **intangible** [inˈtændʒəbl] *a.* 无形的
- **intellectual** [ˌintiˈlektjuəl] *a.* 智力的
- **intellectual property** 知识产权
- **light duty trucks** 轻型卡车
- **liquid** [ˈlikwid] *a.* 液态的，流动的，可变成现金的
- **mineral** [ˈminərəl] *n.* 矿物
- **note** [nəut] *vt.* 注意
- **oil reserves** 石油储备
- **plant** [plɑːnt] *n.* (全部)设备，厂房
- **real estate** 房地产
- **residual** [riˈzidjuəl] *a.* 剩余的，残余的
- **tangible** [ˈtændʒəbl] *a.* 可触摸的，有形的
- **timber** *n.* 木材
- **to date** 到目前为止

11.4 Notes
注释

1) Fixed assets are a long-term, tangible asset held by an organization and not expected to be converted into cash in the current or upcoming fiscal year. 固定资产是企业所持有的长期的有形资产，且预计不会在本财年或下一财年转变成现金的资产。

   held by…是由过去分词引导的短语，做定语，修饰名词短语 tangible asset。

2) Buildings, real estate, equipment and furniture are good examples of fixed assets. 建筑物、地产、设备、家具是固定资产的好例子。

3) Fixed assets are sometimes collectively referred to as "plant". 固定资产有时合称为"厂房"。

4) Fixed assets are also known as a non-current asset or as property, plant, and equipment (PP&E). 固定资产也被称为非流动资产或财产、厂房及设备（PP&E）。

   在会计英语中，经常会用 property, plant, and equipment 来表示"固定资产"，尽管这个

Unit 11　How to depreciate fixed assets?　固定资产如何折旧?

短语的字面意义是"财产、厂房及设备",但是习惯上人们还是直接把它称之为"固定资产"。

5) This can be compared with current assets such as cash or bank accounts, which are described as liquid assets. 这可以和诸如现金或银行账户之类的流动资产相比较,流动资产又被描述成"液体资产"(可变现资产)。

　　句中 which...assets 是非限定性定语从句,对整句进行补充说明。

6) In most cases, only tangible assets are referred to as fixed. 多数情况下,只有有形资产才被称为固定资产。

7) Depreciation is the process by which a company allocates an asset's cost over the duration of its useful life. 折旧是公司把资产成本分摊在其使用寿命期间的程序。

　　句中 by which 是介词加关系词结构,在句中引导一个限定性定语从句,修饰先行词 process。

8) Each time a company prepares its financial statements, it records a depreciation expense to allocate a portion of the cost of the buildings, machines or equipment it has purchased to the current fiscal year. 公司每次准备财务报表时,就会记录一笔折旧费,把其所购买建筑物、机器或设备的部分成本分摊到本财年。

　　句中 it has purchased 是限定性定语从句,前面省略关系词 that,修饰先行词 buildings, machines or equipment。

9) The purpose of recording depreciation as an expense is to spread the initial price of the asset over its useful life. 把折旧记成费用的目的就是要把资产的初始成本平摊在其使用期内。

10) For intangible assets — such as brands and intellectual property — this process of allocating costs over time is called amortization. 对于无形资产——比如品牌和知识产权——按时间分摊成本的这个过程称为摊销。

11) For natural resources — such as minerals, timber and oil reserves — it's called depletion. 对于自然资源——如矿产、木材和石油储备——这一过程称为损耗。

12) the initial cost of the asset　资产的最初(购置)成本

13) the expected useful life of the asset　资产的预期使用寿命

14) the estimated value of the asset at the end of its useful life　资产在使用期末的估计值

15) The initial cost of the asset is the cost to purchase the asset along with any amounts spent to get the asset ready to use. 资产的最初成本是指购买资产的成本加上为使资产投入使用所花费的任何数额。

　　句中 spent to...use 是过去分词短语,做定语,修饰名词。

16) Sales taxes, freight and installation costs are examples of some of the costs that can be included in the cost of the asset for depreciation purposes. 销售税(营业税)、运费及安装费是一些成本的例子,可以包含在资产成本里用于计算折旧。

　　句中 that can...purposes 是限定性定语从句,修饰先行词 costs。

17) The expected useful life should be determined at the time the asset is placed in service. 预期使用寿命在资产投入使用时就应当确定。

18) Generally speaking, most machinery and equipment have a useful life of seven years, while automobiles and light duty trucks have a useful life of five years. 一般讲，多数机器设备有七年使用期，而汽车及轻型卡车有五年使用期。

19) These guidelines are used for income tax purposes. 这些指导方针是用于所得税用途的。

20) …companies may use different guidelines for financial reporting purposes. ……公司可以把不同的指导方针用于财务报告用途。

21) The estimated value at the end of a fixed asset's useful life is typically referred to as the residual value. 某一固定资产使用期末的估计值常常被称之为残值。

22) In order to properly calculate depreciation, the residual value must be determined at the time the asset is placed into service. 为了适当地计算折旧，就必须在资产投入使用时确定其残值。

23) Determining the best method for depreciating tangible fixed assets can be difficult. 要确定有形资产折旧的最佳方法并非易事。

24) the straight-line method 直线法

25) the units-of-production method 单位生产法

26) the double declining balance method 双倍余额递减法

27) A business purchases a new machine for $75,000 on 1 January 2003. 企业于2003年元月1日以75,000美元购买一台新机器。

28) It is estimated that the machine will have a residual value of $10,000 and a useful economic life of (5) years. 这台机器估计会有$10,000的残值及五年的有效经济寿命。

29) The business has an accounting year end of 31 December. 该公司会计年截止于12月31日。

30) Using the straight line depreciation method, the calculation of the annual depreciation charge is as follows. 用直线折旧法，年折旧费计算如下。

31) …where dpn = Annual straight-line depreciation charge 此处，dpn = 年直线折旧费。
   注意，本句中的 where 不是定语从句的关系词，而是连词，表示"在某地，在此"，如：
   a. He lives where the climate is mild.
      他住在一个气候温暖的地方
   b. Where there's smoke, there's fire.
      哪里有烟，哪里就有火

32) In the accounts of the business a depreciation charge of $13,000 will be expensed in the profit and loss account for each of the five years of the asset's useful economic life. 在公司的账户上，该资产在五年有效经济寿命内每年要有$13,000 的折旧费列支在其损益账上。

33) In the annual balance sheet, the machine would be shown at its original cost less the total accumulated depreciation for the asset to date. 在资产负债表上，该机器会显示其原始成本减去该资产迄今为止的总累计折旧。

  注意：less 在此处是介词，不是形容词比较级，意为"减去"。如：
a. a month less two days 一月差两天
b. Your salary less personal income tax is your net salary. 你的工资减去个人所得税就是你的净工资。

34) At the end of the third year of ownership of the machine, the financial accounts of the business would include the following items in relation to the machine. 在拥有机器的第三年末，该公司的财务账目会包括与机器相关的如下科目。

35) The figure for accumulated depreciation of $39,000 at 31 December 2005 represents three years' worth of depreciation at $13,000 per year. 2005 年 12 月 31 日的$39,000 的累计折旧数字表示按每年$13,000 计的三年折旧值。

36) The cost of the machine ($75,000) less the accumulated depreciation charged on the machine ($39,000) is known as the "written-down value"(WDV) or "net book value"(NBV). 机器成本($75,000)减去机器累计折旧费($39,000)就称为"折余值"(WDV)或"净账面值"(NBV)。

37) It should be noted that WDV or NBV is simply an accounting value that is the result of a decision about which method is used to calculate depreciation. 应当注意 WDV 或 NBV 仅仅是一种会计值，这由采用何种方法来计算折旧决定。

  本句有两个定语从句，前一个由 that 引导，是限定性定语从句，修饰先行词 value，后一个是 about which，这是介词加关系词结构，用来修饰先行词 decision。

38) It does not necessarily mean that the machine is actually worth more or less than the WDV or NBV. 这并不一定是说该机器的价值实际上大于或小于其 WDV 或 NBV。

  That 在句中引导一个宾语从句，做动词 mean 的宾语。

11.5 Reinforcement exercise
强化练习

1. Answer the following questions in English.

 1) What is the definition of fixed assets?
 2) What is depreciation?
 3) What's the purpose of depreciation?

4) What are the elements in planning depreciation?
5) What are the methods of depreciation?
6) What is WDV and NBV?
7) Does WDV or NBV represents the actual value of an asset?

2. Put the following into Chinese.

1) fixed assets
2) tangible asset
3) fiscal year
4) real estate
5) non-current asset
6) property, plant and equipment (PP&E)
7) current asset
8) liquid asset
9) depreciation
10) useful life
11) depreciation expense
12) allocate a portion of the cost
13) initial price
14) intangible assets
15) intellectual property
16) amortization

3. Put the following into English.

1) 损耗，耗损，折耗
2) 预期使用寿命
3) 资产的估计值
4) 最初成本，创办费
5) 销售税、运费和安装费
6) 机器设备
7) 所得税
8) 期望值，预期值
9) 残值
10) 直线法
11) 单位生产法
12) 双倍余额递减法
13) 损益账
14) 原始成本，原价，原置成本
15) 总累计折旧
16) 账面值
17) 冲减值，折余值纯账面价

4. Subject for self-study: A depreciation chart

Example 1. Depreciating a machinery by the MACRS 150% declining balance option.

Original Basis = $60,000

Tax Year	Tax depreciation (adjusted) tax	Year-end (adjusted) Depreciation	Tax Basis
1	10.71%	$ 6,425	$53,574
2	19.13	11,478	42,096
3	15.03	9,018	33,078
4	12.25	7,350	25,728
5	12.25	7,350	18,378
6	12.25	7,350	11,028
7	12.25	7,350	3,678
8	6.13	3,678	0

Reminder 提示

modified accelerated cost recovery system (MACRS) 改进加速成本回收法
original basis 原始计算基础
year-end adjusted depreciation 年末调整后折旧
tax basis 计税基础

11.6 Accounting-related knowledge
会计相关知识介绍

固定资产折旧的方法
Methods of fixed assets depreciation

机械设备（machinery and equipment）提取折旧，是通过计提转作生产费用的办法使其在生产经营过程中的有形损耗（tangible depletion）与无形损耗（intangible depletion）得到补偿（compensation）和积累（accumulation）。那么该设备折旧总额在规定的使用期限内（useful life）各期分摊的数额应该与其创造价值的大小成正比，这也是会计配比原则的要求。目前，企业在计提固定资产折旧时多数是采用直线法（straight-line method）平均分配折旧总额在各会计期间的数额，这对于机械设备来说，其折旧额的平均分配是不符合会计配比原则的。

机械设备在购入初期工作性能良好，运转正常，它所创造的价值较大，应多分摊一些折旧额。随着生产的持续进行，机械设备逐渐磨损，设备在维修费和修理费用上较期初逐年增加，所创造的价值逐年减少，应少分摊一些折旧。

我国现行财会制度规定允许使用的加速折旧法（accelerated depreciation method）主要有两种：即年数总和法（sum of the years digits [SYD] method）和双倍余额递减法（double declining balance method）。这两种方法能使机械设备的价值在其使用的前一半时间里有近于 2/3 至 3/4 得到补偿，在后一半时间里不会因为维修费用过高而导致成本过大，使生产协调稳步进行，同时也给企业设备的及时更新累积了足够的资金。

1. 双倍余额递减法

在不考虑固定资产残值的情况下,以平均年限法折旧率(不扣残值)的两倍作为折旧率,乘以每期期初固定资产折余价值求得每期折旧额的一种快速折旧的方法。

年折旧率(annual depreciation)=2/预计使用年限×100%

月折旧率(monthly depreciation)=年折旧率/12

月折旧额(annual depreciation amount)=期初固定资产账面净值
(net book value [NBV])×月折旧率

为了保证固定资产使用年限终了时账面净值与预计净残值(expected net residual value)相等,在该固定资产折旧年限到期的前两年,将固定资产净值扣除预计净残值后的余额平均摊销。

2. 年数总和法

年数总和法又称合计年限法,是将固定资产的原值(original value)减去净残值(net residual value)后的净额乘以一个逐年减低的分数计算每年的折旧额,这个分数的分子代表固定资产尚可使用的年数,分母代表使用年数的逐年数字总和。计算公式如下:

年折旧率=尚可使用年数/预计使用年数的年限总和,或

年折旧率=(预计使用年限—已使用年限)/预计使用年限×(预计使用年限+1)/2×100%

月折旧率=年折旧率/12

月折旧额=(固定资产原值—预计净残值)×月折旧率

11.7 Extended reading
延伸阅读

Amortization and depreciation
摊销与折旧

In accounting terms, amortization and depreciation both refer to the devaluation of assets overtime. As an asset loses its value, the loss in value is charged as an expense. The offsetting reciprocal journal entry to the expense is a decrease in the actual assets value. The main purpose for devaluating assets is to create a reduction in the tax liability by reducing net income.

Intangible Assets and Amortization

Amortization in accounting terms means the devaluation of an *intangible asset*. An intangible asset is something of value to a business that does not have a physical presents. In order to write

down an asset, it must have a useful life. The useful life of an intangible is often difficult to determine. Some examples of intangible assets are:
- Patents
- Goodwill
- Contracts
- License
- Trademarks
- Franchise

Fixed Assets and Depreciation

Depreciation in accounting terms normally means the devaluation of a *fixed asset*. Determining the useful life of a fixed asset is usually much easier than an intangible asset. Since the useful life of fixed assets is much easier to determine, depreciation is much more common than amortization. Some examples of fixed assets are:
- Equipment
- Computers
- Vehicles
- Furniture
- Buildings

Amortization and Depreciation Expense Affect on Net Income

To get a better understanding of how amortization and depreciation affects income, it's best to see how the transaction is posted to the accounting journal. The following is an example of a typical journal asset for depreciation.
- Depreciation expense — Increase with a debit
- Asset (fixed or intangible) — Decrease with a credit

The journal increase of the expense is transferred to the general ledger. Expense general ledger totals are then transferred to the income statement at the end of the month. The result is a decrease to net income (income — expense). Since the result is a decrease in net income, this creates a decrease in the tax liability of the company. The decrease in the asset is transferred to the balance sheet at the end of the month, resulting in a decrease in the company's net worth.

Methods of Amortization and Depreciation

There are several methods of devaluating assets. The most common method is the straight-line method. This method of depreciation (or amortization) divides the value of the asset over the useful life of the asset. This results in equal write down amounts over the useful life of the asset.

There are also accelerated depreciation methods that results in larger write-downs in the early life of an asset. This allows a business a larger decrease in the tax burden in the early life of the asset. This is especially beneficial if an asset produces more income in the early stages of its useful life.

There are many rules as to what types of depreciation methods are used depending on numerous factors. Before choosing and implementing a certain method of depreciation, it's always best to consult a certified public accountant (CPA) to discuss what options are best.

Unit 12
What is liability?
什么是负债?

Core terms reminder
核心术语提示

负债	liability
偿付能力	solvency
资产负债比率	assets-liabilities ratio
	debt to assets ratio
债务产权比率	debt-equity ratio
股本融资	to finance through equity
债务融资	to finance through debt
固定负债	fixed liability
长期负债	long-term liability
流动负债	current liability
商业负债	trade liability
金融负债	financial liability
或有负债	contingent liability

12.1a What is liability?
什么是负债?

In legal terms, the word liability refers to **fault**. The person who is at fault is **liable** to another because of his or her actions or failure to act. One example is in the case of a crime. The liability of the **offending party** may include providing **restitution** for damage to property or paying medical bills in the case of physical injury.

In accounting terms, liability is a debt **assumed** by a business **entity** as a result of its borrowing activities or other **fiscal obligations** (such as **funding pension** plans for its employees). Liabilities are **paid off** under either short-term or long-term arrangements. The amount of time **allotted** to pay off the liability is typically determined by the size of the debt; large amounts of money usually are borrowed under long-term plans.

fault *n.* 过错,缺点
liable *a.* 有责任的,有义务的
be liable to 对……应负责任
offending party 冒犯方,过失方
restitution *n.* 归还,赔偿

assume *vt.* 承担
entity *n.* 实体
business entity 实体企业
fiscal obligation 财政责任,经济责任
fund *vt.* 资助,提供资金
pension *n.* 养老金,退休金
pay off 还清,付清
allot *vt.* 分配,分派

12.1b What is the significance of liabilities?
负债的意义是什么?

A company's liabilities are critical factors in understanding its **status** in any industry in which it is involved. As John Brozovsky noted in *Journal of Commercial Lending*, "a basic understanding of accounting for liabilities is necessary to assess

status *n.* 地位,状况

Journal of Commercial Lending
商业贷款杂志

the **viability** of any company. Companies are required to follow certain accounting rules; however, the rules allow considerable flexibility in how a company **accounts for** liabilities."

viability *n.* 生存能力

account for 说明，解释

12.1c What are the types of liabilities?
债务有哪些种类？

The various types of liabilities are given below:

Fixed liability

The liability which is to be paid of at the time of **dissolution** of a firm is called fixed liability. Examples are **capital**, **reserve** and **surplus**.

Long-term liability

The liability which is not payable within the next accounting period is called long-term liability. Examples are **debentures** of a company, **mortgage loan** etc.

Current liability

The liability which is to be paid off in the next accounting period is current liability. Examples: **sundry charges, bills payable** and **bank overdraft** etc.

Trade liability

Liability which is incurred for goods and services supplied or expenses incurred is called trade liability. Examples: bills payable and **sundry period**.

Financial liability

Liability which is incurred for financial purposes is called financial liability. Examples: bank overdraft, short-term loan, bills payable.

Contingent liability

A **contingent** liability is one which is not an actual liability but which will become an actual one on the happening of some event which is uncertain. Examples: **bills discounted before maturity**, liability of a case **pending** in the court.

Fixed liability 固定负债

dissolution *n.* 分解，解散

capital *n.* 资本
reserve *n.* 储备
surplus *n.* 剩余，盈余
Long-term liability 长期负债

debenture *n.* 债券
mortgage *n.* 抵押
mortgage loan 抵押贷款
Current liability 流动负债
sundry *a.* 杂项的
sundry charge *n.* 杂费
bill payable 应付票据
bank overdraft 银行透支
Trade liability 商业负债
sundry period 杂费期
Financial liability 金融负债

Contingent liability 或有负债
contingent *a.* 临时的，偶然的

bill discounted 贴现票据
before maturity 到期前，未到期
pending *a.* 悬而未决的，待解决的

12.1d What is the assets-liabilities ratio?
什么是资产负债比？

Total liabilities divided by total assets are the assets-liabilities ratio, or debt to assets ratio. The debt/asset ratio shows the **proportion** of a company's assets which are financed through debt. If the ratio is less than one, most of the company's assets are financed through equity. If the ratio is greater than one, most of the company's assets are financed through debt. Companies with high debt/asset ratios are said to be "**highly leveraged**" and could be in danger if creditors start to demand repayment of debt.

proportion *n.* 比例

highly leveraged 高杠杆的

The Debt to Assets, or Debt to Total assets financial ratio measures a company's **solvency**. It is **derived** by taking the company's total liabilities and dividing by the company's total assets, which can both be found on the balance sheet.

solvency *n.* 偿付能力
derive *vt.* 得自，起源

$$\text{Debt to assets ratio} = \frac{\text{total liabilities}}{\text{total assets}}$$

The higher the ratio, the greater risk will be associated with the firm's operation. In addition, high debt to assets ratio may indicate low **borrowing capacity** of a firm, which in turn will lower the firm's financial flexibility.

borrowing capacity 借贷能力

Things to remember
This ratio is very similar to the **debt-equity ratio**.

debt-equity ratio 债务产权比率

A ratio under one means a majority of assets are **financed through equity**, above one means they are financed more by debt. Furthermore you can interpret a high ratio as a "**highly debt leveraged firm**".

finance through equity 股本融资
highly debt leveraged firm 高债务杠杆公司

Figure 1 *The debt-asset ratio of Ace Trading Partners Limited.*

图1 艾思贸易合伙人有限公司的资产负债比率

Debt-asset analysis

Not a particularly exciting ratio, but a useful one. Ace Trading's debt/asset ratio is **fairly** low, meaning that its assets are financed more through equity rather than debt. And notice that Ace Trading has zero long term debt and shouldn't have to worry about creditors getting nervous. Companies with high ratios are placing themselves at risk, especially in an increasing **interest rate** market. Creditors **are bound to** get worried if the company is **exposed to** a large amount of debt and may demand that the company pay some of it back.

fairly *ad.* 相当地，尚可

interest rate 利率
be bound to 一定要
expose *vt.* 暴露
be exposed to 暴露于，招致

12.2 Core accounting terms
核心会计术语

- bank overdraft 银行透支
- before maturity 到期前，未到期
- bill payable 应付票据
- bill discounted 贴现票据
- borrowing capacity 贷款能力
- contingent liability 或有负债
- current liability 流动负债
- debt-equity ratio 债务产权比率
- debt to assets ratio 资产负债比率
- finance through debt 债务融资
- finance through equity 股本融资
- financial liability 金融负债
- fiscal obligation 财政责任，经济责任
- fixed liability 固定负债
- highly debt leveraged firm 高债务杠杆公司
- interest rate 利率
- long-term liability 长期负债
- mortgage loan 抵押贷款
- solvency ['sɔlvənsi] n. 偿付能力
- sundry charge 杂费
- trade liability 商业负债

12.3 Extended words
扩展词汇

- account for 说明，解释
- allot [ə'lɔt] vt. 分配，分派
- assume [ə'sju:m] vt. 承担
- be bound to 一定要
- business entity 实体企业
- capital ['kæpitəl] n. 资本
- contingent [kən'tindʒənt] a. 临时的，偶然的
- creditor ['kreditə] n. 债权人，贷方
- debenture [di'bentʃə] n. 债券
- derive [di'raiv] vt. 得自，起源
- discount ['diskaunt] vt. 打折扣，给（票据等）贴现
- dissolution [disə'lju:ʃən] n. 分解，解散
- entity ['entiti] n. 实体
- expose [iks'pəuz] vt. 暴露
- be exposed to 暴露于，招致
- fairly ['fɛəli] ad. 相当地，尚可
- fault [fɔ:lt] n. 过错，缺点
- fund [fʌnd] vt. 资助，提供资金
- highly leveraged 高杠杆的
- journal of commercial lending 商业贷款杂志
- liable ['laiəbl] a. 有责任的，有义务的
- be liable to 对……应负责任
- mature [mə'tjuə] a. 成熟的，到期的
- mortgage ['mɔ:gidʒ] n. 抵押
- offending party 冒犯方，过失方

- **pay off** 还清，付清
- **pending** ['pendiŋ] *a.* 悬而未决的，待解决的
- **pension** ['penʃən] *n.* 养老金，退休金
- **proportion** [prə'pɔ:ʃən] *n.* 比例
- **reserve** [ri'zə:v] *n.* 储备
- **restitution** [,resti'tju:ʃən] *n.* 归还，赔偿
- **status** ['steitəs] *n.* 地位，状况
- **sundry** ['sʌndri] *a.* 杂项的
- **sundry period** 杂费期
- **surplus** ['sə:pləs] *n.* 剩余，盈余
- **viability** [,vaiə'biliti] *n.* 生存能力

12.4 Notes 注释

1) **In legal terms, the word liability refers to fault.** 在法律术语中，责任一词是指过错。
2) **The person who is at fault is liable to another because of his or her actions or failure to act.** 因为其行为或不作为，过错者应对另一方承担责任。

   …who is at fault 是限定性定语从句，修饰先行词 person。

3) **The liability of the offending party may include providing restitution for damage to property or paying medical bills in the case of physical injury.** 过失方的责任可能包括对财产损失进行赔偿或是在对方身体伤害的情况下支付医疗费。

4) **In accounting terms, liability is a debt assumed by a business entity as a result of its borrowing activities or other fiscal obligations (such as funding pension plans for its employees).** 在会计术语中，责任是指由实体企业在借贷活动或其他财务义务中（如为其雇员的养老金计划提供资金）所承担的债务。

   assumed by…是由过去分词引导的短语，在句中做定语，修饰名词 debt，相当于定语从句 which is assumed…

5) **Liabilities are paid off under either short-term or long-term arrangements.** 负债要么是短期清偿，要么是长期清偿。
6) **The amount of time allotted to pay off the liability is typically determined by the size of the debt.** 清偿负债所分配的时间量通常由债务的大小来确定。
7) **…large amounts of money usually are borrowed under long-term plans.** ……大额资金通常属于长期性借贷。

8) **A company's liabilities are critical factors in understanding its status in any industry in which it is involved.** 在理解公司在其所处行业中的地位时，公司的负债是至关重要的因素。

句中 in which 是介词加关系词结构，引导一个限定性定语从句，修饰先行词 industry。

9) **As John Brozovsky noted in *Journal of Commercial Lending*…** 正如 John Brozovsky 在《商业借贷杂志》中所指出……

10) **A basic understanding of accounting for liabilities is necessary to assess the viability of any company.** 对负债核算的基本理解对于评估任何公司的生存能力都是非常必要的。

11) **…however, the rules allow considerable flexibility in how a company accounts for liabilities.** ……然而，在公司如何解释负债方面，这些规则留有相当的灵活性。

how a company…是宾语从句，做介词 in 的宾语。

12) **The liability which is to be paid off at the time of dissolution of a firm is called fixed liability.** 拟于公司解散时清偿的负债称为固定负债。

which 在句中引导一个限定性定语从句，修饰先行词 liability. 下面注 13）～16）中的结构同本句。

13) **The liability which is not payable within the next accounting period is called long-term liability.** 不拟于下一个会计年度支付的负债称为长期负债。

14) **The liability which is to be paid off in the next accounting period is current liability.** 拟于下一个会计年度偿付的负债称为流动负债。

15) **Liability which is incurred for goods and services supplied or expenses incurred is called trade liability.** 由所供应的商品或服务所发生的负债或发生的费用称为商业负债。

16) **Liability which is incurred for financial purposes is called financial liability.** 金融用途所发生的负债称为金融负债。

17) **A contingent liability is one which is not an actual liability but which will become an actual one on the happening of some event which is uncertain.** 或有负债并非实际负债，但会在某些不确定事件发生时成为实际负债。

本句包含三个由 which 引导的定语从句，第一个是 which…liability，修饰先行词 one，第二个是 which…event，亦修饰先行词 one，第三个是 which is uncertain，修饰先行词 event，三个全部是限定性从句。

18) **Examples: bills discounted before maturity, liability of a case pending in the court.** 例子有：到期前的贴现票据，在法庭上未判决案件的负债。

19) **Total liabilities divided by total assets are the assets-liabilities ratio, or debt to assets ratio.** 总负债除以总资产就是资产负债比，或债务资产比。

20) **The debt-asset ratio shows the proportion of a company's assets which are financed through debt.** 资产负债率显示公司用债务融资的资产比例。

句中 which 引导一个限定性定语从句，修饰先行词 assets。

21) If the ratio is less than one, most of the company's assets are financed through equity. 如果负债率小于一，则公司的多数资产是用股本融资的。

22) If the ratio is greater than one, most of the company's assets are financed through debt. 如果负债率大于一，则公司的多数资产是用债务融资的。

23) Companies with high debt/asset ratios are said to be "highly leveraged," and could be in danger if creditors start to demand repayment of debt. 具有高资产负债比的公司可以说是"具有高杠杆"，并且如果债权人开始要求偿还债务时，公司就会处于危险中。

24) The Debt to Assets, or Debt to Total assets financial ratio measures a company's solvency. 债务对资产，或债务对总资产的财政比率可以衡量公司的偿付能力。

25) It is derived by taking the company's total liabilities and dividing by the company's total assets, which can both be found on the balance sheet. 拿公司的总负债除以公司的总资产就可以得出资产负债比率，二者均可在资产负债表中看到。

句中 which 引导一个非限定性定语从句，对主句作补充说明。

26) The higher the ratio, the greater risk will be associated with the firm's operation. 负债比愈高，公司经营所涉及的风险就愈大。

27) In addition, high debt to assets ratio may indicate low borrowing capacity of a firm, which in turn will lower the firm's financial flexibility. 此外，高资产负债比率可能显示公司的低借贷能力，这又反过来降低了公司的财务灵活性。

句中 which 引导一个非限定性定语从句，对主句作补充说明。

28) A ratio under one means a majority of assets are financed through equity, above one means they are financed more by debt. 负债比率小于一表示多数资产是用股本融资的，大于一表示多数资产是用债务融资的。

29) Furthermore you can interpret a high ratio as a "highly debt leveraged firm". 而且你可以把高负债比率解释成"高债务杠杆的公司"。

30) Ace Trading's debt/asset ratio is fairly low, meaning that its assets are financed more through equity rather than debt. 艾斯贸易公司的资产负债比率还算低，也就是说该公司用股本融资的资产多，用债务融资的资产少。

31) And notice that Ace Trading has zero long term debt and shouldn't have to worry about creditors getting nervous. 并且还要注意到，艾斯贸易公司的长期债务是零，不用担心债权人的不安情绪。

32) Companies with high ratios are placing themselves at risk, especially in an increasing interest rate market. 资产负债比率高的公司正使自身处于危险中，在加息市场中尤甚。

33) Creditors are bound to get worried if the company is exposed to a large amount of debt and may demand that the company pay some of it back. 如果公司大量举债，债权人就会不安，并且可能要求公司偿付部分债务。

句中 that 引导一个宾语从句，做动词 demand 的宾语。

12.5 Reinforcement exercise
强化练习

1. Answer the following questions in English.

1) What is liability?
2) What is the significance of liabilities?
3) What are the types of liabilities?
4) What is the assets-liabilities ratio?
5) What can the debt to assets ratio measure?

2. Put the following into Chinese.

1) assume debt
2) business entity
3) fiscal obligation
4) pay off liabilities
5) viability
6) capital, reserve and surplus
7) fixed liability
8) long-term liability
9) current liability
10) trade liability
11) financial liability
12) contingent liability
13) dissolution of firm
14) mortgage loan

3. Put the following into English.

1) 银行透支
2) 发生费用
3) 法庭未判决的案件
4) 未到期贴现票据
5) 债务资产比
6) 股本融资
7) 债务融资
8) 还债
9) 偿付能力
10) 借贷能力
11) 财务灵活性
12) 债务权益比率
13) 利率
14) 大量举债

4. Subject for self-study: A leverage effect formula.

Leverage effect formula

$$R(E) = R(A) + [R(A) - R(D)] \times [D/E]$$

Where:

R(E) = return on equity capital
R(A) = return on assets
R(D) = required return on borrowed capital

Reminder 提示

leverage effect formula 杠杆效应公式
return on equity capital 股本资本回报率
return on assets 资产回报率
required return on borrowed capital 借贷资本所要求回报率

12.6 Accounting-related knowledge
会计相关知识介绍

如何计算资产负债率？
How to calculate the debt to assets ratio?

资产负债率（asset to liability ratio）是全部负债总额（total liabilities）除以全部资产总额（total assets）的百分比，也就是负债总额与资产总额的比例关系，也称之为债务比率（debt ratio）。资产负债率的计算公式（formula）如下：

资产负债率=(负债总额÷资产总额)×100%

公式中的负债总额指企业的全部负债，不仅包括长期负债（long-term liability），而且也包括流动负债（current liability）。公式中的资产总额指企业的全部资产总额，包括流动资产（current assets）、固定资产（fixed assets）、长期投资（long-term investment）、无形资产（intangible assets）和递延资产（deferred assets）等。

资产负债率是衡量企业负债水平及风险程度的重要标志。

一般认为，资产负债率的适宜水平是40%～60%。对于经营风险（operational risks）比较高的企业，为减少财务风险应选择比较低的资产负债率；对于经营风险低的企业，为增加股东收益（shareholder's income）应选择比较高的资产负债率。

在分析资产负债率时，可以从以下三个方面进行。

1）从债权人（creditors）的角度看，资产负债率越低越好。资产负债率低，债权人提供的资金与企业资本总额相比，所占比例低，企业不能偿债的可能性小。由于企业的风险主要由股东承担，这对债权人来讲，是十分有利的。

2）从股东（shareholders）的角度看，他们希望保持较高的资产负债率水平。站在股东的立场上，可以得出结论：在全部资本利润率高于借款利息率时，负债比例越高越好。

3）从经营者（operators）的角度看，他们最关心的是在充分利用借入资本（borrowed capital）给企业带来好处的同时，尽可能降低财务风险。

12.7 Extended reading
延伸阅读

What is ALM?
什么是资产负债管理?

ALM, short for asset liability management, is the process of responsibly managing the balance between the debts and assets owned by the business or other entity. The idea is to make sure that the liabilities or debt carried by the entity is kept in proportion with the assets on hand. Many businesses engage in the process of asset liability management, including banks, insurance providers, and even small businesses.

With banks, the process of asset liability management is often focused on maintaining an agreeable balance between the amount of customer deposits and the amount of the loans issued by the bank. Ideally, that balance will prevent the bank from overextending the amount of debt it assumes as a result of making loans to various customers. This balance helps protect banks from being especially vulnerable, should any sudden change in interest rates take place, as well as keep the bank solvent in the face of credit changes or unforeseen issues with liquidity.

When it comes to insurance providers, the focus of asset liability management has to do with the relationship between premiums collected on policies and the amount paid out in claims. As with banks, insurance providers seek to make sure enough money is coming in from premium collections that all outstanding claims can be settled quickly and efficiently. Following and managing this relationship effectively helps to ensure that the provider can service all accounts promptly, and also be in a position to write new policies over time.

Businesses of all sizes, including small businesses, pay close attention to asset liability management. This is particularly true when considering the purchase of new equipment needed for the operation of the company. One approach would be to pay cash for the purchase, which in turn would decrease one asset while it created a new one. A second approach would be to take out a loan, making it possible to acquire an asset, but also creating a liability. Depending on the overall balance between existing assets and liabilities, one strategy is likely to be more suitable for the business than the other.

Today, many entities engage in this task with the use of asset liability management software. By using the software to create specific guidelines for the relationship between debts and assets, it is possible to quickly determine the current balance at any given point in time. This can help the entity identify a possible financial crisis before it becomes a major problem, and resolve the issue with a minimum of trouble. Companies that underwrite asset liability management insurance often provide discounts for customers who have this type of resource in place, providing one more reason to make use of software to aid in the process of asset liability management.

Unit 13
What is shareholders' equity?
什么是股东权益?

Core terms reminder
核心术语提示

股本回报率，权益收益率	return on equity
净值回报率，净值收益率	return on net worth
股份资本，股本	share capital
留存收益，未分配利润	retained earnings
库存股份	treasury share
股东权益	stockholders' equity
平均普通股回报率	return on average common equity
普通股东资金回报率	return on ordinary shareholders' funds
股票回购	stock buyback
杜邦公式	DuPont Formula
利润率，边际利润	profit margin
资产周转率	asset turnover
财务杠杆，金融杠杆	financial leverage

13.1a What is shareholders' equity?

什么是股东权益？

Shareholders' equity is a firm's total assets minus its total liabilities. **Equivalently**, it is **share capital** plus **retained earnings** minus **treasury shares**. Shareholders' equity represents the amount by which a company is financed through **common** and **preferred shares**.

Shareholders' equity is also known as "share capital", "net worth" or "**stockholders' equity**".

Shareholders' equity comes from two main sources. The first source is the money that was originally invested in the company, along with any **additional investments** made **thereafter**. The second comes from retained earnings which the company is able to accumulate over time through its operations. In most cases, the retained earnings **portion** is the largest component.

equivalently *ad.* 相等地，同等地
share capital 股份资本，股本
retained earnings 留存收益，未分配利润
treasury share 库存股份
common share 普通股
preferred share 优先股
stockholders' equity 股东权益

additional investment 额外投资
thereafter *ad.* 其后，此后

portion *n.* 一部分，一分

13.1b What is ROE?

什么是ROE？

ROE stands for **return on equity**.

ROE refers to the amount of **net income** returned as a percentage of shareholders' equity. Return on equity measures a firm's **profitability** by revealing how much profit a company generates with the money shareholders have invested.

ROE is expressed as a percentage and calculated as:

$$\text{Return on equity} = \frac{\text{Net income}}{\text{Shareholders' equity}}$$

return on equity 股本回报率，股本收益率
net income 净收入
profitability *n.* 收益性，盈利能力

Net income is for the full fiscal year (before **dividends** paid to common stockholders but after dividends to preferred stock). Shareholders' equity does not include preferred shares.

Return on equity is also known as **return on net worth** (RONW), **return on average common equity**, or **return on ordinary shareholders' funds**.

dividend *n.* 股息，红利

return on net worth 净值回报率，净值收益率

return on average common equity 平均普通股回报率

return on ordinary shareholders' funds 普通股东资金回报率

13.1c How to calculate the ROE?

如何计算 ROE？

Return on Equity (ROE) is one of the **financial ratios** used by stock investors in analyzing stocks. It indicates how effective the management team is in converting the **reinvested** money into profits. The higher the ROE, the more money a company is able to generate for the same dollar amount spent.

financial ratios 财务比率

reinvest *vt.* 再投资

Step 1

Calculate Shareholders' Equity (SE) by **subtracting** the Total Liabilities (TL) from the Total Assets (TA)

$$SE = TA - TL$$

subtract *vt.* 减去

Step 2

Calculate the average shareholders' equity from the beginning (SE_1) and the ending (SE_2) of financial year

$$SE\ (avg) = (SE_1 + SE_2) / 2$$

Step 3

Find the Net Profits (NP) as listed on the company's **annual report**.

annual report 年度报告

Step 4

Calculate ROE by dividing the net profits by the average of shareholders' equity

$$ROE = NP / SE\ (avg)$$

13.1d Caution: ROE can be misleading!

小心：ROE 可能有误导性！

While ROE is a useful **measure**, it does have some **flaws** that can give you a **false picture**, so never rely on it alone. For example, if a company carries a large debt and **raises funds** through borrowing rather than **issuing stock** it will reduce its book value. A lower book value means you're dividing by a smaller number so the ROE is **artificially** higher. There are other situations such as taking **write-downs** or **stock buybacks** that reduces book value, which will produce a higher ROE without improving profits.

It may also be more meaningful to look at the ROE over a period of the past five years, rather than one year to **average out** any **abnormal numbers**.

measure *n*. 尺度，测量
flaw *n*. 缺点，瑕疵
false picture 虚假的画面

raise fund 集资
issue stock 发行股票

artificially *ad*. 人工地，人为地
write-down *n*. 调低账面价值，资产减值
stock buyback 股票回购

average out 达到平均数，最终得到平衡
abnormal number 异常数目

Given that you must look at the total picture, ROE is a useful tool in **identifying** companies with a competitive advantage. All other things roughly equal, the company that can **consistently** **squeeze out** more profits with their assets, will be a better investment in the long run.

identify *vt*. 识别，鉴别
consistently *ad*. 一贯地，始终如一地
squeeze out 挤压，挤窄

13.1e What is the DuPont Formula?

什么是杜邦公式?

The **DuPont Formula** integrates elements of both the **income statement** and balance sheet. At the simplest level the DuPont Formula **equates** Return on Equity (ROE) with profitability, **asset utilization** and leverage.

The DuPont Formula is also known as the **DuPont Analysis**, **DuPont Identity**, **DuPont Model** or **DuPont Method**. It is an expression which breaks ROE (Return On Equity) into three parts.

- **Profit margin** (used to measure operating efficiency)
- **Asset turnover** (used to measure asset utilization)
- **Equity multiplier** (used to measure **financial leverage**)

DuPont Formula 杜邦公式

income statement 收益表,损益表

equate *vt.* 使相等,等同

asset utilization 资产利用率
DuPont Analysis 杜邦分析法
DuPont Identity 杜邦识别法
DuPont Model 杜邦模型
DuPont Method 杜邦法
profit margin 利润率,边际利润
asset turnover 资产周转率
equity multiplier 权益乘数
financial leverage 财务杠杆,金融杠杆

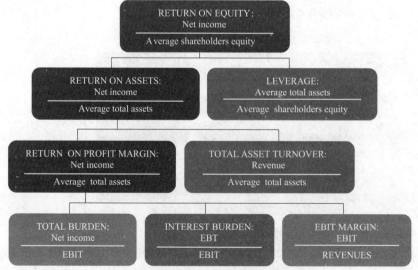

Figure 1 *ROE and its variables*
图 1 ROE 及其变体

13.2 Core accounting terms
核心会计术语

- annual report 年度报告
- asset turnover 资产周转率
- asset utilization 资产利用率
- common share 普通股
- dividend ['dividend] n. 股息，红利
- DuPont Formula 杜邦公式
- financial leverage 财务杠杆，金融杠杆
- financial ratios 财务比率
- income statement 收益表，损益表
- issue stock 发行股票
- net income 净收入
- preferred share 优先股
- profit margin 利润率，边际利润
- raise fund 集资
- retained earnings 留存收益，未分配利润
- return on average common equity 平均普通股回报率
- return on equity 股本回报率，权益收益率
- return on net worth 净值回报率，净值收益率
- return on ordinary shareholders' funds 普通股东资金回报率
- share capital 股份资本，股本
- stock buyback 股票回购
- stockholder's equity 股东权益
- treasury share 库存股份
- write-down 调低账面价值，资产减值

13.3 Extended words
扩展词汇

- **abnormal number** 异常数目
- **additional investment** 额外投资
- **artificially** [ˌɑːtiˈfiʃəli] ad. 人工地，人为地
- **average out** 达到平均数，最终得到平衡
- **consistently** [kənˈsistəntli] ad. 一贯地，始终如一地
- **DuPont Analysis** 杜邦分析法
- **DuPont Identity** 杜邦识别法
- **DuPont Method** 杜邦法
- **DuPont Model** 杜邦模型
- **equate** [iˈkweit] vt. 使相等，等同
- **equity multiplier** 权益乘数
- **false picture** 虚假的画面
- **flaw** [flɔː] n. 缺点，瑕疵
- **identify** [aiˈdentifai] vt. 识别，鉴别
- **measure** [ˈmeʒə] n. 尺度，测量
- **equivalently** [iˈkwivələntli] ad. 相等地，同等地
- **portion** [ˈpɔːʃən] n. 一部分，一分
- **profitability** [ˌprɔfitəˈbiliti] n. 收益性，盈利能力

- □ **reinvest** ['riːin'vest] *vt.* 再投资
- □ **squeeze out** 挤压，挤窄
- □ **subtract** [səb'trækt] *vt.* 减去
- □ **thereafter** [ðɛər'ɑːftə] *ad.* 其后，此后

13.4 Notes 注释

1) **Shareholders' equity is a firm's total assets minus its total liabilities.** 股东权益是公司的总资产减去其总负债所得出的。
2) **Equivalently, it is share capital plus retained earnings minus treasury shares.** 它等同于股本加留存收益减去库存股票。
3) **Shareholders' equity represents the amount by which a company is financed through common and preferred shares.** 股东权益表示一个公司用普通股和优先股所融资的金额。

    句中 by which 是介词加关系词结构，引导一个限定性定语从句，修饰先行词 amount。

4) **The first source is the money that was originally invested in the company, along with any additional investments made thereafter.** 第一个来源是原本投资于公司的资金，再加上此后所做的任何追加投资。

    句中，that 引导一个限定性定语从句，修饰先行词 money。
5) **The second comes from retained earnings which the company is able to accumulate over time through its operations.** 第二个来源于公司随时间推移通过其经营所积累起来的留存收益。

    句中，which 引导一个限定性定语从句，修饰名词短语 retained earnings。
6) **In most cases, the retained earnings portion is the largest component.** 多数情况下，留存收益部分是最大的构成成分。
7) **ROE refers to the amount of net income returned as a percentage of shareholders equity.** ROE 是指由股东权益的一定百分比所回报的净收入数额。

    句中 returned as...是过去分词短语引导的定语，修饰名词短语 net income。
8) **Return on equity measures a firm's profitability by revealing how much profit a company generates with the money shareholders have invested.** 通过显示公司用股东所投入的资金能够产生多少利润，权益收益率可以衡量一家公司的赢利能力。

    句中 how much profit...是宾语从句，做动词 reveal 的宾语。
9) **Net income is for the full fiscal year (before dividends paid to common stock holders but after dividends to preferred stock).** 净收入是对整个财务年度而言的（在给普通股东派发

红利前但在给优先股派发红利后）。

　　　　句中 after dividends to…是省略句，after 后省略 paid。

10) **Return on equity is also known as return on net worth (RONW), return on average common equity, or return on ordinary shareholders' funds.** 权益收益率又称为净值回报率（RONW）、平均普通股权回报率或普通股东资金回报率。

11) **Return on Equity (ROE) is one of the financial ratios used by stock investors in analyzing stocks.** 权益收益率是股票投资者用来分析股票的财务比率之一。

12) **It indicates how effective the management team is in converting the reinvested money into profits.** 它表示管理团队在把再投入资金转化成利润时有多大的效果。

　　　　句中 how 引导一个宾语从句，做动词 indicate 的宾语。

13) **The higher the ROE, the more money a company is able to generate for the same dollar amount spent.** ROE 愈高，公司就愈能为所花费的同样的美元数额产生出更多的钱。

14) **Calculate Shareholders' Equity (SE) by subtracting the Total Liabilities (TL) from the Total Assets (TA).** 把总负债(TL)从总资产(TA)中减去就可以计算出股东权益(SE)。

15) **Calculate the average shareholders' equity from the beginning (SE_1) and the ending (SE_2) of financial year.** 计算出财政年度的平均股东权益的年初值(SE_1)和年末值(SE_2)。

16) **Find the Net Profits (NP) as listed on the company's annual report.** 找出列在公司年度报告中的净利润(NP)。

17) **Calculate ROE by dividing the net profits by the average of shareholders' equity.** 用净利润除以平均股东权益就可计算出 ROE。

18) **While ROE is a useful measure, it does have some flaws that can give you a false picture, so never rely on it alone.** ROE 一方面是有用的尺度，同时它的确有瑕疵，会给人提供虚假的图画，所以绝不要单独地依赖它。

　　　　句中 that can…picture 是限定性定语从句，修饰先行词 flaws。

19) **For example, if a company carries a large debt and raises funds through borrowing rather than issuing stock, it will reduce its book value.** 例如，如果一家公司背有大量的债务，它通过借贷而不是通过发行股票来募资，这样公司就减少了账面值。

20) **A lower book value means you're dividing by a smaller number, so the ROE is artificially higher.** 账面值的减少就意味着你除以一个较小的数目，这就人为地提高了 ROE。

　　　　句中 you're dividing…是宾语从句，做动词 mean 的宾语，其前省略关系词 that。

21) **There are other situations such as taking write-downs or stock buybacks that reduces book value, which will produce a higher ROE without improving profits.** 也有其他情况如使用资产减值或进行股票回购来降低账面值，这就会在利润没有提高的情况下把 ROE 调高。

22) **It may also be more meaningful to look at the ROE over a period of the past five years, rather than one year to average out any abnormal numbers.** 按照过去五年的时间段，而不是按一年来审视 ROE 可能更有意义，这样就可以得出平均数字以抵消任何异常的数目。

23) **Given that you must look at the total picture, ROE is a useful tool in identifying companies with a competitive advantage.** 考虑到必须审视总体财务数据，ROE 在判定公

司的竞争性优势时是有用的工具。

　　注意 given that 是一个短语，其用法相当于连词，意为"考虑到，假设"。

24) **All other things roughly equal, the company that can consistently squeeze out more profits with their assets, will be a better investment in the long run.** 如果其他指标相同，能够用其资产始终挤出更高利润的公司从长远来看就是更佳的投资对象。

　　　a. all other things roughly equal 是独立结构，在句中做伴随性状语，相当于条件从句 if all other things are roughly equal.

　　　b. that can…assets 是限定性定语从句，修饰先行词 company。

25) **The DuPont Formula integrates elements of both the income statement and balance sheet.** 杜邦公式把收益表和资产负债表二者的要素整合在一起。

26) **At the simplest level the DuPont Formula equates Return on Equity (ROE) with profitability, asset utilization and leverage.** 从最简单的层次讲，杜邦公式把权益收益率等同于赢利能力、资产利用率及杠杆。

27) **Profit margin (used to measure operating efficiency)** 边际利润（用来衡量经营效率）

28) **Asset turnover (used to measure asset utilization)** 资产周转率（用来衡量资产利用率）

29) **Equity multiplier (used to measure financial leverage)** 权益乘数（用来衡量财务杠杆）

13.5 Reinforcement exercise

强化练习

1. Answer the following questions in English.

1) What is shareholders' equity?
2) What are the two main sources of shareholders' equity?
3) What is ROE?
4) What are the other names for return on equity?
5) What do you think of ROE? Is it reliable?
6) What is the DuPont Formula?
7) What are the other names for the DuPont Formula?

2. Put the following into Chinese.

1) share capital
2) retained earnings
3) treasury share
4) common share
5) preferred share
6) net worth
7) stockholders' equity
8) additional investment
9) return on equity
10) net income

11) profitability
12) generate profit
13) dividend
14) return on net worth
15) return on average common equity
16) return on ordinary shareholders' funds

3. Put the following into English.

1) 年度报告
2) 集资
3) 发行股票
4) 平均股东权益
5) 调低账面价值，资产减值
6) 股票回购
7) 异常数目
8) 挤出更多的利润
9) 竞争性优势
10) 杜邦公式
11) 收益表，损益表
12) 资产利用率
13) 利润率，边际利润
14) 资产周转率
15) 权益乘数
16) 财务杠杆，金融杠杆
17) 再投资
18) 财务比率

4. Subject for self-study: An ROE chart.

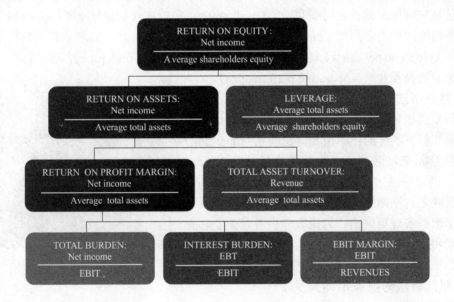

return on assets 资产收益率
return on profit margin 利润边际收益率
total burden 总负担

interest burden 利息负担
EBIT = earnings before interest and tax 付息及税前收益额
EBT = earnings before tax 纳税前收益额

13.6 Accounting-related knowledge
会计相关知识介绍

杜邦分析法
The DuPont Analysis

杜邦分析法的概念

杜邦分析法最早由美国杜邦公司使用，故名杜邦分析法。杜邦分析法利用几种主要的财务比率（financial ratios）之间的关系来综合地分析企业的财务状况（financial position），这种分析方法是一种用来评价公司赢利能力（profitability）和股东权益回报水平（return on equity），并从财务角度评价企业绩效（enterprise performance）的经典方法。其基本思想是将企业净资产收益率（return on net assets）逐级分解为多项财务比率乘数（multiplier），这样有助于深入分析比较企业的经营业绩（operating performance）。

杜邦分析法的特点

杜邦模型最显著的特点是将若干个用以评价企业经营效率和财务状况的比率按其内在联系（inner link）有机地结合起来，形成一个完整的指标体系（index system），并最终通过权益收益率（return on equity）来综合反映之。采用这一方法，可使财务比率分析的层次更清晰、条理更突出，为报表分析者全面了解企业的经营和盈利状况提供方便。

杜邦分析法的财务指标关系

在杜邦体系中，包括以下四种主要的指标关系。

（1）净资产收益率（return on net assets）是整个分析系统的起点和核心。该指标的高低反映了投资者的净资产获利能力的大小。净资产收益率是由销售报酬率（return on sales）、总资产周转率和权益乘数决定的。

（2）权益乘数(equity multiplier)表明了企业的负债程度。该指标越大，企业的负债程度越高，它是资产权益率的倒数。

（3）总资产收益率（return on total assets）是销售利润率（sales profit ratio）和总资产周转率的乘积，是企业销售成果和资产运营的综合反映。要提高总资产收益率，必须增加销售收入（sales revenue），降低资金占用额。

（4）总资产周转率(total assets turnover)反映企业资产实现销售收入的综合能力。分析时，必须综合销售收入分析企业资产结构（asset structure）是否合理，即流动资产（current assets）和长期资产（long-term assets）的结构比率关系。同时还要分析流动资产周转率、存货（inventory）周转率、应收账（account receivable）周转率等有关资产使用效率的指标，找出总资产周转率高低变化的确切原因。

13.7 Extended reading
延伸阅读

Return on equity
股本收益率

ROE is equal to a fiscal year's net income (after preferred stock dividends but before common stock dividends) divided by total equity (excluding preferred shares), expressed as a percentage.

But not all high-ROE companies make good investments. Some industries have high ROE because they require no assets, such as consulting firms. Other industries require large infrastructure builds before they generate a penny of profit, such as oil refiners. You cannot conclude that consulting firms are better investments than refiners just because of their ROE.

Generally, capital-intensive businesses have high barriers to entry, which limit competition. But high-ROE firms with small asset bases have lower barriers to entry. Thus, such firms face more business risk because competitors can replicate their success without having to obtain much outside funding. As with many financial ratios, ROE is best used to compare companies in the same industry.

High ROE yields no immediate benefit. Since stock prices are most strongly determined by earnings per share (EPS), you will be paying twice as much (in Price/Book terms) for a 20% ROE company as for a 10% ROE company. The benefit comes from the earnings reinvested in the company at a high ROE rate, which in turn gives the company a high growth rate.

ROE is presumably irrelevant if the earnings are not reinvested.
- The sustainable growth model shows us that when firms pay dividends, earnings growth lowers. If the dividend payout is 20%, the growth expected will be only 80% of the ROE rate.
- The growth rate will be lower if the earnings are used to buy back shares. If the shares are bought at a multiple of book value (say 3 times book), the incremental earnings returns will be only "that fraction" of ROE (ROE/3).

- New investments may not be as profitable as the existing business. Ask "What is the company doing with its earnings?"
- Remember that ROE is calculated from the company's perspective, on the company as a whole. Since much financial manipulation is accomplished with new share issues and buyback, always recalculate on a "per share" basis, i.e., earnings per share/book value per share.

Unit 14
What is a cash flow statement?
什么是现金流量表？

Core terms reminder
核心术语提示

现金流量表	cash flow statement
流入资金	incoming money
流出资金	outgoing money
正现金流	positive cash flow
负现金流	negative cash flow
经营活动	operating activities
投资活动	investing activities
筹资活动	financing activities

14.1a What is a cash flow statement?

什么是现金流量表?

In financial accounting, a **cash flow statement (CFS)** is a financial statement that shows a company's **incoming** and **outgoing money** (sources and uses of cash) during a time period (often monthly or quarterly). The statement shows how changes in balance sheet and **income accounts** affected cash and **cash equivalents**, and breaks the analysis down according to operating, investing, and financing activities.

A cash flow statement is also known as statement of cash flows or **funds flow statement**. Figure one is a sample of cash flow statement.

Figure 1 *A simple sample of cash flow statement*
图1 简单现金流量表

cash flow statement 现金流量表

incoming money 流入资金
outgoing money 流出资金

income accounts 收益账目
cash equivalent 现金等价物

funds flow statement 资金流量表

14.1b What is the role played by CFS?

现金流量表的作用是什么?

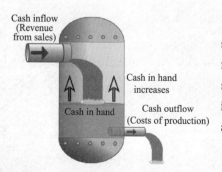

The **balance sheet** is a **snapshot** of a firm's financial resources and obligations at a single point in time, and the **income statement** summarizes a firm's **financial transactions**

balance sheet 资产负债表
snapshot *n.* 快照,简单描述

income statement 收益表,损益表
financial transaction 财务往来
accrual *n.* 获利,增长
accrual basis accounting 应计制核算

Unit 14　What is a cash flow statement? 什么是现金流量表?

over an interval of time. These two financial statements reflect the **accrual basis accounting** used by firms to match revenues with the expenses associated with generating those revenues. The cash flow statement includes only inflows and outflows of cash and cash equivalents; it **excludes** transactions that do not directly affect **cash receipts and payments**. These **non-cash transactions** include **depreciation** and **write-offs** on **bad debts**.

exclude *vt.* 排除，不包括
cash receipt and payment 现金收支
non-cash transaction 非现金交易
depreciation *n.* 折旧
write-off *n.* 勾销，注销，冲销
bad debt *n.* 坏账

14.1c What is the structure of a CFS?
现金流量表的结构是什么？

The CASHFLOW quadrant

Cash flow is divided into three components: cash flows resulting **respectively** from **operating activities**, investing activities and **financing activities**.

respectively *ad.* 分别地
operating activities 经营活动
financing activities 筹资活动

Operating activities

Operating activities include the production, sales and delivery of the company's product as well as **collecting payment** from its customers. This could include purchasing raw materials, building inventory, advertising and **shipping the product**.

collect payment 收款

ship the product 发运产品

Operating cash flows include
- receipts from the sale of goods or services
- receipts for the sale of loans, debt or **equity instruments** in a **trading portfolio**
- interest received on loans
- **dividends** received on **equity securities**
- payments to suppliers for goods and services
- payments to employees or on behalf of employees
- tax payments
- interest payments
- payments for the sale of loans, debt or equity instruments in a trading portfolio

equity instrument 权益工具，股权工具
trading portfolio 交易组合
dividend *n.* 红利，股息
equity security 股票

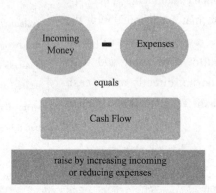

Items which are added back to the net income figure (which is found on the Income Statement) to arrive at cash flows from operations generally include:
- depreciation (loss of **tangible asset** value over time) **deferred tax**
- **amortization** (loss of intangible asset value over time)
- any **gains or losses** associated with an asset sale (unrealized gains/losses are also added back from the income statement)

tangible asset 有形资产
deferred tax 递延税金
amortization *n.* 摊销
gain or loss 损益

Investing activities

Changes in equipment, assets or investments relate to cash from investing. Usually cash changes from investing are a **"cash out" item**, because cash is used to buy new equipment, buildings or short-term assets such as **marketable securities**. However, when a company **divests of** an asset, the transaction is considered "cash in" for calculating cash from investing.

"cash out" item 现金流出项目

marketable securities 有价证券
divest *vi.* 剥夺，剥离
divest of 剥离

Financing activities

Changes in debt, loans or dividends are accounted for in cash from financing. Changes in cash from financing are "cash in" when capital is raised, and they are "cash out" when dividends are paid. Thus, if a company **issues a bond** to the public, the company receives cash financing; however, when interest is paid to **bondholders**, the company is reducing its cash.

issue a bond 发行债券

bondholder *n.* 债券持有人

Unit 14 What is a cash flow statement? 什么是现金流量表?

	Cash Flow Statement	
	For the Year Ending	Dec. 31, 2009
	Cash at Beginning of Year	15,700
Operations		
	Cash receipts from customers	693,200
	Cash paid for	
	Inventory purchases	(264,000)
	General operating and administraive expenses	(112,000)
	Wage expenses	(123,000)
	Interest	(13,500)
	Income taxes	(32,800)
Net Cash Flow from Operations		147,900
Investing Activities		
	Cash receipts from	
	Sale of property and equipment	33,600
	Collection of principal on loans	
	Sale of investment securities	
	Cash paid for	
	Purchase of property and equipment	(75,000)
	Making loans to other entities	
	Purchase of investment securities	
Net Cash Flow from Invesing Activities		(41,400)
Financing Activities		
	Cash receipts from	
	Issuance of stock	
	Borrowing	
	Cash paid for	
	Repurchase of stock (treasury stock)	
	Repayment of loans	(34,000)
	Dividends	(53,000)
Net Cash Flow from Financing Activities		(87,000)
Net Increase in Cash		19,500
	Cash at End of Year	35,200

Figure 2 *A cash flow statement classified in operating, investing and financing activities*
图 2 分类为经营、投资和筹资活动的现金流量表

14.1d Analyzing a sample CFS
分析现金流量样表

Let's take a look at this CFS sample:

Cash flow statement	
ABC Company FY ended December 31, 2009 All figures in USD	
Cash flow from operations	
Net earnings	2,000,000
Additions to cash	
Depreciation	10,000
Decrease in accounts receivable	15,000
Increase in accounts payable	15,000
Increase in taxes payable	2,000
Subtractions from cash	
Increase in inventory	(30,000)
Net cash from operations	2,012,000
Cash flow from investing	
Equipment	(500,000)
Cash flow from financing	
Notes payable	10,000
Cash flow for FY ended 31 Dec. 2009	1,522,000

From this CFS, we can see that the cash flow for FY 2009 was $1,522,000. The **bulk** of the **positive cash flow** stems from cash earned from operations, which is a good sign for investors. It means that **core operations** are generating business and that there is enough money to buy new inventory. The purchasing of new equipment shows that the company has cash to invest in inventory for growth. Finally, the amount of cash available to the company should **ease** investors' minds regarding the notes payable, as cash is plentiful to cover that future **loan expense**.

Cash flow is *key to success*

Of course, not all cash flow statements look this healthy, or **exhibit** a positive cash flow. But a **negative cash flow** should not automatically raise a **red flag** without some further analysis. Sometimes, a negative cash flow is a result of a company's decision to expand its business at a certain point in time, which would be a good thing for the future.

bulk *n*. 大部分，大块

positive cash flow 正现金流

core operation 核心经营业务

ease [i:z] *vt*. 使安心，使放松

loan expense 贷款费用

exhibit *vt*. 展示，展现
negative cash flow 负现金流
red flag 红旗，危险信号

14.2 Core accounting terms
核心会计术语

- accrual basis accounting 应计制核算
- amortization [əˌmɔːtiˈzeiʃən] n. 摊销
- bad debt 坏账
- balance sheet 资产负债表
- bondholder [ˈbɔndˌhəuldə] n. 债券持有人
- cash equivalent 现金等价物
- cash flow statement 现金流量表
- cash receipt and payment 现金收支
- "cash out" item 现金流出项目
- collect payment 收款
- core operation 核心经营业务
- deferred tax 递延税金
- depreciation [diˌpriːʃiˈeiʃən] n. 折旧
- dividend [ˈdividend] n. 红利，股息
- equity instrument 权益工具，股权工具
- financing activity 筹资活动
- financial transaction 财务往来
- funds flow statement 资产流量表
- gain or loss 损益
- income account 收益账目
- equity security 股票
- income statement 收益表，损益表
- incoming money 流入资金
- issue a bond 发行债券
- loan expense 贷款费用
- marketable securities 有价证券
- negative cash flow 负现金流
- non-cash transaction 非现金交易
- operating activity 经营活动
- outgoing money 流出资金
- positive cash flow 正现金流
- tangible asset 有形资产
- trading portfolio 交易组合
- write-off n. 勾销，注销，冲销

14.3 Extended words
扩展词汇

- accrual [əˈkruːəl] n. 获利，增长
- bulk [bʌlk] n. 大部分，大块
- divest [daiˈvest] vi. 剥夺，剥离
- divest of 剥离
- ease [iːz] vt. 使安心，使放松
- exclude [iksˈkluːd] vt. 排除，不包括
- exhibit [igˈzibit] vt. 展示，展现
- red flag 红旗，危险信号
- respectively [riˈspektivli] ad. 分别地
- ship the product 发运产品
- snapshot [ˈsnæpʃɔt] n. 快照，简单描述

14.4 Notes 注释

1) **In financial accounting, a cash flow statement (CFS) is a financial statement that shows a company's incoming and outgoing money (sources and uses of cash) during a time period (often monthly or quarterly).** 在财务会计中，现金流量表是指显示公司在一个时间段内（通常为一个月或一个季度）的流入及流出的资金（现金的来源及使用）。

   句中 that shows...是限定性定语从句，修饰前面的名词短语 financial statement。

2) **The statement shows how changes in balance sheet and income accounts affected cash and cash equivalents.** 这个报表显示在资产负债表和收益账目中的变化是如何影响现金及现金等价物的。

   How 在句中引导一个宾语从句，做动词 show 的宾语。

3) **…and breaks the analysis down according to operating, investing, and financing activities.** 并且把这一分析按照经营活动、投资活动和筹资活动进行细分。

   break sth. down 是固定短语，意为"分解，把……细分为"。

4) **The balance sheet is a snapshot of a firm's financial resources and obligations at a single point in time.** 资产负债表是公司财务资源及负债在一个单一时间点的简短描述。

5) **…and the income statement summarizes a firm's financial transactions over an interval of time.** ……而收益表则概括公司在一段时间间隔的财务往来。

6) **These two financial statements reflect the accrual basis accounting used by firms to match revenues with the expenses associated with generating those revenues.** 这两个财务报表反映了公司用来把收入以及产生这些收入的相关费用进行对照的权责发生制核算。

   本句包含两个过去分词结构，第一个是 used by firms，做定语，修饰名词短语 accrual basis accounting；第二个是 associated...revenues，亦是定语，修饰名词 expenses。

7) **The cash flow statement includes only inflows and outflows of cash and cash equivalents.** 现金流量表仅包括现金及现金等价物的流入及流出。

8) **…it excludes transactions that do not directly affect cash receipts and payments.** 它不包括对现金收支没有直接影响的往来业务。

   句中 that...payments 是限定性定语从句，修饰名词短语 transactions。

9) **These non-cash transactions include depreciation and write-offs on bad debts.** 这些非现金交易包括折旧以及坏账的注销。

10) Operating activities include the production, sales and delivery of the company's product as well as collecting payment from its customers. 经营活动包括公司产品的生产、销售、交付以及向客户收款。
11) This could include purchasing raw materials, building inventory, advertising and shipping the product. 这可能包括原材料采购、建立存货、广告宣传和发运产品。
12) receipts from the sale of goods or services 来自销售商品或服务的收款
13) receipts for the sale of loans, debt or equity instruments in a trading portfolio 来自出售贷款、债务或交易组合中的权益工具的收款
14) interest received on loans 所收到的贷款利息
15) dividends received on equity securities 所收到的股票红利
16) payments to suppliers for goods and services 向供应商支付商品及服务
17) payments to employees or on behalf of employees 给员工支付或代员工支付
18) tax payments 税金支付
19) interest payments 利息支付
20) payments for the sale of loans, debt or equity instruments in a trading portfolio 来自出售贷款、债务或交易组合中的权益工具的付款
21) Items which are added back to the net income figure (which is found on the Income Statement) to arrive at cash flows from operations generally include. 反加给净收益表数字（可在收益表中找到）以便得出经营活动现金流的项目一般包括。

  句中 which...figure 是限定性定语从句，修饰先行词 items. 括号中的 which...statement 也是限定性定语从句，修饰名词短语 income figure。

22) depreciation (loss of tangible asset value over time) 折旧（有形资产随时间而发生的价值损失）
23) deferred tax 递延税金
24) amortization (loss of intangible asset value over time) 摊销（有形资产随时间而发生的价值损失）
25) any gains or losses associated with an asset sale (unrealized gains/losses are also added back from the income statement) 和资产出售相关联的任何损益（未实现的损益也要从收益表中反加回来。）
26) Changes in equipment, assets or investments relate to cash from investing. 设备、资产或投资方面的变化均和来自投资的现金相关联。
27) Usually cash changes from investing are a "cash out" item, because cash is used to buy new equipment, buildings or short-term assets such as marketable securities. 通常，来自于投资的现金变化属于"现金支出"项目，原因是现金用于购买新设备、建筑物或短期资产，如有价证券。

28) However, when a company divests of an asset, the transaction is considered "cash in" for calculating

cash from investing. 然而，当公司剥离资产时，这一交易被认为是计算来自投资方面的"现金收入"。

29) **Changes in debt, loans or dividends are accounted for in cash from financing.** 债务、贷款或红利方面的变化要算作来自筹资的现金。

30) **Changes in cash from financing are "cash in" when capital is raised.** 在筹集资本时，来自筹资的现金变化是"现金收入"项目。

31) **...and they are "cash out" when dividends are paid.** 而在支付红利时，这些变化就成了"现金支出"项目。

32) **Thus, if a company issues a bond to the public, the company receives cash financing.** 因此，如果公司公开发行债券，公司就收到了现金筹资。

33) **...however, when interest is paid to bondholders, the company is reducing its cash.** ……然而，在给债券持有人支付利息时，公司的现金就减少了。

34) **From this CFS, we can see that the cash flow for FY 2009 was $1,522,000.** 从这个现金流量表中，我们可以看出2009财年的现金流是$1,522,000。

  句中 that 引导一个宾语从句，做动词 see 的宾语。

35) **The bulk of the positive cash flow stems from cash earned from operations, which is a good sign for investors.** 现金流的大头来自于经营所得的现金，这对投资人来说是好兆头。

  句中 which 引导一个非限定性定语从句，对整个句子补充说明。

36) **It means that core operations are generating business and that there is enough money to buy new inventory.** 这意味着核心经营业务有买卖可做，并且有足够的钱来购买新的存货。

  本句中的两个 that 从句均为宾语从句，它们共同做动词 mean 的并列宾语。

37) **The purchasing of new equipment shows that the company has cash to invest in inventory for growth.** 新设备的采购表明公司有现金为了成长而投资于库存。

  句中 that 引导一个宾语从句，做动词 show 的宾语。

38) **Finally, the amount of cash available to the company should ease investors' minds regarding the notes payable, as cash is plentiful to cover that future loan expense.** 最后，就应付票据而言，公司当前可用的现金量应该能让投资者安心，因为有足够的现金来应付未来的贷款费用。

39) **Of course, not all cash flow statements look this healthy, or exhibit a positive cash flow.** 当然，并不是所有的现金流量表都看上去这样的健康，或展现出正现金流。

40) **But a negative cash flow should not automatically raise a red flag without some further analysis.** 但是，如果不做进一步的分析，就不应该自动地给负现金流亮起红牌。

41) **Sometimes, a negative cash flow is a result of a company's decision to expand its business at a certain point in time, which would be a good thing for the future.** 有时，负现金流是公司在某个时间点扩大业务的决定所致，而这对未来是好事情。

  句中 which 引导一个非限定性定语从句，对整个句子补充说明。

14.5 Reinforcement exercise
强化练习

1. Answer the following questions in English.

1) What is a cash flow statement?
2) What is the other name for cash flow statement?
3) What is the role played by CFS?
4) What is the structure of a CFS?

2. Put the following into Chinese.

1) operating activities
2) investing activities
3) financing activities
4) cash flow statement
5) incoming money
6) outgoing money
7) cash equivalent
8) funds flow statement
9) income statement
10) financial resources and obligations
11) financial transaction
12) accrual basis accounting
13) match revenues with the expenses
14) inflows and outflows of cash
15) cash receipt and payment
16) non-cash transaction
17) depreciation
18) write-off
19) bad debt
20) collect payment

3. Put the following into English.

1) 产品的生产、销售及交付
2) 发运产品
3) 权益工具，股权工具
4) 交易组合
5) 红利，股息
6) 股票
7) 有形资产
8) 递延税金
9) 摊销
10) 损益
11) 现金流出项目
12) 有价证券
13) 发行债券
14) 债券持有人
15) 正现金流
16) 现金流的大头
17) 核心经营业务
18) 贷款费用
19) 负现金流
20) 扩张业务

4. Subject for self-study: A CFS chart.

		C	D
		Cash Flow Statement	
		For the Year Ending	Dec. 31, 2009
		Cash at Beginning of Year	15,700
		Operations	
		Cash receipts from customers	693,200
		Cash paid for	
		Inventory purchases	(264,000)
		General operating and administraive expenses	(112,000)
		Wage expenses	(123,000)
		Interest	(13,500)
		Income taxes	(32,800)
		Net Cash Flow from Operations	147,900
		Investing Activities	
		Cash receipts from	
		Sale of property and equipment	33,600
		Collection of principal on loans	
		Sale of investment securities	
		Cash paid for	
		Purchase of property and equipment	(75,000)
		Making loans to other entities	
		Purchase of investment securities	
		Net Cash Flow from Invesing Activities	(41,400)
		Financing Activities	
		Cash receipts from	
		Issuance of stock	
		Borrowing	
		Cash paid for	
		Repurchase of stock (treasury stock)	
		Repayment of loans	(34,000)
		Dividends	(53,000)
		Net Cash Flow from Financing Activities	(87,000)
		Net Increase in Cash	19,500
		Cash at End of Year	35,200

inventory purchases 存货采购
wage expenses 工资开支
property ['prɔpəti] *n.* 财产
principal on loans 贷款利息

investment securities 投资性证券
making loans to other entities 向其他实体提供贷款
issuance of stock 发行股票
borrowing ['bɔrəuiŋ] n. 借款
repurchase [riː'pɜːtʃis] n. 再采购
treasury stock 库存股票

14.6 Accounting-related knowledge
会计相关知识介绍

如何编制现金流量表？
How to prepare a cash flow statement?

现金流量表（cash flow statement）的编制一直是企业报表编制的一个难点，如果对所有的会计分录（accounting entries），按现金流量表准则的要求全部调整为收付实现制（accrual basis system），这等于是重做一套会计分录，无疑将大大增加财务人员的工作量，在实践中也缺乏可操作性。许多财务人员因此希望仅根据资产负债表（balance sheet）和利润表（profit statement）两大主表来编制出现金流量表，但这是一种奢望，实际上仅根据资产负债表和利润表是无法编制出现金流量表的，还需要根据总账（ledger）和明细账（detailed ledger）获取相关数据。

本文提出的编制方法从重要性原则出发，牺牲精确性，以换取速度。编制现金流量表按以下由易到难顺序快速完成编制。

首先，填列补充资料中"现金及现金等价物（cash and cash equivalent）净增加情况"各项目，并确定"现金及现金等价物的净增加额"。

第二，填列主表中"筹资活动（financing activities）产生的现金流量"各项目，并确定"筹资活动产生的现金流量净额"。

第三，填列主表中"投资活动（investing activities）产生的现金流量"各项目，并确定"投资活动产生的现金流量净额"。

第四，计算确定经营活动（operating activities）产生的现金流量净额，计算公式是：

经营活动产生的现金流量净额＝现金及现金等价物的净增加额－筹资活动产生的现金流量净额－投资活动产生的现金流量净额

编制现金流量表的难点在于确定经营活动产生的现金流量净额，由于筹资活动和投资活动在企业业务中相对较少，财务数据（financial data）容易获取，所以这两项活动的现金流量项目容易填列，并容易确保这两项活动的现金流量净额结果正确，从而根据该公式计算得出的经营活动产生的现金流量净额也容易确保正确。这一步计算的结果，可以验证主表和补充资料中"经营活动产生的现金流量净额"各项目是否填列正确。

第五，填列补充资料中"将净利润调节为经营活动现金流量"各项目，并将计算结果与第四步公式得出的结果进行验证，看看是否一致，如不相符，再进行检查，以求最终一致。

第六，最后填列主表中"经营活动产生的现金流量"各项目，并将计算结果与第四步公式计算的结果进行验证，如不相符，再进行检查，以求最终一致。由于本项中"收到的其他与经营活动有关的现金"项目是倒挤产生，因此主表和附加资料中"经营活动产生的现金流量净额"是相等的，从而快速完成现金流量表的编制。

14.7 Extended reading
延伸阅读

The preparation methods of a CFS
现金流量表的编制方法

There are two methods in preparing a CFS. The direct method of preparing a cash flow statement results in a more easily understood report. The indirect method is almost universally used, because a supplementary report similar to the indirect method is generally required if a company chooses to use the direct method.

Direct method

The direct method for creating a cash flow statement reports major classes of gross cash receipts and payments. For example, dividends received may be reported under operating activities or under investing activities. If taxes paid are directly linked to operating activities, they are reported under operating activities; if the taxes are directly linked to investing activities or financing activities, they are reported under investing or financing activities.

Indirect method

The indirect method uses net-income as a starting point, makes adjustments for all transactions

Sample cash flow statement using the direct method

Sample cash flow statement using the direct method

Cash flows from operating activities	
Cash receipts from customers	$27,500
Cash paid to suppliers and employees	(20,000)
Cash generated from operations (sum)	7,500
Interest paid	(2,000)
Income taxes paid	(2,000)
Net cash flows from operating activities	$3,500
Cash flows from investing activities	
Proceeds from the sale of equipment	7,500
Dividends received	3,000
Net cash flows from investing activities	10,500
Cash flows from financing activities	
Dividends paid	(12,000)
Net cash flows used in financing activities	(12,000)
Net increase in cash and cash equivalents	2,000
Cash and cash equivalents, beginning of year	1,000
Cash and cash equivalents, end of year	$ 3,000

for non-cash items, then adjusts for all cash-based transactions. An increase in an asset account is subtracted from net income, and an increase in a liability account is added back to net income. This method converts accrual-basis net income (loss) into cash flow by using a series of additions and deductions.

Rules

The following rules are used to make adjustments for changes in current assets and liabilities, operating items not providing or using cash and non-operating items.

- Decrease in non-cash current assets are added to net income
- Increase in non-cash current asset are subtracted from net income
- Increase in current liabilities are added to net income
- Decrease in current liabilities are subtracted from net income
- Expenses with no cash outflows are added back to net income
- Revenues with no cash inflows are subtracted from net income (depreciation expense is the only operating item that has no effect on cash flows in the period)
- Non-operating losses are added back to net income
- Non-operating gains are subtracted from net income

Citigroup Cash Flow Statement (all numbers in thousands)			
Period ending	12/31/2006	12/31/2005	12/31/2004
Net income	21,538,000	24,589,000	17,046,000
Operating activities, cash flows provided by or used in:			
Depreciation and amortization	2,790,000	2,592,000	2,747,000
Adjustments to net income	4,617,000	621,000	2,910,000
Decrease (increase) in accounts receivable	12,503,000	17,236,000	--
Increase (decrease) in liabilities (A/P, taxes payable)	131,622,000	19,822,000	37,856,000
Decrease (increase) in inventories	--	--	--
Increase (decrease) in other operating activities	(173,057,000)	(33,061,000)	(62,963,000)
Net cash flow from operating activities	13,000	31,799,000	(2,404,000)
Investing activities, cash flows provided by or used in:			
Capital expenditures	(4,035,000)	(3,724,000)	(3,011,000)
Investments	(201,777,000)	(71,710,000)	(75,649,000)
Other cash flows from investing activities	1,606,000	17,009,000	(571,000)
Net cash flows from investing activities	(204,206,000)	(58,425,000)	(79,231,000)
Financing activities, cash flows provided by or used in:			
Dividends paid	(9,826,000)	(9,188,000)	(8,375,000)
Sale (repurchase) of stock	(5,327,000)	(12,090,000)	133,000
Increase (decrease) in debt	101,122,000	26,651,000	21,204,000
Other cash flows from financing activities	120,461,000	27,910,000	70,349,000
Net cash flows from financing activities	206,430,000	33,283,000	83,311,000
Effect of exchange rate changes	645,000	(1,840,000)	731,000
Net increase (decrease) in cash and cash equivalents	$2,882,000	$4,817,000	$2,407,000

Unit 15
What tasks does an accountant do?
会计师的工作范围是什么?

Core terms reminder
核心术语提示

会计员，会计师	accountant
职能经理	functional manager
注册会计师	certified public accountant (CPA)
财务健康	financial health
做财务记录	keep financial records
内部审计	internal audit
预算计划	budgetary plans
国家认证	state certification
风险管理	risk management

15.1a What is an accountant?

什么是会计师？

An **accountant** is a person who performs accounting tasks for individuals or companies. The exact material that an accountant handles varies **depending on** the size of the company and the accountant's **specialization**, but generally includes **financial records**, taxes, and responsibility for the **issuing** of financial reports. An accountant is one of the **primary figures** in a business that he/she works for, whether it is a **multinational corporation** or a small family owned business. Requirements to become an accountant vary upon specialization and nation, but generally include certification through a professional agency and a basic college degree in accounting and finance.

accountant *n.* 会计员，会计师

depend on 信赖，取决于
specialization *n.* 专门化，专业化，专长
financial record 财务记录
issuing *n.* 发行，发布

primary figure 首要人物
multinational corporation 跨国公司

15.1b What tasks does an accountant do?

会计师的工作范围是什么？

In a small firm, an accountant may be responsible for **keeping** all **financial records**. These records include **payroll** information, **accounts payable**, **accounts receivable**, **retail sales**, and information regarding investments held by the company. These accounts are kept and organized in **ledgers** which are used to assess the

keep financial records 做财务记录
payroll *n.* 薪水册
account payable 应付账
account receivable 应收账
retail sales 零售额

ledger *n.* 分类账，总账

financial health of a company. Ledgers are always kept **up to date**, and may be **consulted** by managers and **high ranking** members of a company when they are making major business decisions.

In larger firms, accountants also perform **internal audits**, to ensure that the financial records of the company are accurate. Because of **bias concerns**, an internal audit cannot be handled by an accountant who regularly handles the material concerned, and many companies hire outside accounting firms to perform audits. When this is the case, the hired firm should not be **contracted** to handle any of the company's other financial material, as this may represent a **conflict of interest**.

financial health 财务健康
up to date 最新的，最近的
keep sth. up to date 保持更新
consult vt. 商量，请教
high ranking 高级别的
audit n. 审计
internal audit 内部审计
bias concern 偏见关系
contract vt. 签订合同，缔结合同

conflict of interest 利益冲突

In most cases, an accountant will choose to specialize in a particular field such as audits, **bookkeeping**, or taxes. In other instances, an accountant may acquire a wide range of skills to better serve his/her clients. This is common with a **certified public accountant** (CPA) who handles the books for several small businesses at once. In both instances, the accountant must have strong math skills, as well as an education in accounting.

bookkeeping n. 减

certified public accountant (CPA) 注册会计师

Depending on the type of accounting being performed, certification by the state may be required. **State certification** is usually required for accountants who perform audits and other **sensitive** accounting tasks, while it is not as vitally necessary for **accounting clerks** who work under certified accountants. Commonly, an accountant is also a member of a professional organization of accountants, and takes advantage of meetings and seminars to keep up with advances in the field.

state certification 国家认证

sensitive a. 敏感的

accounting clerk 会计职员

Unit 15　What tasks does an accountant do? 会计师的工作范围是什么？　177

15.1c　Why important?
为什么重要？

Accountants or financial managers in a company are the most important **functional managers**. They make the financial decisions which can support the clients and the employees. They help in making decisions about the short term and the long term **budgetary plans** of the company. They act as the business **analyst** for any company therefore. They also help in making decisions about the right **allocation of resources**. Some of the decision areas in which they actively participate include the **interpretation** of financial information and then **highlighting** the important areas which must be taken under consideration. They also play an important role in the business **modeling** and **forecasting**. They are responsible for improving the performance of the finances of the company through their wise decisions. Financial managers have to make important decisions about the **risk management**. They can also make important suggestions about the **pricing** of the products and make decisions on the basis of complex financial situation. The selection of the right **loanable funds** and investments are also accomplished according to the suggestions given by financial managers.

functional manager 职能经理

budgetary plans 预算计划
analyst *n.* 分析家

allocation *n.* 分配，配置
allocation of resources 资源配置
interpretation *n.* 解释，阐明
highlight *vt.* 突出，强调
modeling *n.* 建立模型
forecasting *n.* 预测
risk management 风险管理
pricing *n.* 定价

loanable fund 可贷出资金

15.2　Core accounting terms
核心会计术语

□ **accountant** [ə'kauntənt] *n.* 会计员，会计师
□ **account payable** 应付账款
□ **account receivable** 应收账
□ **accounting clerk** 会计职员
□ **audit** ['ɔːdit] *n. vt.* 审计

- functional manager 职能经理
- financial health 财务健康
- financial record 财务记录
- internal audit 内部审计
- keep financial records 做财务记录
- ledger ['ledʒə] n. 分类账，总账
- loanable fund 可贷出资金
- multinational corporation 跨国公司
- risk management 风险管理
- specialization [ˌspeʃəlaiˈzeiʃən] n. 专门化，专业化，专长
- state certification 国家认证
- payroll ['peirəul] n. 薪水册
- certified public accountant (CPA) 注册会计师
- budgetary plans 预算计划
- bookkeeping ['bukˌki:piŋ] n. 簿记

15.3 Extended words 扩展词汇

- allocation [ˌæləuˈkeiʃən] n. 分配，配置
- analyst ['ænəlist] n. 分析家
- bias concern 偏见关系
- contract ['kɔntrækt] vt. 签订合同，缔结合同
- conflict of interest 利益冲突
- consult [kənˈsʌlt] vt. 商量，请教
- depend on 信赖，取决于
- forecasting ['fɔ:kɑ:stiŋ] n. 预测
- highlight ['hailait] n. 突出，强调
- high ranking 高级别的
- interpretation [inˌtə:priˈteiʃən] n. 解释，阐明
- issuing ['isju:iŋ] n. 发行，发布
- keep sth. up to date 保持更新
- modeling ['mɔdliŋ] n. 建立模型
- pricing ['praisiŋ] n. 定价
- primary figure 首要人物
- retail sales 零售额
- sensitive ['sensitiv] a. 敏感的
- up to date 最新的，最近的

15.4 Notes 注释

1) **An accountant is a person who performs accounting tasks for individuals or companies.** 会计师是为个人或公司履行核算任务的人。
   句中，who 引导一个限定性定语从句，修饰先行词 person。
2) **The exact material that an accountant handles varies depending on the size of the company and the accountant's specialization.** 会计师所处理的准确材料取决于公司的规

模以及会计师的专长。

  句中，that...handles 是限定性定语从句，修饰先行词 material。

3) **An accountant is one of the primary figures in a business that he/she works for.** 会计师是其所供职公司的首要人物之一。

  句中，that 引导一个限定性定语从句，修饰先行词 figures。

4) **Requirements to become an accountant vary upon specialization and nation, but generally include certification through a professional agency and a basic college degree in accounting and finance.** 成为会计师的要求因专长及国家不同而异，但是一般包括经由职业机构或财会专业的基本大学学位而获得的认证。

5) **These records include payroll information, accounts payable, accounts receivable, retail sales, and information regarding investments held by the company.** 这些财务记录包括薪水册信息、应付账、应收账、零售额以及有关公司所持有的投资方面的信息。

6) **These accounts are kept and organized in ledgers which are used to assess the financial health of a company.** 这些账目收录在用来评估公司财务健康的分类账里。

  句中，which 引导一个限定性定语从句，修饰先行词 ledgers。

7) **Ledgers are always kept up to date, and may be consulted by managers and high ranking members of a company when they are making major business decisions.** 分类账总是在更新，而且可能在做出重大业务决定时与公司经理或高级别成员协商。

8) **In larger firms, accountants also perform internal audits, to ensure that the financial records of the company are accurate.** 在大公司里，为确保公司财务记录的准确性，会计师也履行内部审计业务。

9) **Because of bias concerns, an internal audit cannot be handled by an accountant who regularly handles the material concerned, and many companies hire outside accounting firms to perform audits.** 由于偏见关系，内部审计不能由经常处理相关材料的会计师来办理，因此许多公司雇佣外部会计事务所来做审计。

  句中，who...concerned 是限定性定语从句，修饰先行词 accountant。

10) **When this is the case, the hired firm should not be contracted to handle any of the company's other financial material, as this may represent a conflict of interest.** 在这种情况下，所雇佣的事务所不应该被赋予处理公司的其他财务材料的合同义务，因为这可能形成利益冲突。

11) **This is common with a certified public accountant (CPA) who handles the books for several small businesses at once.** 这种情况对于同时为数家小公司做账的注册会计师（CPA）来说是很常见的。

  句中，who 引导一个限定性定语从句，修饰名词短语 certified public accountant。

12) **State certification is usually required for accountants who perform audits and other sensitive accounting tasks, while it is not as vitally necessary for accounting clerks who work under certified accountants.** 做审计业务和其他具有敏感性的核算任务的会计师通常要求有国家认证，而这一点对于在注册会计师手下工作的会计职员来说就不是非常必要的。

本句包含两个由 who 引导的定语从句，分别是 who...tasks 和 who...accountants，前者修饰名词 accountants，后者修饰名词短语 accounting clerks。二者均为限定性从句。

13) **Commonly, an accountant is also a member of a professional organization of accountants, and takes advantage of meetings and seminars to keep up with advances in the field.** 通常，会计师也是某个会计师职业组织的成员，并能够利用会议及研讨会来跟上该领域内的进展。

14) **They make the financial decisions which can support the clients and the employees.** 他们做出能够支持客户和雇员的财务决定。

句中，which 引导一个限定性定语从句，修饰名词短语 financial decisions。

15) **They help in making decisions about the short term and the long term budgetary plans of the company.** 他们也帮助做出关于公司长期及短期预算计划的决定。

16) **Some of the decision areas in which they actively participate include the interpretation of financial information and then highlighting the important areas which must be taken under consideration.** 他们积极参与的一些决策领域包括说明财务信息，然后突出需要考虑的重要领域。

本句包含两个由 which 引导的定语从句，前一个是 in which...participate，这是介词加关系词结构，修饰名词短语 decision areas；后一个是 which...consideration，修饰名词 areas，二者均为限定性定语从句。

17) **They can also make important suggestions about the pricing of the products and make decisions on the basis of complex financial situation.** 他们也可以就产品定价提出重要建议并依据复杂的财务形势做出决策。

18) **The selection of the right loanable funds and investments are also accomplished according to the suggestions given by financial managers.** 对适当的可贷出资金和投资的选择也是根据财务经理提出的建议所完成的。

句中 given by...是由过去分词引导的短语，做定语，修饰名词 suggestions。

15.5 Reinforcement exercise
强化练习

1. Answer the following questions in English.

1) What is an accountant?
2) What kind of materials does an accountant handle?
3) What tasks does an accountant do?

Unit 15 What tasks does an accountant do? 会计师的工作范围是什么?

4) Why do companies hire outside accounting firms to perform audits?

2. Put the following into Chinese.

1) accountant
2) accounting firm
3) specialization
4) financial record
5) multinational corporation
6) family owned business
7) professional agency
8) keep financial records
9) payroll
10) account payable
11) account receivable
12) retail sales
13) ledger
14) financial health
15) high ranking members
16) audit

3. Put the following into English.

1) 内部审计
2) 处理有关材料
3) 利益冲突
4) 簿记
5) 注册会计师
6) 国家认证
7) 会计职员
8) 跟上本领域的进步
9) 职能经理
10) 预算计划
11) 资源配置
12) 建立模型及预测
13) 风险管理
14) 定价
15) 可贷出资金

4. Subject for self-study: A bookkeeping chart.

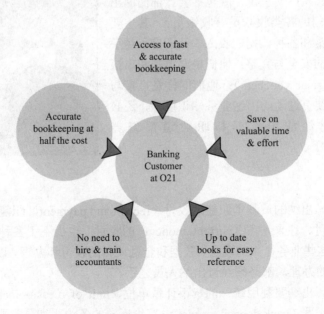

access to 进入，可以使用
books *n.* 账册，账簿
for reference 供参考
at half the cost 以一半的成本

15.6 Accounting-related knowledge
会计相关知识介绍

什么是出纳？
What is a cashier?

出纳的概念：

（1）出纳工作。顾名思义，出即支出（payment），纳即收入（receipt）。出纳工作是管理货币资金（pecuniary resources）、票据（bills）、有价证券（marketable resources）进进出出的一项工作。

（2）出纳人员。从广义上讲，既包括会计部门的出纳，也包括业务部门的各类收款员（收银员）。其主要工作是办理货币资金和各种票据的收入，保证自己经手的货币资金和票据的安全与完整；他们也要填制和审核许多原始凭证（original vouchers）；他们同样是直接与货币打交道，除了要有过硬的出纳业务知识以外，还必须具备良好的财经法纪素养和职业道德修养（professional ethics）。

出纳的职能

（1）收付职能。出纳的最基本职能是收付（receipt and payment）职能。企业经营活动少不了货物价款的收付、往来款项（current money）的收付，也少不了各种有价证券以及金融业务往来的办理。这些业务往来的现金、票据和金融证券的收付和办理，以及银行存款（bank deposit）收付业务的办理，都必须经过出纳人员之手。

（2）反映职能。出纳要利用统一的货币计量单位（unit of measurement），通过其持有的现金与银行存款日记账（bank deposit journal）、有价证券的各种明细分类账（detailed ledger），

Unit 15　What tasks does an accountant do? 会计师的工作范围是什么？

对本单位的货币资金和有价证券进行详细的记录与核算，以便为经济管理和投资决策（investment decision-making）提供所需的完整、系统的经济信息。因此，反映职能是出纳工作的主要职能之一。

（3）监督职能。出纳要对企业的各种经济业务，特别是货币资金收付业务的合法性、合理性和有效性进行全过程的监督（supervision）。

（4）管理职能。出纳还有一个重要的职能是管理职能。对货币资金与有价证券进行保管，对银行存款和各种票据进行管理，对企业资金的使用效益进行分析研究，为企业投资决策提供金融信息，甚至直接参与企业的方案评估（assessment）、投资效益预测分析（forecasting and analysis）等都是出纳的职责所在。

15.7 Extended reading
延伸阅读

What is a bank teller?
什么是银行出纳？

　　A bank teller is a member of the staff of a bank who deals directly with the public and handles routine banking transactions like deposits, withdrawals, and so forth. For many people, bank tellers are iconic figures, since they represent the face of the bank to the public. Employment in this profession is actually shrinking, because some people have turned to Automated Teller Machines (ATMs) and online banking since they find these services more convenient.

　　The job requirements for becoming a bank teller are fairly minimal. He/she must have a high school diploma and exhibit an ability to perform basic math functions. Bank tellers must also be comfortable with members of the public and with handling large amounts of money. They are also expected to be extremely attentive and discreet, and in some regions a bank teller may need to pass a law enforcement background check before he/she can be hired.

　　In a workday, a bank teller might accept cash or checks for deposit, cash checks drawn on his/her bank, issue funds like money orders and traveler's checks, and handle transactions related to savings accounts. A bank teller also usually promotes services offered by the bank, such as loans, retirement accounts, and insurance; if a customer expresses interest in these services, the teller refers him/her to another bank employee who specializes in these offerings. A bank teller might also provide access to safe deposit boxes, if a bank offers this service.

　　Classically, the tellers at a bank are managed by a single head teller who usually walks the bank floor to ensure that customer transactions are running smoothly. Each teller has a window or booth, and typically tellers are assigned their own cash drawers which no other teller handles. This ensures that each teller can manage his/her transactions for the day, and at the end of the day, each teller counts out the drawer to ensure that it matches the transaction records.

Unit 16
How to calculate shareholders' dividend?
如何计算股东股息？

Core terms reminder
核心术语提示

红利，股息	dividend
股息收益率	dividend yield
现金股息	cash dividend
股票股息	stock dividend
股息支付率	dividend payout ratio
固定利率	fixed rate
蓝筹股，绩优股	blue chip, blue chip stock
普通股	common stock
优先股	preferred stock
每股股息	dividend per share
每股平均收益	earnings per share

16.1a What is a dividend?

什么是股息？

Dividends are a small slice of the income pie

Total personal income: $9.078 trillion*
- $5.102 Trillion Wages and salaries
- $1.149 Trillion Other
- $1.309 Trillion Retirement, disability, other benefits
- $1.074 Trillion Interest income
- $0.444 Trillion Dividend income

A **dividend** is a portion of corporate **earnings** paid out to **shareholders**. Most dividends are paid quarterly.

The primary purpose of any business is to create profit for its owners, and the dividend is the most important way the business fulfills this mission. When a company earns a profit, some of this money is typically reinvested in the business and called **retained earnings**, and some of it can be paid to its shareholders as a dividend. Paying dividends reduces the amount of cash available to the business, but the distribution of profit to the owners is, after all, the purpose of the business.

Some stocks, especially **blue chips**, pay dividends. This means that for every share you own, you are paid a portion of the company's earnings. For example, for every share of **Coca Cola** you own, you will be sent $0.15 every year. Most companies pay dividends quarterly (four times a year), meaning at the end of every business quarter, the company will send a check for 1/4 of $0.15 for each share you own.

This may not seem like a lot, but when you have built your **portfolio** up to thousands of shares, and use those dividends to buy more stock in the company, you can make a lot of money over the years.

dividend *n.* 红利，股息
earnings *n.* 所得，收益
shareholder *n.* 股东

retained earnings 留存收益

blue chip 蓝筹股，绩优股

Coca Cola 可口可乐公司

portfolio *n.* 有价证券组合

16.1b How does a dividend work?

股息是如何起作用的？

Dividends are payments in cash or stock made to shareholders of a company. A dividend may be declared (authorized by the company's **board of directors**) or it can be a **guaranteed fixed rate** in the case of **preferred stock**. Strictly speaking, dividends are issued, rather than calculated. However, investors calculate **dividend yield**, **payout ratio** and the amount of income a particular stock provides as part of analyzing a stock's performance. Knowing the return dividends provide is a major concern for stockholders who are primarily interested in income-producing investments. Investors whose investment strategy is aimed at **equity growth** tend to place less importance on dividends.

The first step in analyzing a company's dividends is to find how much income the dividend represents. All that is necessary is to **multiply** the number of shares by the **dividend amount** per share. Dividends are normally paid quarterly. Divide by 4 to find the income that is paid every three months. For example, if you have 800 shares of stock that pay an **annual dividend** of $2 per share, the **annual income** is 800 times $2, or $1,600. Divided by 4, this comes to a quarterly payment of $400.

- **board of directors** 董事会
- **guaranteed** *a.* 保证的
- **fixed rate** 固定利率
- **preferred stock** 优先股
- **dividend yield** 股息收益率
- **payout ratio** 股息支付率
- **equity growth** 股本增长
- **multiply** *vt.* 乘以
- **dividend amount** 股息额
- **annual dividend** 年股息
- **annual income** 年收入，岁入

16.1c How to calculate dividend yield and payout ratio?

如何计算股息收益率和股息支付率？

DIVIDEND YIELD

To **figure** yield, divide the dividend amount per share by the

- **dividend yield** 股息收益率
- **figure** *vt.* 计算

price paid for a **share of the stock**. For instance, if the stock was purchased for $25 per share and the dividend is $2 per share, the yield is $2 divided by $25 or 0.08 (8 percent).

share of stock 股份，每份股票

ABC Company			
Balance sheet before a stock dividend			
Current assets	$100,000	Current liabilities	$50,000
Fixed assets	$200,000	Long term liabilities	50,000
		Equity: common stock $1 per 100,000 shares outstanding	100,000
		Additional paid-in capital	30,000
		Retained earnings	70,000
		Total equity	200,000
Total assets	$300,000	Total liabilities and equity	$300,000
After 10 percent stock dividend (market price: $5 per share)			
Current assets	$100,000	Current liabilities	$50,000
Fixed assets	$200,000	Long term liabilities	50,000
		Equity: common stock $1 per 100,000 shares outstanding	110,000
		Additional paid-in capital	70,000
		Retained earnings	20,000
		Total equity	200,000
Total assets	$300,000	Total liabilities and equity	$300,000

Figure 1　*A sample balance sheet before and after a stock dividend*
图1　股息前及股息后的资产负债表样本

PAYOUT RATIO

Management cutting dividends is always a DANGER！

The dividend payout ratio is the ratio of how much profit is paid in dividends compared with the total profit earned by the company. Divide the **earnings per share** (which tells you how much profit per share the company made) by the **dividend per share**. For instance, if earnings per share are $2/50 and the dividend is $0.50, the dividend payout ratio works out to 5:1. A high payout ratio indicates the company is retaining most of its profit (usually to expand or **pay off debts**) while a low payout ratio shows the company is devoting much of its profit to paying dividends.

Payout ratio 股息支付率

earnings per share 每股平均收益率

dividend per share 每股股息

pay off debts 清偿债务

16.1d Why stock dividend instead of cash dividend?
为什么是股票股息而不是现金股息？

Sometimes a company **issues** additional **shares** to stockholders **in lieu of** a cash dividend. This can allow a company to **issue a dividend** while retaining cash profits to reinvest. Since the stock may **appreciate**, it may also be a good deal for investors, especially with **growth-oriented** companies. A company might issue a 4 percent **stock dividend**, for example, by giving each stockholder an extra 4 shares for every 100 shares owned. To find out how much the dividend is actually worth, multiply the number of shares by the market price of the shares. If the stock is selling for $25 per share, that 4 percent dividend would be 4 percent of $25, or $1 per share.

issue *vt.* 发行
issue share 发行股票，派股
in lieu of 代替
cash dividend 现金股息
issue a dividend 派息
appreciate *vt.* 增值
growth-oriented 成长面好的
stock dividend 股票股息

16.2 Core accounting terms
核心会计术语

- **annual dividend** 年股息
- **annual income** 年收入，岁入
- **cash dividend** 现金股息
- **blue chip** 蓝筹股，绩优股
- **dividend** ['dividend] *n.* 红利，股息
- **dividend amount** 股息额
- **dividend per share** 每股股息
- **dividend yield** 股息收益率
- **earnings** ['ə:niŋz] *n.* 所得，收益
- **earnings per share** 每股平均收益
- **equity growth** 股本增长

- **issue a dividend** 派息
- **issue shares** 发行股票，派股
- **fixed rate** 固定利率
- **pay off debt** 清偿债务
- **payout ratio** 股息支付率
- **portfolio** [pɔ:t'fəuljəu] *n.* 有价证券组合
- **preferred stock** 优先股
- **retained earnings** 留存收益
- **shareholder** ['ʃɛəhəuldə] *n.* 股东
- **share of stock** 股份，每份股票
- **stock dividend** 股票股息

16.3 Extended words
扩展词汇

- **appreciate** [ə'priːʃieit] *vt.* 增值
- **board of directors** 董事会
- **Coca Cola** 可口可乐公司
- **figure** ['figə] *vt.* 计算
- **growth-oriented** 成长面好的
- **guaranteed** [ˌgærən'tiːd] *a.* 保证的
- **in lieu of** 代替
- **issue** ['isjuː] *vt.* 发行
- **multiply** ['mʌltiplai] *vt.* 乘以

16.4 Notes
注释

1) **A dividend is a portion of corporate earnings paid out to shareholders.** 股息是支付给股东的公司收益的一部分。

   句中 paid out to shareholders 是过去分词短语做定语，修饰其前的名词短语 corporate earnings。

2) **…and the dividend is the most important way the business fulfills this mission.** ……而且股息是公司实现这一使命的最重要的方法。

   句中 the business fulfills this mission 是限定性定语从句，前面省略关系词 that，修饰名词 way。

3) **When a company earns a profit, some of this money is typically reinvested in the business and called retained earnings.** 当公司赢利时，一些资金常常被再投资于业务中，这就是所谓的留存收益。

4) **This means that for every share you own, you are paid a portion of the company's earnings.** 这就是说对于你所拥有的每一份股票，你都可以得到公司收益的一部分。

   a) 句中 that for…earnings 是宾语从句，做动词 mean 的宾语。

   b) you own 是限定性定语从句，省略关系词 that，修饰名词短语 every share。注5)和注6)中的 you own 同本例。

5) **For example, for every share of Coca Cola you own, you will be sent $0.15 every year.** 例如，对于你所拥有的每一份可口可乐公司的股票，你将每年得到$0.15 的红利。

6) **Most companies pay dividends quarterly (four times a year), meaning at the end of every**

business quarter, the company will send a check for 1/4 of $0.15 for each share you own. 多数公司按季度分红（一年四次），也就是说在每个营业季末尾，公司将会按$0.15 的 1/4 来向你所拥有的每份股票派发支票。

    a) 句中 meaning 是 V-ing 形式，在句中引导一个伴随性状语。

    b) the company…own 是宾语从句，其前省略关系词 that，做动词 mean 的宾语。

7) **This may not seem like a lot, but when you have built your portfolio up to thousands of shares, and use those dividends to buy more stock in the company, you can make a lot of money over the years.** 这可能看上去没有多少，但是当你把证券组合积累到数千股时，并且用这些红利购买公司更多的股票时，你就会在数年中赚到很多钱。

8) **Dividends are payments in cash or stock made to shareholders of a company.** 股息是以现金或股票形式支付给公司股东的。

9) **A dividend may be declared (authorized by the company's board of directors).** 股息可以被宣布（由公司的董事会授权）发放。

10) **…or it can be a guaranteed fixed rate in the case of preferred stock.** ……或者也可以是在优先股情况下的保证固定股息率。

11) **Strictly speaking, dividends are issued, rather than calculated.** 严格地讲，股息是派发的、而不是计算出来的。

12) **However, investors calculate dividend yield, payout ratio and the amount of income a particular stock provides as part of analyzing a stock's performance.** 然而，作为分析股票绩效的一部分工作，投资人会计算股息收益率、股息支付率以及某一特定股票的收益额。

    句中 a particular stock provides 是限定性定语从句，其前省略关系词 that，修饰名词短语 amount of stock。

13) **Knowing the return dividends provide is a major concern for stockholders who are primarily interested in income-producing investments.** 了解股息所提供的回报率是那些对创收性投资有重大兴趣的股东们主要关注的事情。

    a) 句中 dividends provide 是限定性定语从句，其前省略关系词 that, 修饰先行词 dividend。

    b) who…investments 也是限定性定语从句，修饰先行词 stockholders。

14) **Investors whose investment strategy is aimed at equity growth tend to place less importance on dividends.** 那些投资策略着眼于股本增长的投资人不把红利看得很重要。

    句中 whose…growth 是限定性定语从句，修饰名词短语 equity growth。

15) **The first step in analyzing a company's dividends is to find how much income the dividend represents.** 分析公司股息的第一步就是找出股息占收益的多大比例。

    句中 how much 引导一个宾语从句，做动词 find 的宾语。

16) **All that is necessary is to multiply the number of shares by the dividend amount per share.** 所有必要的事情就是用股票数量乘以每股红利额。

　　句中 that is necessary 是限定性定语从句，修饰代词 all。

17) **Divide by 4 to find the income that is paid every three months.** 除以 4 就可以得出每三个月所支付的收益。

　　句中 that…months 是限定性定语从句，修饰名词 income。

18) **For example, if you have 800 shares of stock that pay an annual dividend of $2 per share, the annual income is 800 times $2, or $1,600.** 例如，如果你有 800 份股票，每年支付股息$2/股，那么，年收益就是 800 乘以 2，即$1,600。

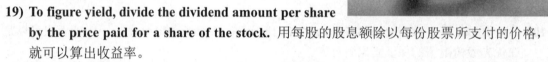

　　句中 that…share 是限定性定语从句，修饰名词短语 shares of stock。

19) **To figure yield, divide the dividend amount per share by the price paid for a share of the stock.** 用每股的股息额除以每份股票所支付的价格，就可以算出收益率。

20) **For instance, if the stock was purchased for $25 per share and the dividend is $2 per share, the yield is $2 divided by $25 or 0.08 (8 percent).** 例如，如果股票的购买价为每股$25，而股息是每股$2，那么股息收益率就是$2 除以$25 即 0.08（百分之八）。

21) **The dividend payout ratio is the ratio of how much profit is paid in dividends compared with the total profit earned by the company.** 股息支付率是有多少利润用来支付股息与公司所获得的总利润相比较的比率。

　　a) 句中 how much…dividends 是宾语从句，做介词 of 的宾语。

　　b) compared 和 earned 均为过去分词引导的短语，做定语，分别修饰名词 dividends 和 profit。

22) **Divide the earnings per share (which tells you how much profit per share the company made) by the dividend per share.** 可以用每股平均收益（这表明公司每股赚了多少利润）除以每股股息来计算。

　　a) 本句包含两个定语从句，第一个 which…made 是限定性定语从句，修饰名词短语 earnings per share；第二个 the company made，也是限定性从句，其前省略关系词 that, 修饰名词 profit。

　　b) how much…made 是宾语从句，做动词 tell 的宾语。

23) **For instance, if earnings per share are $2/50 and the dividend is $0.50, the dividend payout ratio works out to 5:1.** 例如，如果每股平均收益是$2/50，而股息是 $0.50，那么就可以算出股息支付率是 5:1。

24) **A high payout ratio indicates the company is retaining most of its profit (usually to expand or pay off debts).** 高股息支付率表明公司留存了多数的利润（通常用于扩张或偿债）。

　　句中 the company…profit 是宾语从句，其前省略关系词 that, 做动词 indicate 的

宾语。

25) **...while a low payout ratio shows the company is devoting much of its profit to paying dividends.** ...而低股息支付率则表明公司把利润的很大部分用来支付股息。

句中 the company...dividends 是宾语从句，做动词 show 的宾语。

26) **Sometimes a company issues additional shares to stockholders in lieu of a cash dividend.** 有时，公司会给股东派发额外股份来代替现金股息。

27) **This can allow a company to issue a dividend while retaining cash profits to reinvest.** 这就能够使公司在发放股息的同时还能够留存现金利润用来再投资。

28) **Since the stock may appreciate, it may also be a good deal for investors, especially with growth-oriented companies.** 由于股票会升值，这对于投资人来说可能也是一笔好买卖，尤其对于成长面向好的公司更是如此。

29) **A company might issue a 4 percent stock dividend, for example, by giving each stockholder an extra 4 shares for every 100 shares owned.** 公司可能会派发4%的股票股息，例如，通过向每个股东所持有的每100份股票派发4股。

句中 owned 是过去分词后置，做定语，修饰名词 shares，相当于定语从句 which are owned。

30) **To find out how much the dividend is actually worth, multiply the number of shares by the market price of the shares.** 要计算出这笔股息实际价值是多少，可以用股票数量乘以股票的市场价。

句中 how much...worth 是宾语从句，作动词短语 find out 的宾语。

31) **If the stock is selling for $25 per share, that 4 percent dividend would be 4 percent of $25, or $1 per share.** 如果股票每股卖$25，那么4%的股息就是$25的4%即每股$1。

16.5 Reinforcement exercise

强化练习

1. Answer the following questions in English.

1) What is a dividend?
2) How does a dividend work?
3) How do we calculate the dividend yield?
4) How do we calculate dividend payout ratio?
5) Why do companies issue stock dividend instead of cash dividend?

2. Put the following into Chinese.

1) dividend
2) earnings
3) shareholder
4) retained earnings
5) pay dividends
6) distribution of profit to the owners
7) blue chip, blue chip stock
8) a portion of the company's earnings
9) pay dividends quarterly
10) portfolio
11) board of directors
12) fixed rate
13) preferred stock
14) dividend yield
15) payout ratio

3. Put the following into English.

1) 分析股票的绩效
2) 创收性投资
3) 股本增长
4) 股息额
5) 年股息
6) 年收入，岁入
7) 股份，每份股票
8) 每股的股息额
9) 每股平均收益
10) 每股股息
11) 清偿债务
12) 留存多数利润
13) 发行股票，派股
14) 成长面向好的公司
15) 股票股息
16) 现金股息

4. Subject for self-study: A balance sheet chart.

ABC Company

Balance sheet before a stock dividend

Current assets	$100,000	Current liabilities		$50,000
Fixed assets	$200,000	Long term liabilities		50,000
		Equity: common stock	100,000	
		$1 per 100, 000 shares outstanding		
		Additional paid-in capital	30,000	
		Retained earnings	70,000	
		Total equity		200,000
Total assets	$300,000	Total liabilities and equity		$300,000

After 10 percent stock dividend
(market price: $5 per share)

Current assets	$100,000	Current liabilities		$50,000
Fixed assets	$200,000	Long term liabilities		50,000
		Equity: common stock	110,000	
		$1 per 100,000 shares outstanding		
		Additional paid-in capital	70,000	
		Retained earnings	20,000	
		Total equity		200,000
Total assets	$300,000	Total liabilities and equity		$300,000

Unit 16　How to calculate shareholders' dividend?　如何计算股东股息？

Reminder 提示

current asset　流动资产
fixed asset　固定资产
total assets　总资产
liability [ˌlaiə'biliti] n.　负债
equity ['ekwiti] n.　权益，股本
common stock　普通股
outstanding [aut'stændiŋ] a.　未付清的
additional paid-in capital　追加投入资本
total equity　总股本，全部股本
total liabilities and equity　总负债及权益

16.6 Accounting-related knowledge
会计相关知识介绍

什么是股息率？
What is the dividend yield?

　　股息率又称为股息收益率（dividend yield），是一年的总派息额（total dividend payout amount）与当时市价（market price）的比例。
　　以占股票最后销售价格的百分数表示年度股息（annual dividend），该指标是投资收益率的简化形式。股息率是股息（dividend）与股票价格（stock prices）之间的比率。在投资实践中，股息率是衡量企业是否具有投资价值的重要标尺之一。

股息率的意义
　　股息率是挑选收益型股票的重要参考标准，如果连续多年年度股息率超过一年期银行存款利率（interest rate of bank deposits），则这只股票基本可以视为收益型股票，股息率越高越吸引人。
　　股息率也是挑选其他类型股票的参考标准之一。决定股息率高低的不仅是股利（stock bonus）和股利发放率的高低，还要视股价来定。例如两支股票，A股价为10元，B股价为20元，两家公司同样发放每股0.5元股利，则A公司5%的股息率显然要比B公司2.5%的股息率诱人。

16.7 Extended reading
延伸阅读

How to calculate the annual dividend on preferred shares?
如何计算优先股的年股息？

Preferred shares of stock are ownership equity securities just as regular (common) stock shares. However, preferred shareholders don't have voting rights at stockholder's meetings and preferred shares usually have less growth potential. Investors buy preferred shares because they pay guaranteed annual dividends. Strictly speaking, you don't calculate the annual dividend on preferred shares because it is determined when the shares are first issued. However, you should be able to calculate the income and yield provided by a preferred stock.

Step 1

Look in the prospectus of the preferred stock issue you are interested in to find the annual dividend. There may be more than one issue of preferred shares for a particular company. These will be listed according to their dividend rate or date of issue in the annual report. You can obtain the annual report and preferred stock prospectus online on the company's Investor Relations website or by asking your broker.

Step 2

Calculate the annual dividend for a given number of preferred shares. For example, if the shares were originally issued at $50 a share with a 6 percent dividend, the annual dividend per share is 0.06×$50 = $3.00. If you have 1,000 shares, that works out to $3,000 in dividend income per year. Dividends are usually paid quarterly, so you would get a check for $750 every four times each year.

Step 3

Calculate the annual yield of the preferred shares. The price of preferred stock varies depending on market conditions. The yield is the actual rate of interest you earn and depends on the price paid for the stock. If the shares in the example in Step 3 are purchased for $40 a share instead of the original $50 a share, the yield is $3.00 a share divided by $40, or 0.075. Multiply by 100 to express as percentage yield (7.5 percent).

Tips & Warnings

- Although preferred shares carry less risk than common stock, they are not risk-free. Always read the company annual report carefully and research any company thoroughly before investing.
- Check the terms and conditions of the preferred shares as described in the prospectus. Preferred stock can have a number of features you should be aware of before investing. For example, some preferred shares can be converted into common stock. Others can get additional dividends over and above the guaranteed amount if company performance warrants the additional payment.

Unit 17
How to maintain a healthy cash flow in a small business?
小企业如何保持健康的现金流？

Core terms reminder
核心术语提示

cash flow management	现金流管理
cash flow position	现金状况
access to cash	获得现金
expense forecast	费用预测
budget cash inflow and outflow	预算现金流入量与流出量
beginning cash balance	期初现金余额
debtor management	债务人管理
billing term	付费条款，出单条款
prompt payment	立即付款
credit check	信用检查
tie up money	占压资金
free up cash	释放现金

Unit 17　How to maintain a healthy cash flow in a small business? 小企业如何保持健康的现金流?

17.1a　Why is a healthy cash flow vital for business survival?
为什么健康的现金流对企业生存是重要的?

With tough economic times **prevailing**, businesses should be aware of the importance of healthy cash flow to **thrive** and survive through this period. In view of this, cash flow management should be the **top priority** for businesses of our time.

Cash flow is the **lifeblood** of a business, so smart **debtor management** is **crucial** to success. Therefore it is important to organize debtor payments and creating a steady cash flow.

Constantly **reviewing** and managing cash flows, particularly in this environment, is the key to avoiding **financial strain** and ultimately preventing business failure.

As an expert put it, "It's no secret that businesses that have cash or **access to cash** will have a better chance of survival than those businesses that need to borrow to **keep their doors open**."

There are many ways to **accelerate** the flow of cash from customers to the business to **stay afloat**, even for those currently without a cash-flow budget.

"One of the most important things is to put together key data such as sales and **expense forecasts** and then set up a simple budget **worksheet** that **tabulates** cash flows, such as your **beginning cash**

---

prevail *vi.* 盛行，流行

thrive *vi.* 兴旺

top priority 最高优先，头等大事

lifeblood *n.* 生命的血液，生命线
debtor management 债务人管理
crucial *a.* 至关紧要的
be crucial to 对……至关紧要

review *vt.* 回顾，检查

financial strain 财务紧张

access to cash 获得现金
keep one's door open 保持营业，不至于关门
accelerate *vt.* 加速，促进
afloat *a.* 飘浮的，能航行的
stay afloat 保持航行，保持运营
expense forecast 费用预测
worksheet *n.* 工作表
tabulate *vt.* 列表，制成表格
beginning cash balance 期初现金余额

balance and your **budget cash inflows and outflows**."

budget cash inflow and outflow 预算现金流入量与流出量

17.1b What is a stress test?

什么是压力测验？

In tough economic times, many small businesses struggle to manage their cash flow **adequately**. Where they once thought they were **cruising along** nicely, a **bump** appears in the road and they are **thrown off course**. All business owners should undertake what the experts call a "stress test" of the business and have risk management strategies in place to ensure the business survives bumps along the way.

adequately ad. 恰当地

cruise vi. 巡游，航行
cruise along 行进
bump n. 碰撞，颠簸
throw off course 脱离赛道，出局

A stress test is a way for you to analyze your past, present and future **cash flow position**. It involves you, as the business owner, putting together detailed reports covering off everything from Key Performance Indicators (KPI), to cash flow forecasting and drawing up **hypothetical** "WHAT IF" **scenarios** to ensure you are prepared for anything. Do this regularly and make it standard procedure in your business.

cash flow position 现金状况
hypothetical a. 假设的

scenario n. 剧本，情节，说明

17.1c 10 cash flow management tips

10 个现金流管理提示

Maintaining a healthy bank account is **top of mind** with every small business owner. How can you improve your cash flow and reduce common money management headaches as well? The below tips will help you stay ahead:

1. Invoice regularly

Be direct with your customers about your **billing terms** —

top of mind 心中的头等大事

invoice regularly 定期开发票
billing term 付费条款，出单条款

upfront a. 在前面的，预付的

whether it's a **deposit upfront**, invoicing based on percentage of work complete, or immediately after completion of a project. Timely billing will help you maintain a more consistent cash flow.

2. Reward prompt payment

Rewarding customers who pay quickly is a great way to keep the cash coming in. Even a relatively small reward, such as a 1~2 percent discount for customers who pay within the first ten days, is usually enough of an **enticement** to **get the ball rolling**.

3. Enforce credit checks

Knowing that your clients are capable of paying you is key to keeping a steady **influx** of cash. Don't **give credit to** or work with those who are not qualified.

4. Invest excess cash

Don't let large sums of cash sit in your business cheque account. When your business has excess cash — invest it. **Savings accounts**, **money market accounts**, and **term deposits** are all great financial options to keep that cash working for you.

5. Set a budget

And **stick to** it. A budget will help forecast the future of your business as well as assist you in maintaining the best schedule for paying bills.

6. Take your time

An important aspect of maintaining a **positive cash flow** is to **hold on to** your money as long as possible. Pay all bills on time so as not to incur **late fees**, but take advantage of longer payment periods and don't pay too far in advance.

7. Raise your prices

A simple solution that is often **overlooked**. If you find it difficult to pay bills regularly, or if you haven't raised prices in the last five years, consider raising them. **Benchmark** your pricing against your competitors and see if you can afford to raise your

deposit upfront 预付押金

reward prompt payment 奖励立即付款

enticement n. 诱惑
get the ball rolling 开始活动，使蓬勃发展
enforce vt. 推行，实施
enforce credit check 实行信用检查
influx n. 流入
give credit to 让……赊账
excess cash 过剩现金
invest excess cash 把过剩现金投资出去
savings account 储蓄账户
money market account 金融市场账户
term deposit 定期存款
set a budget 设定预算
stick to 坚持
take your time 从容不忙
positive cash flow 正现金流
hold on to 抓住，不放
late fee 滞纳金，超时附加费
raise your prices 提高价格
overlook vt. 忽略

benchmark vt. 设定基准点，检测

rates. You cannot stay in business if you don't make a profit.

8. Prepare plan B

Set up **a line of credit** with your bank to cover your business expenses in an emergency.

9. Avoid excess inventory

Although many vendors offer discounts for **bulk purchases**, **excess inventory ties up your money**. Manage your inventory closely and you can **free up cash**.

10. Be efficient

The faster you deliver your product or service, the quicker you get paid. Examine your **business model/supply chain** closely and look for ways to cut out wasted time. Unnecessary delays **disrupt** your cash flow.

prepare plan B 准备 B 计划
a line of credit 一种信贷
avoid excess inventory 避免过剩存货
bulk purchase 批量采购
excess inventory 过剩存货
tie up one's money 占压资金
free up cash 释放现金
be efficient 讲求效率
business model 业务模式
supply chain 供应链
disrupt *vt.* 使中断，使混乱

17.2 Core accounting terms
核心会计术语

- **access to cash** 获得现金
- **a line of credit** 一种信贷
- **beginning cash balance** 期初现金余额
- **billing term** 付费条款，出单条款
- **budget cash inflow and outflow** 预算现金流入量与流出量
- **bulk purchase** 批量采购
- **business model** 业务模式
- **cash flow position** 现金状况
- **credit check** 信用检查
- **debtor management** 债务人管理
- **deposit upfront** 预付押金
- **excess cash** 过剩现金
- **excess inventory** 过剩存货
- **expense forecast** 费用预测
- **financial strain** 财务紧张
- **free up cash** 释放现金
- **keep one's door open** 保持营业，不至于关门
- **late fee** 滞纳金，超时附加费
- **money market account** 金融市场账户
- **positive cash flow** 正现金流
- **prompt payment** 立即付款
- **savings account** 储蓄账户
- **term deposit** 定期存款
- **tie up one's money** 占压资金

17.3 Extended words
扩展词汇

- **accelerate** [æk'seləreit] *vt.* 加速，促进
- **adequately** ['ædikwitli] *ad.* 恰当地

Unit 17 How to maintain a healthy cash flow in a small business? 小企业如何保持健康的现金流? 203

- afloat [ə'fləut] *a.* 飘浮的，能航行的
- stay afloat 保持航行，保持运营
- benchmark ['bentʃmɑ:k] *vt.* 设定基准点，检测
- bump [bʌmp] *n.* 碰撞，颠簸
- crucial ['kru:ʃəl] *a.* 至关紧要的
- be crucial to 对……至关紧要
- cruise [kru:z] *vi.* 巡游，航行
- cruise along 行进
- disrupt [dis'rʌpt] *vt.* 使中断，使混乱
- enforce [in'fɔ:s] *vt.* 推行，实施
- enticement [in'taismənt] *n.* 诱惑
- get the ball rolling 开始活动，使蓬勃发展
- give credit to 让……赊账
- hold on to 抓住，不放
- hypothetical [haipə'θetikl] *a.* 假设的
- influx ['inflʌks] *n.* 流入

- lifeblood ['laifblʌd] *n.* 生命的血液，生命线
- overlook [,əuvə'luk] *vt.* 忽视
- prevail [pri'veil] *vi.* 盛行，流行
- review [ri'vju:] *vt.* 回顾，检查
- scenario [si'nɑ:riəu] *n.* 剧本，情节，说明
- stick to 坚持
- supply chain 供应链
- tabulate ['tæbjuleit] *vt.* 列表，制成表格
- thrive [θraiv] *vi.* 兴旺
- throw off course 脱离赛道，出局
- top priority 最高优先，头等大事
- top of mind 心中的头等大事
- upfront [ʌp'frʌnt] *a.* 在前面的，预付的
- worksheet ['wə:kʃi:t] *n.* 工作表

17.4 Notes
注释

1) **With tough economic times prevailing, businesses should be aware of the importance of healthy cash flow to thrive and survive through this period.** 由于经济形势普遍艰难，企业应当意识到健康现金流的重要性，以便在这段时间内能够生存并兴旺发展。

2) **In view of this, cash flow management should be the top priority for businesses of our time.** 考虑到这一点，现金流管理应当成为当今企业的头等要务。

3) **Cash flow is the lifeblood of a business, so smart debtor management is crucial to success.** 现金流是企业的命脉，所以精明的债务人管理对成功是至关紧要的。

4) **Therefore it is important to organize debtor payments and creating a steady cash flow.** 因此组织债务人付款并创造稳定的现金流是非常重要的。

5) Constantly reviewing and managing cash flows, particularly in this environment, is the

key to avoiding financial strain and ultimately preventing business failure. 经常检查并管理现金流，尤其是在这样的环境中，是避免财务紧张并最终防止生意失败的关键所在。

6) **It's no secret that businesses that have cash or access to cash will have a better chance of survival than those businesses that need to borrow to keep their doors open.** 有现金或能够获得现金的企业比那些需要靠举债来维持营业的企业会具有更好的生存机会，这不是秘密。

　　本句包含三个由 that 引导的从句，第一个是 that businesses…open，这是一个真实主语，句首的 it 是形式主语，代替这个 that 从句。第二个是 that have cash or access to cash，这是限定性定语从句，修饰名词 businesses。第三个是 that need…open，也是限定性定语从句，修饰名词 businesses。

7) **There are many ways to accelerate the flow of cash from customers to the business to stay afloat, even for those currently without a cash-flow budget.** 有许多方法可以加快从客户到企业的现金流，以便使企业稳定发展，即使对于那些当前没有现金流预算的企业来说也是如此。

8) **One of the most important things is to put together key data such as sales and expense forecasts.** 最重要的事情之一就是把关键数据如销售额和费用预测汇总到一起。

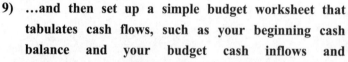

9) **…and then set up a simple budget worksheet that tabulates cash flows, such as your beginning cash balance and your budget cash inflows and outflows.** ……并建立一份简单的制成现金流表格的预算工作表，比如期初现金余额以及预算现金流入量与流出量。

　　句中 that…flows 是限定性定语从句，修饰名词短语 budget worksheet。

10) **Where they once thought they were cruising along nicely, a bump appears in the road and they are thrown off course.** 在他们一度认为自己还能够轻松行进的地方，路上出现了颠簸，他们也就被抛离了道路。

　　句中 where 是连词，意为"在……某地，在某处"，引导一个状语从句。

11) **All business owners should undertake what the experts call a "stress test" of the business and have risk management strategies in place to ensure the business survives bumps along the way.** 所有企业主应当着手对企业进行一种专家所讲的"压力测试"，并把风险管理安排到位以确保企业能在发展过程中渡过难关。

　　句中 what…business 是宾语从句，做动词 undertake 的宾语。

12) **A stress test is a way for you to analyze your past, present and future cash flow position.** 压力测试是让您分析过去、现在及未来的现金流。

13) **It involves you, as the business owner, putting together detailed reports covering off everything from Key Performance Indicators (KPI), to cash flow forecasting.** 这个测试涉及您——作为企业主——把涵盖一切事情的报告汇总在一起，从关键绩效指标（KPI）到

现金流预测。

14) **…and drawing up hypothetical "WHAT IF" scenarios to ensure you are prepared for anything.** ……并且拟定假设性的"如果什么"情景以确保准备好应对任何事情。

15) **Be direct with your customers about your billing terms— whether it's a deposit upfront, invoicing based on percentage of work complete, or immediately after completion of a project.** 在讲述收费条款时要向客户直接讲明——无论这是预付押金，还是根据已完成工作的百分比来出具发票，还是根据项目完成就立即付款来出具发票。

16) **Timely billing will help you maintain a more consistent cash flow.** 及时出票将有助于维持更加连贯的现金流。

17) **Rewarding customers who pay quickly is a great way to keep the cash coming in.** 奖励那些快速付款的客户是保持现金流入的很好方法。

   句中 who 引导一个限定性定语从句，修饰名词 customers。

18) **Even a relatively small reward, such as a 1~2 percent discount for customers who pay within the first ten days, is usually enough of an enticement to get the ball rolling.** 即使相对较小的奖励，如给在头 10 天内付款的客户打 1%~2%的折扣，通常足以能让事情顺利发展。

19) **Don't give credit to or work with those who aren't qualified.** 不要赊账给那些不够资格的人，也不要和他们共事。

   句中 who 引导一个限定性定语从句，修饰代词 those。

20) **A budget will help forecast the future of your business as well as assist you in maintaining the best schedule for paying bills.** 预算将有助于预测企业的未来，同时也有助于维持支付账单的最佳时间表。

21) **An important aspect of maintaining a positive cash flow is to hold on to your money as long as possible.** 维持正现金流的一个重要方面就是要尽可能长时间地紧抓现金。

22) **Pay all bills on time so as not to incur late fees, but take advantage of longer payment periods and don't pay too far in advance.** 按时支付所有账单以便不产生滞纳金，但是要利用较长的付款期，不要过于提前支付。

23) **A simple solution that is often overlooked.** （这是）一个经常被忽略的简单解决方案。

句中 that 引导一个限定性定语从句，修饰名词 solution。

24) Benchmark your pricing against your competitors and see if you can afford to raise your rates. 对照竞争对手来测定自己定价，看看是否能够经受住提价的影响。

25) Set up a line of credit with your bank to cover your business expenses in an emergency. 和银行确定一种信贷方式，以便能处理应急性的业务费用。

26) Although many vendors offer discounts for bulk purchases, excess inventory ties up your money. 虽然许多供货商会为批量采购打折，但是存货过剩会占压资金。

17.5 Reinforcement exercise
强化练习

1. Answer the following questions in English.

1) Why is a healthy cash flow vital for business survival?
2) What is a stress test?
3) How can we encourage prompt payment by customers?
4) Why should we take our time in paying bills?

2. Put the following into Chinese.

1) cash flow management
2) top priority
3) debtor management
4) financial strain
5) access to cash
6) accelerate the flow of cash
7) cash-flow budget
8) expense forecast
9) beginning cash balance
10) budget cash inflow and outflow
11) cash flow position
12) billing term

3. Put the following into English.

1) 立即付款
2) 信用检查
3) 过剩现金
4) 储蓄账户
5) 金融市场账户
6) 定期存款
7) 正现金流
8) 滞纳金，超时附加费
9) 批量采购
10) 过剩存货
11) 占压资金
12) 释放现金
13) 预付押金

4. Subject for self-study: A cash flow statement chart.

Cash Flow Statement
For the month ended January 31, 2002

Operating Activities.	
Net Income.	$ 7,000
Plus Depreciation Expense.	1,000
Less Gain on Sale of Stock.	(500)
Less Increase in Accounts Rec.	(10,000)
Less Increase in Inventory.	(5,000)
Plus Increase in Accounts Pay.	(20,000)
Plus Increase in Interest Pay.	(500)
Cash flow from operating activities	$ 13,000
Investing Activities	
Purchase of equipment	$(60,000)
Purchase of securities	(3,000)
Sale of securities	3,500
Cash flow from investing activities	$(59,500)
Financing Activities	
Issuarce of stock	$ 200,000
Increase in notes payable	50,000
Repurchase of treasury stock	(100)
Cash flow from financing activities	$ 249,900
Total cash flow	$ 203,400
Beginning cash	0
Ending cash	$ 203,400

Reminder 提示

depreciation [di,pri:ʃi'eiʃən] *n.* 折旧
gain on sale of stock 出售股票收益
accounts rec. = accounts receivable 应收账款
accounts pay. = accounts payable 应付账款
interest pay. = interest payable 应付利息
securities [si'kjuəritiz] *n.* 证券
notes payable 应付票据
treasury stock 库存股票

17.6 Accounting-related knowledge
会计相关知识介绍

卡桑国际的瘦身计划
Kaseng International's downsizing scheme

全球经济下滑（slowdown）尚未见底，眼看着营业收入（operating revenue）大幅下降、存货积压（overstock of inventory）尚未根本解决，而客户又在延长付款周期，企业主们有了雪上加霜之感。

面对这种不利的局面，企业应当争分夺秒地回收账款，去库存化，削减成本，获取流动性（liquidity），是存活的大前提。对此，波士顿咨询公司的建议是：企业首先必须建立一系列经济下滑的情境（scenario），然后基于当前的成本结构为每个情境制定相应的成本削减目标；高管层应该建立侧重不同职能的多个 SWAT 团队，并由这些团队设定大胆的成本削减目标；企业必须建立确定优先级的行动计划，并在项目管理办公室的带领下利用结构化的方式确保这一计划最终形成一个严谨的成本节约机制（cost-saving mechanism）。

经济衰退时期的现金流管理（cash flow management），最简单的原则就是开源节流，比如减少应收（accounts receivable）、存货（inventory），增加应付（accounts payable），缩减费用（reduce costs），以及由此衍生的各式各样的技巧。

果断瘦身

位于浙江海宁的卡森国际，是中国最大的皮革家具 OEM 供应商，已经错失了"不要套牢"的最佳时期。之前，卡森一直致力于"成为全球最大的软体家具产品及汽车皮革生产商"，并为此进行了广泛的生产能力（production capacity）布局，其 2004 年、2005 年资本支出分别为 7.4 亿元和 2.3 亿元。

卡森的扩张，具有中国制造企业扩张路径的典型性：重资产（assets），高折旧（depreciation），高负债率（liability）(特别是短期负债多)，高利息费用（interest charges），或者短期的商业交易融资多，短期现金流出压力大。在 2005 年香港 IPO 之前，资产负债率达到 70%，一年内到期的银行借贷（bank borrowings）相对于总资产的比值是 36.5%。

自 2006 年，卡森开始遭遇一系列外部宏观因素的打击，人民币升值（appreciation of RMB Yuan）、原材料涨价、出口退税减少，最沉重的打击来自发生次贷危机的美国，美国市场曾占据卡森超过 70%的收入。2007、2008 财年，卡森分别巨亏 1.9 亿元和 2.78 亿元。

从 2007 年，卡森开始正视产能利用不充分的问题，并迅速开展了"瘦身"（downsizing）运动。2007 年 1—8 月，卡森出售了两间沙发制造附属公司的权益，并关闭了位于上海的另一家工厂，获得了资产净值加出售收益共 8 620 万元。2008 年，卡森再次分批出售了两间附属公司的股权，出售所得超过 5 000 万元。

卡森曾经有进军地产的计划，其合营公司（卡森拥有 60%股权）曾以总成本 2.6 亿元购得长沙一块土地，准备兴建皮革以及家具的零售市场，2009 年，卡森退回了土地，直接套现 2.8 亿元；在公司总部所在地海宁，还将一块工业用地退还给当地政府，套现 5 亿元。据卡森副总裁兼 CFO 钟剑粗略估计，两年间，卡森累计回收现金约在 10 亿元。

"去资产化"在卡森最近公布的 2008 年报中得到了直接体现，其中"物业、厂房及设备"（property, plant and equipment）一项，从 2006 年的 11.73 亿元，迅速下降到 5.72 亿元。截至 2008 年年底，卡森的雇员总数已下降至 5 400 余名，而其高峰雇工人数是 28 000 名。

有人比喻，中国企业生产设施（production facility）的利用，就像沾水的毛巾，还有大量的潜在产能可以挤出来。业内人士指出，中国不少制造型企业增加资产属于战略失误，"新增加的资产往往并没有带来更大的增量效应"，资产总额越大，回报率越低。在这样的情况下，企业即使主营业务衰退，通过合理的现金筹划，短期内可转危为安，其中最简单有效的办法就是瘦身运动，专家说"只要把闲置的、多余的资产换成现金，让臃肿的身体瘦下来，提高资产报酬率（return on assets），公司自然也就有了新的希望。"

17.7 Extended reading
延伸阅读

Perceive cash flow problems closely
密切注意现金流问题

What are the evidences of poor cash flows?

Every business owner must be proactive as opposed to reactive. The companies that get stuck in tough times are those that start to work on a problem after it has already happened. By this time, their cash flow has already been severely damaged and can take a long time to recover.

More often than not there are warning signs that all is not right in your business financially. Financial experts would identify the following as evidence of poor cash flow:

- Margin erosion
- Overtrading
- High gearing
- Under capitalization
- Lack of cash flow forecasting

- Need for regular capital/loans injections
- Lack of financial information

FAQs concerning the cash flow

Here are some suggestions for things you can do to prevent these scenarios from occurring in the first place.

The first step is to ask the hard questions in order to find an appropriate solution. In speaking with business recovery experts, the most common questions a business owner should ask when it comes to maintaining a healthy cash flow include:

- What is the new break-even level for the business? How does this differ from the previous level?
- What is the impact to revenue and earnings if you lose a major customer?
- What is your tipping point? For example, how far are you willing to go to maintain earnings and are you prepared to lose customers in the process?
- How is cash flow affected if debtors take extra days to settle their accounts?
- What changes will you require to your banking facilities and what would be your bank's attitude to an increase in lending?
- Are stuff cuts needed and how will you deal with this?
- Do you have the required cash flow to fund redundancies?
- What overheads will you reduce and what measures will you take to preserve cash?
- What non-core assets could be sold to reduce debt and provide additional cash flow?
- What do you have to do to meet ATO tax requirements?

By doing this, you will be able to react quickly if conditions change suddenly and show financers you are prepared for any challenges that may arise. By asking the "what if" questions and creating strategies to deal with given scenarios to minimize risk, you will be able to maximize the potential and opportunity for the business. As a direct result, key stakeholders will have increased confidence in your company's abilities and knowing possible outcomes will minimize the stress on the business when tough decisions have to be made.

Tips to improve cash flow

If you are looking for a way to loosen the restraints your business is facing, start by easing your cash flow. Dun & Bradstreet offers the following debtor management tips to get you started.

- Set clear policies at the outset of a credit agreement
- Get a signed contract
- Always conduct a credit check prior to the extension of credit
- Issue invoices promptly
- Monitor your accounts receivable on an ongoing basis
- Gradually escalate pressure on your debtors

- Be prepared to address individual circumstances
- Start the collection process the day after the account becomes due
- Cease the extension of credit on overdue accounts
- Never be afraid to ask for help and do not wait too long to call in the experts

Unit 18
What is cost accounting?
什么是成本核算？

Core terms reminder
核心术语提示

成本核算	cost accounting
绝对成本	absolute cost
相对成本	relative cost
可变成本	variable cost
固定成本	fixed cost
机会成本	opportunity cost
生产单位	unit of production
最低总成本	minimum total cost
盈亏临界成本点公式	breakeven cost-point formula
生产成本	production cost
底线利润	bottom line profit

18.1a What are absolute costs and relative costs?
什么是绝对成本和相对成本？

Cost is important to all industry. Costs can be divided into two general classes: **absolute costs** and **relative costs**. Absolute cost measures the loss in value of assets. Relative cost involves a comparison between the chosen **course of action** and the course of action that was **rejected**. This cost of the **alternative action** — the action not taken — is often called the "**opportunity cost**".

absolute cost 绝对成本
relative cost 相对成本
course of action 行动步骤
reject vt. 拒绝
alternative action 选择性行动，变通行动
opportunity cost 机会成本

18.1b What are variable costs and fixed costs?
什么是可变成本和固定成本？

Costs are divided into two types: **variable costs** and **fixed costs**. Variable costs vary **per unit of production**. For example, they may be the cost per **cubic meter** of wood **yarded**, per cubic meter of **dirt excavated**, etc. Fixed costs, on the other hand, are incurred only once and as additional units of production are produced, the unit costs fall. Examples of fixed costs would be equipment **move-in costs** and **road access costs**.

variable cost 可变成本
fixed cost 固定成本
per prep. 每，由，经
unit of production 生产单位
cubic metre 立方米
yard vt. 堆放，码放
dirt n. 土
excavate vt. 挖掘
move-in cost 搬进成本
road access cost 道路通行成本

18.1c What are the total cost and unit cost formulas?

什么是总成本和单位成本公式？

As harvesting operations become more complicated and involve both fixed and variable costs, there usually is more than one way to accomplish a given task. It may be possible to change the quantity of one or both types of cost, and thus to arrive at a **minimum total cost**. Mathematically, the relationship existing between **volume of production** and costs can be expressed by the following equations:

minimum total cost 最低总成本
volume of production 生产量，产量

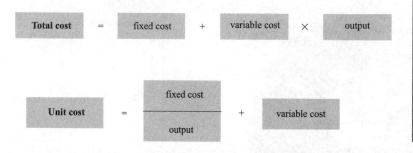

18.1d What is the unit cost equation?

什么是单位成本等式？

The use of **breakeven** and **minimum-cost-point formulas** require the collection of unit costs. Unit costs can be divided into **subunits**, each of which measures the cost of a certain part of the total. A typical unit cost formula might be

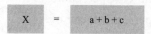

where **X** is the cost **per unit volume** such as dollars per cubic meter and the subunits a, b, c will deal with distance, volume, area, or weight. Careful selection of the subunits to express the factors controlling costs is the key to success in all cost studies.

breakeven *a.* 盈亏相抵的，无亏损的
breakeven-cost-point formula 盈亏临界成本点公式
minimum-cost-point formula 最低成本点公式
subunit *n.* 亚单位，二级单位
volume *n.* 体积
per unit volume 每单位体积

18.1e What is cost accounting?

什么是成本核算？

Cost accounting is an approach to **evaluating** the overall costs that are associated with **conducting business**. Generally based on **standard accounting practices**, cost accounting is one of the tools that managers utilize to determine what type and how much expenses is involved with maintaining the current business model. At the same time, the principles of cost accounting can also be utilized to **project** changes to these costs in the event that specific changes are implemented.

When it comes to measuring how wisely company resources are being utilized, cost accounting helps to provide the data relevant to the current situation. By **identifying production costs** and further defining the cost of production by three or more **successive business cycles**, it is possible to note any trends that indicate a rise in production costs without any **appreciable** changes or increase in production of goods and services. By using this approach, it is possible to identify the reason for the change, and take steps to contain the situation before **bottom line profits** are impacted to a greater degree.

Product development and marketing strategies are also informed by the utilization of cost accounting. In terms of product development, it is possible to determine if a new product can be produced at a reasonable price, considering the cost of raw materials and the labour and equipment necessary to produce a **finished product**. At the same time, marketing **protocols** can make use of cost accounting to project if the product will sell enough units to make production a **viable** option.

Cost accounting is helpful in making a number of business decisions. By **weighing** the actual costs **versus** the **anticipated**

cost accounting 成本核算
evaluate vt. 评估，评价
conduct business 做业务
standard accounting practices 标准核算惯例
project vt. 设计，预测

identify vt. 识别，鉴别
production cost 生产成本
successive a. 连续的
business cycle 商业周期
appreciable a. 可感知的

bottom line profit 底线利润

finished product 成品
protocol n. 草案，计划
viable a. 可行的
weigh vt. 称重量，权衡
versus prep. 对，与……相对
anticipated benefit 预期效益

benefit, cost accounting can help a company to avoid **launching a product** with no real market, prevent the purchase of unnecessary goods and services, or **alter** the current operational model in a manner that will decrease efficiency. Whether utilized to evaluate the status of a department within the company or as a tool to project the **feasibility** of opening new locations or closing older ones, cost accounting can provide important data that may impact the final decision.

launch a product 推出产品

alter *vt.* 变更，改变

feasibility *n.* 可行性

18.2 Core accounting terms
核心会计术语

- **absolute cost** 绝对成本
- **anticipated benefit** 预期效益
- **bottom line profit** 底线利润
- **breakeven-cost-point formula** 盈亏临界成本点公式
- **business cycle** 商业周期
- **cost accounting** 成本核算
- **fixed cost** 固定成本
- **minimum-cost-point formula** 最低成本点公式
- **minimum total cost** 最低总成本
- **production cost** 生产成本
- **relative cost** 相对成本
- **standard accounting practices** 标准核算惯例
- **unit of production** 生产单位
- **volume of production** 生产量，产量

18.3 Extended words
扩展词汇

- **alter** [ˈɔːltə] *vt.* 变更，改变
- **alternative action** 选择性行动，变通行动
- **appreciable** [əˈpriːʃiəbl] *a.* 可感知的
- **breakeven** [ˈbreikˈiːvən] *a.* 盈亏相抵的，无亏损的
- **conduct business** 做业务
- **course of action** 行动步骤
- **cubic metre** 立方米
- **dirt** [dəːt] *n.* 土
- **evaluate** [iˈvæljueit] *vt.* 评估，评价
- **excavate** [ˈekskəveit] *vt.* 挖掘
- **feasibility** [ˌfiːzəˈbiləti] *n.* 可行性
- **finished product** 成品
- **identify** [aiˈdentifai] *vt.* 识别，鉴别
- **launch a product** 推出产品
- **move-in cost** 搬进成本

- opportunity cost 机会成本
- per [pə:] *prep.* 每，由，经
- per unit volume 每单位体积
- project [prə'dʒekt] *vt.* 设计，预测
- protocol ['prəutəkɔl] *n.* 草案，计划
- reject [ri'dʒekt] *vt.* 拒绝
- road access cost 道路通行成本
- subunit [sʌb'ju:nit] *n.* 亚单位，二级单位
- successive [sək'sesiv] *a.* 连续的
- variable cost 可变成本
- versus ['və:səs] *prep.* 对，与……相对
- viable ['vaiəbl] *a.* 可行的
- volume ['vɔlju:m] *n.* 体积
- weigh [wei] *vt.* 称重量，权衡
- yard [jɑ:d] *vt.* 堆放，码放

18.4 Notes 注释

1) **Absolute cost measures the loss in value of assets.** 绝对成本检测资产价值的损失。
2) **Relative cost involves a comparison between the chosen course of action and the course of action that was rejected.** 相对成本涉及所选择行动步骤与所拒绝行动步骤之间的对比。
   句中，that was rejected 是限定性定语从句，修饰其前的名词短语 course of action。
3) **This cost of the alternative action — the action not taken — is often called the "opportunity cost".** 替代性行动——即未采取的行动——的成本经常被称之为"机会成本"。
   句中 not taken 是过去分词短语后置做定语，修饰其前的名词 action，相当于定语从句 that is not taken 或 that has not been taken。
4) **Variable costs vary per unit of production.** 可变成本随生产单位而异。
5) **For example, they may be the cost per cubic meter of wood yarded, per cubic meter of dirt excavated, etc.** 例如，它们可以是堆放在一起的每立方米木头、挖掘出来的每立方米土的成本等。
   句中 yarded 和 excavated 均为过去分词后置做定语，分别修饰其前的名词 wood 和 dirt，相当于定语从句 that is yarded 和 that is excavated。
6) **Fixed costs, on the other hand, are incurred only once and as additional units of production are produced, the unit costs fall.** 另一方面，固定成本仅发生一次，而且随着额外生产单位的产出，单位成本会降低。
7) **Examples of fixed costs would be equipment move-in costs and road access costs.** 固定成本的例子有设备搬入费用以及道路通行费用。
8) **As harvesting operations become more complicated and involve both fixed and variable costs, there usually is more than one way to accomplish a given task.** 由于收获运作变得更加复杂并且涉及固定成本和可变成本，在完成一个特定任务时通常有不止一种方法。
9) **It may be possible to change the quantity of one or both types of cost, and thus to arrive at a minimum total cost.** 有可能改变一种或两种成本，由此来获得最低总成本。

10) **Mathematically, the relationship existing between volume of production and costs can be expressed by the following equations.** 从数学角度讲，存在于产量和成本之间的关系可以用下列等式表达。

11) **The use of breakeven and minimum-cost-point formulas require the collection of unit costs.** 盈亏平衡成本点及最低成本点公式的使用需要收集单位成本。

   句中 breakeven and minimum-cost-point formulas 相当于 breakeven-cost-point formula and minimum-cost-point formula。

12) **Unit costs can be divided into subunits, each of which measures the cost of a certain part of the total.** 单位成本可以分为次级单元，每个次级单元都可以测量总成本的某一部分成本。

   句中，each of which 引导一个非限定性定语从句，对 subunits 进行补充说明。each of which 相当于 each of the subunits。

13) **…where X is the cost per unit volume such as dollars per cubic meter and the subunits a, b, c will deal with distance, volume, area, or weight.** ……在此，X 是每单位体积的成本，如每立方米多少美元，而且次级单元 a, b, c 将涉及距离、体积、区域或重量。

14) **Careful selection of the subunits to express the factors controlling costs is the key to success in all cost studies.** 仔细选择表示成本控制因素的次级单元是所有成本研究成功的关键所在。

15) **Cost accounting is an approach to evaluating the overall costs that are associated with conducting business.** 成本核算是评估与进行业务活动相关联的总体成本的途径。

   句中 that are…business 是限定性定语从句，修饰其前的名词短语 overall costs。

16) **Generally based on standard accounting practices, cost accounting is one of the tools that managers utilize to determine what type and how much expenses is involved with maintaining the current business model.** 成本核算一般基于标准核算惯例，是经理们用来确定维持当前业务模式所涉及的费用是何种类以及有多少费用的一种工具。

   a) 句中 that 引导一个限定性定语从句，修饰其前的名词 tools。
   b) what type and how much…model 是宾语从句，作动词 determine 的宾语。

17) **At the same time, the principles of cost accounting can also be utilized to project changes to these costs in the event that specific changes are implemented.** 同时，倘若实施特定的变化时，成本核算的原则还可以用来预测这些成本的变化。

   in the event that…意为"万一，倘若"，后面接从句。如：In the event that adverse weather conditions may affect the progress of the project, the contractor can apply for an extension of the duration. 万一不利的天气条件影响工程进度，承包商可以申请延期。

18) **When it comes to measuring how wisely company resources are being utilized, cost accounting helps to provide the data relevant to the current situation.** 当涉及衡量公司资源是否得到明智的利用时，成本核算有助于提供与当前情形相关的数据。

   句中 how…utilized 是宾语从句，做动词 measure 的宾语。

19) **By identifying production costs and further defining the cost of production by three or more successive business cycles…** 通过识别生产成本并进一步把生产成本确定为三、四种连续的业务周期……

20) **…it is possible to note any trends that indicate a rise in production costs without any**

appreciable changes or increase in production of goods and services. ……就有可能注意到在商品或服务的生产没有明显改变或增加的情况下却出现生产成本增加的趋势。

句中 that…services 是限定性定语从句，修饰先行词 trends。

21) **By using this approach, it is possible to identify the reason for the change, and take steps to contain the situation before bottom line profits are impacted to a greater degree.** 通过使用这个方法，有可能找出改变的原因，并采取步骤来控制形势，以免让底线利润向更深的程度下滑。

22) **Product development and marketing strategies are also informed by the utilization of cost accounting.** 产品开发和市场策略也是通过利用成本核算来获取信息的。

23) **In terms of product development, it is possible to determine if a new product can be produced at a reasonable price, considering the cost of raw materials and the labor and equipment necessary to produce a finished product.** 就产品开发而言，在考虑到生产制成品所必要的原材料成本、人工成本和设备成本后，就有可能确定一个新产品是否能够以合理价格来生产。

  a. if a new…price 是宾语从句，做动词 determine 的宾语。

  b. considering 是介词，意为"考虑到，鉴于"。

  c. necessary…product 是形容词短语后置做定语，修饰其前的名词短语 cost of raw materials and the labor and equipment。

24) **At the same time, marketing protocols can make use of cost accounting to project if the product will sell enough units to make production a viable option.** 与此同时，营销方案也可以利用成本核算来预测产品是否能够销售足够的单位以便让生产成为可行的选择。

  if…option 是宾语从句，做动词 project（预测）的宾语。

25) **By weighing the actual costs versus the anticipated benefit…** 通过权衡实际成本对照预期成本……

动词 weigh 原意是"称……重量"，引申为"权衡，掂量"。如：

We must carefully weigh the plus and minus of each investment decision. 我们必须小心地权衡每一个投资决策的利弊。

26) **…cost accounting can help a company to avoid launching a product with no real market, prevent the purchase of unnecessary goods and services, or alter the current operational model in a manner that will decrease efficiency.** 成本核算能够帮助公司避免在没有真实市场的情况下推出产品，防止采购不必要的商品或服务，或避免因改变当前的运营模式却出现效率降低的情况。

27) **Whether utilized to evaluate the status of a department within the company or as a tool to project the feasibility of opening new locations or closing older ones, cost accounting can provide important data that may impact the final decision.** 不论是利用成本核算来评估公司内部一部门的情况或是作为预测开设新地点或关闭老地点的可行性，成本核算都能够提供影响最后决策的重要数据。

句中 that 引导一个限定性定语从句，修饰其前的名词 data。

18.5 Reinforcement exercise
强化练习

1. Answer the following questions in English.

1) What are absolute costs and relative costs?
2) What are variable costs and fixed costs?
3) What is cost accounting?

2. Put the following into Chinese.

1) absolute cost
2) relative cost
3) course of action
4) alternative action
5) opportunity cost
6) variable cost
7) fixed cost
8) unit of production
9) move-in cost
10) road access cost

3. Put the following into English.

1) 盈亏临界成本点公式
2) 最低成本点公式
3) 亚单位，次级单位
4) 每单位体积
5) 成本核算
6) 标准核算惯例
7) 生产成本
8) 商业周期
9) 底线利润
10) 预期效益
11) 推出产品
12) 最低总成本
13) 生产量，产量

4. Subject for self-study: A cost accounting chart.

Traditional cost accounting			
Vs			
Activity-based costing			
Traditional cost accounting		Activity-based costing	
Salaries	$200,000	Enrolling new students	$100,000
On costs	$40,000	Designing new courses	$50,000
Consumables	$80,000	Teaching engineering	$150,000
Travel	$20,000	Tutoring students	$20,000
Depreciation	$60,000	Assessing students	$30,000
		Graduating students	$50,000
Total	$400,000	Total	$400,000

Reminder 提示

on cost 间接成本，间接费用
consumable [kən'sju:məbl] *n.* 消费品
depreciation [di,pri:ʃi'eiʃən] *n.* 折旧
enroll [in'rəul] *vt.* 招收
tutor ['tju:tə] *vt.* 辅导
assess [ə'ses] *vt.* 评估
graduate ['grædjueit] *vt.* 使毕业

18.6 Accounting-related knowledge
会计相关知识介绍

中小企业如何进行成本核算？
How to conduct cost accounting in small and medium-sized businesses?

成本核算（cost accounting）是企业管理和财务决策中最重要的一个环节，在市场经济条件下，企业要想在竞争中取胜，必须降低生产成本（reduce production cost），做好成本核算，着力提高利润水平（profit level）。

一、核算方法（accounting methods）的选择

中小型企业一般指资产规模较小、生产工艺流程和产品结构及所用原材料大部分相同的、管理人员（财务人员）相对精简的企业，管理结构通常是垂直管理（vertical management）体系。中小型企业因数量多而在经济结构链中起着不可或缺的作用。随着全球经济一体化（global integration）时代的到来，具备先进技术的人员创办新兴的科技型企业将不断地增加。中小型企业因受到财力、物力和人力的瓶颈（bottleneck），企业内部管理水平、财务决策能力、成本核算制度、财务控制制度等基本制度一般不完整、不系统，这种现象使得会计基础工作薄弱、会计信息数据采集不准确。

二、中小企业的管理模式决定其应使用简易的成本核算方法

中小型企业，无论其生产什么类型的产品，也不论其管理标准如何，最终目标都是要按照产品品种算出产品成本。按产品品种计算成本，是产品成本计算（cost calculation）的最基本要求，品种法是最基本的成本计算方法。若有需要或管理上要求按订单生产（make to order — MTO），也可采用分批法。

三、基本科目设置和成本核算思路

1. 不分别设置基本生产成本（production cost）和辅助生产成本两大科目，将其合并为一个生产成本科目，不再按产品设明细账（detailed ledger），直接设原材料、工资薪酬、动力费用、制造费用等几个二级明细科目对大项费用进行归集。

2. 原材料范围，在满足生产需要的前提下，只把产品构成比例较大的几种作为原材料，把非主要的原材料提前进入成本，这样既能降低工作量，也符合会计原则重要性原则。

3. 中小企业因车间划分不明显或虽明显但传递手续不完全，制造费用科目很难按车间设明细账，只好直接设置材料费（material cost）、修理费（repair cost）、折旧（depreciation）等几个二级明细科目对车间费用进行归集。

4. 若管理上或生产工艺上非常有必要，可设立制半成品科目。否则不设。

5. 设立低值易耗品科目或不设直接记入制造费用——机物料或修理费明细科目，同时设备查账以备管理需要，采用一次摊销法，入账同时即进行分配。

7. 关于固定资产折旧，采用符合税法规定的年限计算，可省去纳税调整的麻烦，又可以及时掌握交税额度。税法没有明确规定的，应按税法的一般要求进行折旧核算。

18.7 Extended reading
延伸阅读

What is a relevant cost?
什么是相关成本？

Relevant cost is any type of cost that is subject to change, depending on what kind of decision is made. Considered a key function within management accounting, the idea behind this type of cost definition is to determine how the budget will be impacted if a particular course of action is pursued. In order to properly evaluate the situation, it is necessary to look at all current costs, and determine which ones would change as a result of the decision, and which ones would remain constant. Those that will change are said to be relevant to the consideration of that course of action.

Assessing the relevant cost is not a particularly difficult process. All that is required is to project the chain of events that will take place should a particular action be taken. For example, a restaurant that wishes to attract more customers for lunchtime may consider implementing a lunchtime special that is only available for a few hours each day. Before actually implementing this new offering, the owner will look closely at what type of impact the project will have on labor, supplies, and utilities.

If it is determined that the number of servers on duty is sufficient to handle the larger lunch crowd, that cost factor is not relevant, as it changes nothing from what already takes place. Should it be determined that an additional laborer in the kitchen is needed to prepare food during the lunchtime period, this does constitute a change in labor costs and would be considered a relevant cost. Since more food would likely be required to manage the additional lunchtime customers, that cost would also be relevant.

The same general principal can be applied to just about any decision. Investors may look at what choosing a given investment scheme would mean in terms of additional expense or demand of their time, and determine if the effort is worth the expected outcome. Shopkeepers can decide if adding a specific product to the items they carry is likely to result in an increase of sales volume that will offset the cost of ordering that additional product. Understanding what the decision will change as far as the normal state of operations always makes it easier to determine if the decision is ultimately beneficial, or likely to have a negative impact.

Understanding the type and nature of a relevant cost can make it much easier to use the accounting process to effectively manage expense, thus increasing the opportunity for earning a profit. Should the amount of relevant cost be so great that the potential for earning profit is greatly diminished, it may be determined that the course of action under consideration is not viable, and is abandoned. From this perspective, identified a relevant cost or costs in any given situation not only enhances the potential for increasing profits, but also prevents the deterioration of the current level of profit.